AN AMERICAN MESSIAH

DAVID MICHAEL

Outskirts Press, Inc.
Denver, Colorado

The opinions expressed in this manuscript are solely the opinions of the author and do not represent the opinions or thoughts of the publisher. The author represents and warrants that s/he either owns or has the legal right to publish all material in this book. If you believe this to be incorrect, contact the publisher through its website at www.outskirtspress.com.

An American Messiah
All Rights Reserved
Copyright © 2006 David Michael

This book may not be reproduced, transmitted, or stored in whole or in part by any means, including graphic, electronic, or mechanical without the express written consent of the publisher except in the case of brief quotations embodied in critical articles and reviews.

Outskirts Press
http://www.outskirtspress.com

ISBN-10: 1-59800-280-5
ISBN-13: 978-1-59800-280-5

Outskirts Press and the "OP" logo are trademarks belonging to
Outskirts Press, Inc.

Printed in the United States of America

DEDICATION

This book is being dedicated to anyone who has battled mental illness, including the following:

Abraham Lincoln
Virginia Woolf
Lionel Aldridge
Gaetano Donizetti
Leo Tolstoy
Vincent Van Gogh
John Keats
Earnest Hemingway
Michelangelo
Vivian Leigh
Jimmy Piersall
Charles Dickens
Eugene O'Neill
Beethoven
Robert Schumann
Uaslov Nijinsky
Tennessee Williams
Isaac Newton
Sylvia Plath
Winston Churchill
Emperor Norton I
Patty Duke

This autobiography is intended to be a true and accurate depiction, as well as, an account of my travels and thoughts as I struggle and cope with mental illness. The pages cover from the spring of 1995 to the fall of 2004.

As one reads I ask they keep a quote that has always stuck with me and made writing this book a little less difficult. These may not be his exact worlds, but a famous author, Alexander Pope once wrote:

'It is not how something is written, it is what is written.'

CHAPTER 1

Early the third or last Saturday in April, I rose early to do some design work at the new Multi-Media Lab. The Fraternity All Day Party would be starting around noon, therefore, getting to a computer and completing this project before the vast majority of students rolled out of bed, would create some time to enjoy the days events. The project involved the coordinating of a layout for the campuses Flower Gardens web page. The year was 1995 and computers where blossoming globally with the advent of the internet. Graphic design was quickly evolving with this new machine, more so than almost any other walk of life.

After giving a knock on the door to this lab, allowing access to Art majors only, I settled in front of one of the Macintosh units. Ones student ID was registered with the design department allowing the identification card to lend a student access with a swipe of the card at the door. Not having the time to register for the new facility, up until that point, left me locked out at the entrance. Depending on another to understand the newness of the studio had locked me out and just knowing of its existence would be enough qualification, paid off. The same passage was allowed to others while I motioned the mouse across it's pad, clicking at points, and altering colors on the fields of flowers I was preparing to occupy the Gardens web site.

Through out the morning, two female Art Education collegians buzzed about the majors' curriculum and the evening before. It was a minor distraction, but something most attending Penn State University grow accustom to as they gather their education. After some time the stories they spun occupied the hole in which ones mind is set drifting away from the task at hand and onto topics like an All Day Party.

Spring sneaks into central Pennsylvania creating energy around the campus. Commencement fills the Alumni in waiting with hope and optimism and this pear of coeds seemed to be part of this class from the way they where analyzing their stay at Happy Valley. This is something I was making note of. For some time I was experiencing and monitoring what I believed to be a change in my physiology. I rationalized it as part of a natural maturation process into an older person. The understanding of my world, through the mass of past experiences, had begun to guide or direct my life into its future. The blooming and blossoming of the spring cycle of nature tangled with my rationalization of growth, I felt was underway. I proceeded in this exercise hoping to be in tune and together, with no clue of what was to follow.

It didn't take more than a few hours to complete the project for the next graphics class. Once the layouts where saved to disk and printed, my focus turned back to the fraternity house. The trip from the computer lab to the Chi Phi house is approximately a third of a mile or so. I would estimate the walk to be six to nine minutes depending on what you're carrying, the time of year, and the pace you need to travel to be on time. I mention these factors for two reasons: first, times and distances and how they are traveled will play an important factor in my development later in this Autobiography. Secondly this day quickly becomes a blur of activity and paranoia. I can only attempt to convey the events and emotions with spots of activity and memory. This experience is such that only a small percentage of its chronology can be draw from. The following segment will consist of the pieces my memory can find from that late April day.

It's hard to say when one of these annual All-Day Parties kick-off. Some time in the early afternoon most gather and a proud few carry the party from the previous night, kick things off the next morning. A vague first memory of moving around the backyard through the horseshoe pits and the sofas, the furniture is dragged out for the day, doesn't aid in recalling an exact time of day. The large back yard of the Chi Phi House is composed of two levels of earth. Running parallel to the driveway one finds a top tear of 40-50 yard in length with 15-20 yards in width. A dramatic 3-4 foot slope connects the lower tear of 40-50 yards in length and a width of 30-35 yards. The upper bar supported a social area, sand volleyball court and barbeque area. The lower stretch held the horseshoe pits with extra room for the dogs staying at the house to chase one another. For an official start a live band would be added on the driveway, followed by another band in the house. On the back veranda you could find drinking games. Finding a seat at the table would be more difficult than finding a drink.

The first true happening I recall is with my pledge brother, Jamie. He was asking to use my room to entertain a group of his friends from home. Jamie lived in the apartment complex next to mine while we pledged the house back in 1993. On the weekends, as pledges, we would have the duty to get the house cleaned early in the morning. I passed his apartment window and woke him almost every weekend. It became expected and part of our routine and we gained a strong relationship.

Jamie decided to live outside the house his senior year, not uncommon for upper classman. He really didn't have to ask, it was implied he could use my room. It was more of a courtesy; I knew what he would be doing, nothing we hadn't done before. His friends on the other hand I wasn't sure about, but I had seen most of them before. Two were students at PSU and I had partied with them on a few different occasions. 'Lucky', as some called Jamie, gave a few shouts out my window, while looking over the back yard, letting me know he was up in my third floor room. Lucky would also graduate this spring. As a member of a Greek system you watch many upper classman graduate Keith and Chris are two meaningful Brothers that were missed. Keith and Chris would be visiting this weekend and any time you have a graduated Brother they are attempting to party for the entire year in one weekend.

Now that I've mentioned Keith, I'll give the story linked to the nickname 'Lucky'. Keith tagged Jamie with the moniker after his lazy cat 'Lucky', who he said took long cat-knaps. Keith found both his cat Lucky and Jamie to have the same propensity toward napping and sleep. For example I had the duty of waking Jamie on pledge weekends.

After some socializing, I spotted someone I was in a study group with. She would also be graduating this spring. I knew her from a few social circles all the way through school, but grew to know Shannon through our Philosophy class. She was on the back veranda (back porch) attempting to get a seat at the drinking table. It was tough even for an attractive girl like her. We gave a wave to one another, and I made it a point to go up to see her and then check into what Jamie and his friends where up to in my room.

DAVID MICHAEL

From what I remember, I had a few worlds with Shannon. We both complained how our Philosophy class was difficult to understand. It was somewhat awkward talking to her. We had started to see one another for a good amount of time, but it was through our studies. I had grown to enjoy her company and we had become good friends. We would see one another through the buzz of humanity Penn State produces at events, until now.

My memory fails to gather any of our conversation. I just remember Shannon waving and then going to chat with her. I told her I was on my way to my room and would see her later. As I proceeded, I bumped into Chris, Keith and some others gathering numbers to hit the bar scene. In the raucous group they had become I received an invitation to join them in there celebration. "Maybe" was the reply. I wasn't holding a job that semester and the money I had build up last summer was withering with the ending of the second semester. They advanced to wherever they headed, as I took aim at what Jamie was doing with his lent space.

The rooms in the Fraternity where small, therefore Jamie and his people where all sandwiched in. When I arrived they had four people on the couch, one standing, one in a chair, and one in my loft bed (a bed elevated, supported a few feet to the ceiling). I was fine with almost everything but I was immediately disturbed with the person I didn't know very well lying in my bed. I waved him down and entered my room with a hit from a bowl. The few hits of weed plus and beer I had consumed was like the routine of any other party, but there was something more powerful controlling me for the past few months or so.

Something was altering my state. Something was happening but I didn't know what. I gathered a seat and for a half an hour or so spent some leisure time with the group that invaded the room. They left in the group they came, after that half hour, most likely pursuing the weekend warriors at the bars. Around this time the day party began changing to the night parties. I took one spin around the fraternity house and then headed to my third floor room. I'd spend the rest of the night there struggling to stay comfortable, focused, or rational.

Taking a nap to refresh didn't work as a quick remedy. Lack of funds was not entirely the truth for staying in instead of meeting old friends at the bars. A credit card could have served the night. The

AN AMERICAN MESSIAH

anxiety and uneasy feelings I was experiencing where the real culprits keeping me from going out. It's difficult to explain what was transpiring. I was attempting to rest myself, but I became more and more strung out as the minutes and hours pasted. There was constant activity in the House, making it more difficult to gain piece of mind. I had mentioned this instability to no one, keeping everyone in the dark. Now the minor changes I had noted began rushing and flooding. This was like no other experience I had ever encountered. At this point any kind of relaxation was a chore.

This night will never be forgotten. The band of brothers from the bars arrived to the house late and in a disruptive manor. They were loud, unruly and unpredictable but after some time they found their way to the room next door to mine. This room belonged to our former Alpha, President, Andy leading them to his space. He had obviously joined the bar hoppers. His area consisted of two rooms and was now becoming the place the graduated brothers crashed for the night. Having this crew on the other side of the plaster made the unrest more difficult to manage, only if it where manageable at all.

They made the goofy noises and loud comments for a few irritating hours. Some appeared to be sent in my direction. As I snubbed their party invitation earlier they sounded as if they wanted to keep the good time (that I had missed) going. This all seemed at my expense. And if that was not enough to deepen the paranoia, there was another bunch at a lower level of the house. They wanted everyone in the house to know they where going to keep the all day party going into the next day. They seemed to be playing video games and partying by the groaning disturbances of failed attempts at the games. The music they played was at a lower decibel to keep conversation around them continuous.

This group seemed to be made up of brothers in my pledge class and others living in the house at that age, but to guess anyone as definitely being there is something I can't do. The two gatherings developed a strange question. Go and see what was going on around Chi Phi or try and keep my struggling self together in my room? With my present condition taking first priority I decided to weather the storm in my room. I didn't want to appear as wired and high strung as I was. I anticipated the sun rolling over the mountains of 'Happy Valley' the next day. Hopefully to awake me from this, now, haunting nightmare.

As the night continued I felt trapped in my room. There was genuine fear that someone could actually come to my door wondering why I didn't party as I usually would. A representative could have come from either party. I knew the people in the next room could hear me in my rickety loft. They sent a comment or so as I moved around. I registered some comments when I changed the sheets on my bed as I found them irritating.

The logic for changing my sheets was simple. There was someone, other than myself whom I did not know, laying in my bed earlier in the day. It was possible he may have left or dropped a few tabs of acid or something in my bed accidentally and I chose to eliminate that chance. I had had my first experience with a tab a few weeks earlier and the feel was not far from that. The problem with the theory was both the dull and ecstatic drain was different from acid. After exchanging the linens the time remained long and annoying. My logic began to falter as I felt the gathering on the other side of the wall was looking into my room throw the light fixture, late that night. Several digits of the clock changed before I removed the bulbs.

I was doing anything to put my mind at ease. The problem: Nothing worked. Logic and reality began slipping in an attempt to desperately solve the dilemma or possibly a bi-product of the present condition. The paranoia continued with no breaks. After several hours, I could see the darkness of night being beaten away by the sun. This was the first relaxing or calming event linked to my ordeal. As morning broke most brothers began to finally give in to the end of the All Day Party. There was some clambering and noise, but for the most part activity was at a stand still. The next round of business would be the pledges coming out to clean the house. Though things quieted down I was still on edge. I can recall looking at myself for the first time that morning. I couldn't look myself in the face. I know something was very wrong, but I had no one or no way to alleviate any anxiety. I sensed the unrest was on the left side. When I say left I mean left side head to toe. My movements where natural but my thought process was bent or tangled or skewed, which ever helps one understand?

The morning gave me new hope. This hope would be extinguished with some passing. I held fast in the room hoping for some change. It seemed to be a nice day, present condition excluded. I originated my game plan through the long difficult night when I chose to stay in. "To tough it out and not show panic would get you out of this mess" I said to myself. Nothing really was wrong with me in anyone else's mind. It wasn't hurting them not to know.

What I did in my room that morning is a blur. I more than likely spent most of my time in my bed, while other moments checking if the look in my eyes would tip someone off. Personally, I could see a change in the tilt or position in my stare. I'd have them call my bluff.

I needed to act as I normally would on any given day. This would be a major task, because one has many different relationships and act differently with each one. I always used a little humor, but I could rule that out at the risk of sounding strange or not funny and getting into an exchange. I would stick to small factual talk, cut and dry. I was anticipating my first encounter, to use as a barometer of how functional I was. Weather I was ready or not my tests where fast approaching.

CHAPTER 2

As mentioned previously, many seniors spend there final year living out of the fraternity. I also elected to be one of those upper classman. With three weeks left in the semester, I had to give the final performance hopefully none of the brothers would remember, before I moved into an apartment next fall. I hoped they would buy my statues quo act. Things would be quiet with finals in two weeks. I had more than my finals to pass. First I had to get through this morning, followed by the final three weeks of this semester, then final exams and another hurdle summer break (back in Rhode Island) with out raising any red flags. My performance would be done without a net or support group. It was not that I didn't want any help; it was the fact I didn't know how to ask or explain what was happening.

The first face-to-face encounter came some time in the early afternoon. Two of my pledge brothers Roger and Tommy swung by my room to see if I wanted to take the walk to get some subs. This was a perfect first test. Two brothers I'd pledged with. You get to know your pledge brothers better than the majority of the others. The fact is you share the awful and ridiculous experience of pledging. I believe Tommy would be another close brother graduating this semester. I accepted the offer willingly. I felt the sooner I had interaction the quicker I could try to assimilate. I hoped for no questions.

The walk was a good first step. I didn't have to look them straight in the face on the journey. The distance was about half a mile each way, which is short distance for a Penn State student. Nothing came from the ordering or selecting of what to eat. We made it there and back with nothing I can recall and nothing mentioned. I can only remember Roger and Tommy coming to my door and then eating in my room. I truly have a blank for the walk and ordering, but I do recall the bookend events. Then again it wasn't my memory in crisis it was disassociation with myself.

The strange thing is they didn't notice any thing was wrong, though I did. While there was unease and angst in me, they ate and I ate with them. There are not many communal activities like eating and that's what I recall the most and it was something that stuck with me. The first task was a success. The whole event may have taken my mind off the ailment and in all fairness that's what I wanted nothing memorable.

Nothing came in very eventful for the final three weeks. I had some nights that where long and full of unease, but as it goes, "…the sun will come up tomorrow…" Days were also long. I had some trouble with focusing on my studies. The good news was my finals only numbered two. I must confess, as an Art major I never had more than two finals any semester my entire way through Penn State. For me semesters endings where filled with portfolio reviews and this semester would carry a review. They exhaust a lot of time in redoing projects. I would do them when I had the time. I didn't have a lot to redo, so I would get my portfolio in without delay.

Both finals were awful in my mind: philosophy and Italian. In addition I had to work on a paper for Commentary on Art. The paper would encompass three pages while focusing on one of my own personal works'. I had a Jim Morrison poster I constructed from colored paper. I used Andy Warhols' silk screens of icons as a comparative style. The three pages where easy to finish by its deadline and drop off. The finals on the other hand were two jumbled messes, to me any way. I understood some of each of the two still the lot of it was like fishing for answers with no hook.

I'm going to shift gears to acknowledge a professor who was making an impact on me that semester. I elected to take swimming as a PE class, yes swimming. I forget the professors' name, more importantly from day one he was off the beaten path. It was common for him to begin the class by reading a quote, a song, or a story. The class started at 9 am and if you are keeping track the semester started in January. For me it was not difficult to get to the indoor pool in the frigged winter months, rather I failed to make the last two classes. I missed them both due to my state at the end of this semester.

Back to the professor who was at one time an Olympiad from the University of Michigan, so I recall. He was tall, lean and marked with tattoos. He taught from his experiences and knowledge of how the swimming motions where done properly. The class learned the four competitive strokes; the butterfly, the backstroke, the breaststroke, and the freestyle. Do to his approach, I found myself giving more than I had expected. How often do you honestly come across an athlete at such a level he is finding different ways to compete and influence others? This is one of the gifts that made my Penn State experience something I'll always miss.

I still had a year and three weeks to fill my credits at PSU. This was my senior year, but it was going to take me another year to graduate. They call this extra time a super senior year. Most important was to get by philosophy and Italian in this last three weeks. I had flash cards I used for Italian. I could never get them down. I can now wonder if my lack of comprehension was linked to the change I was now ailing from. I had special trouble with philosophy as well. In my defense most of our class struggled with philosophy. The professor acknowledged this after each test when putting it to a curve. He tried to make the tests easier by giving nine or so questions to be studied. He would then take four or five for the exam questions. The nine questions would create the next study group and meeting with Shannon and two others. The next obstacle was then put into place. This would be a sharing, learning, and studying environment to challenge my psyche.

We scheduled this final time at Shannon's apartment. Usually four of us would meet but I don't recall the other two showing up. I remember just us two going through the questions we had finished before hand. I could tell she had no idea there was anything affecting me. She was talking a lot as she usually did. When we got to the questions we shared what we had. I don't recall any heavy question we where stuck on. It was more of a friendly get together at the end of the semester. I'll remind you that Shannon would be graduating this semester and had caught the excitement.

Through all the information in that philosophy class that semester, or for that round of testing one philosopher captured my attention. The philosophers name was Nitzia. Reading his book was like eating soup with a knife. Though when the professor of the class broke him down he explained him from this angle, which I took as personal philosophy and I will explain as best I can.

Nitzia was portrayed as a small and tortured man, but could see the goodness in men. He could also recognize the bad and evil in man. I recall his belief this way. The man that was good was divine or an Adonis and when made to be bad or evil was even more evil and or bad than the person with evil or bad at heart. This is how order was established. Of all the philosophers, I believe in his theory. I hope I explained it well enough using word of mouth. This will save you the reading of his inch and a half thick book. The first time I heard or saw Nitzia I had a sense I would like or enjoy him. At that time I theorized perhaps I had succumbed to the affliction that had tortured Nitzia and having my good tested.

I began to associate with someone known as tortured, and I had begun making a mental list of things that could explain my ailment. I stumbled to the word 'broken'. The way an animal is broken or a man under severe direst. That long night felt like something was slowly robed or stolen. Pulled away while I was aware of every second. I felt broken: I was exhausted mentally, emotionally, and physically. I was exhausted and couldn't rest or sleep. I can recall the weeks and days leading up to that night. Answering questions to myself, which I had always done. For example: leading up to that never ending day, I would answer the question: "Insanity?" … 'Inner sanity?' I felt one would be sane on the inside and shouldn't be something to worry about.

Beforehand, I tried making it part of my maturation process in growing into an older male. Leading up to that night I had been monitoring my feelings, emotions, and what I believed to be growth. There was a consistent warmth or activity in the back of my neck which then occupied the majority of my back. It was a good and positive feeling I recall thinking to myself, "I feel like I'm 10 feet tall." I felt if this were a physical stage of development there would have to be someone else going through, or finishing this phase. One way I tried to do this was by looking at others to see if they had been through the same experience and maybe they would be helpful in getting through this if they could notice any symptoms. It didn't take long before I gave up this search. I didn't find others that lent themselves as comforting or remotely experiencing the same stage of life.

Looking back on the past few days before that late April night I wondering when exactly did this change begin to happen? There where things dating back before I even left for Penn State. I recall a vision or a dream with me struggling to gain peace in my bedroom because there was too much happening around me. I associated fear with this vision from day one and in my mind it had come to fruition. I felt this was that long night in my bedroom. Was this a glimpse of my future and a controlling event that was a guiding force to that day? This questioned, when did this start?

During that semester, I had something telling me and I would reaffirm, "You're David Garcia". I heard this a few times before I wanted to show who I was. I definitely had become something very different. All I had to do is look at the few football awards I had introduced to my fraternity room. This may have sparked my inner clash. Combining who I had been with who I had become. Looking at myself at that present, I wasn't weight training that spring semester. Something I had been doing religiously since middle school. That had then fallen by the wayside and was replaced with drinking and experimenting with some drugs. Alcohol and drugs where not even in my vocabulary during high school. In fact this semester I introduced my system to acid and mushrooms.

I also was not working for the first time while in school. I had acquired a part time job each of the semesters leading to this one. This is probably when I first stood up and took notice of what was happening. I was out of control and lazy I was always active in some way. Now I was being taken apart. My grades were sinking. At best I hope for a D in Italian, only because Italian was out side the major and the D would get me past the equivalency level as passing for an Art major. I had always struggled with the subject, even dropping it one semester. I needed Italian I through III. I dropped the second level only to retake it. My struggles with this class could trace my stumbling along the past few years.

I did commit myself to more study time and taking pride in myself. Now facing the end of the semester the self-renovation didn't really work. I was facing lots of confusion. Study time was now up and it was time for the real thing. I got my paper out for Commentary on Art easily, half a day, and dropped it off in the right place. Italian is where I needed the best show. In philosophy, I had been getting B's with the curve. In Italian I was a C or D, with little room above. I'm uncertain of the orders I took the exams, but I'll start with the Italian. I recall the exam was in a class I had had Art History classes in. I sat close to the front in the class. I struggled with words I should have known and found the order of word tenses and sentence structures as difficult as never having studied. With that said I believed I did O.K.

Philosophy was gathered in the same room as the class was taken. I sat in the same spot next to Shannon and Charity. Charity also attended our study sessions. I was equipped with the blue book to be passed to the front only to be sent back in a random fashion to deter cheating. Two pencils also accompanied. The exam consisted of a number of questions from the earlier supplied sheet of questions. I did my best with my pre-answered memorized questions. I always felt the professor graded easy because he taught in a high-minded fashion. After filling the blue book as best I could I passed it in to the professors' assistant and my semester had finished. The remainder of this semester also vanished.

Now that I had fulfilled the requirements given by the Pennsylvania State University I could redirect my attention to the people from the smallest state in the union, Rhode Island with specificity to the town of West Warwick. This in large would cover my family and close friends whose eyes I hoped to pass through without being detected as out of the ordinary. The same type of blind eye the brothers never turned to sight. With this lack of vision, I commenced to an out of house brother. I would be sharing a townhouse with Andy, Keefe, and Brad after summer break. First, I had to get past the people that knew me best, the ones from back home.

CHAPTER 3

The distance between State College and West Warwick is roughly 400 miles, eight to ten hours, or two full tanks of gas, but the people at Penn State seemed to range even further from the individuals in Rhode Island than those distances. They would have an enormous amount of trouble picking one another out of a line-up even if they wore name badges. Only a single friend, Mark, from West Warwick visited Penn State and that was during the summer, Arts Fest, not a true depiction of the Happy Valley seen. He had invited me to his school in Maine last summer, so I returned the favor. My parents did come for a Parents Weekend at Chi Phi, making them the most seasoned social lights. They got to meet many brothers at this event. This is the most the crowds' would mix. I had grown to be an Island, no one fully knew me any more.

No matter how great the distance, my friends in West Warwick were ready to invite me back into the fold. This was a good thing considering my present malady. I wasn't going to say anything, just like at PSU. I'd let someone else make the diagnosis of strange behavior. I was looking closely for any hint that someone else had lived through some kind of developmental phase. Maybe it could come from someone out of West Warwick. It's always good to see my good friends Eddy and Wally. If one of them came to me troubled about my behavior, I don't know what I'd do. The excitement of summer was marked with the arrival of college students returning home. This fever gave me the room to settle in with out too much analysis.

My greatest gap to bridge would be the sea of mistrust and miscommunication, which sent my high school sweetheart and myself drifting from one another. The 400 miles had really taken its toll on our relationship. We needed to see one another more than just on school breaks. I was mailing letters before my ordeal, but was getting no response. Michele was graduating this summer, and I received no invite. We were pretty much over before I tried writing letters to keep things going. At the time, I wanted to share some things and she was the one I tried reaching out to. I could see she was trying to severe the relationship by her lack of response. Michele would most likely see something wrong the quickest. She knew me best. Though it became more and more clear I would 'not' have to face her. This summer she would be getting a step ahead going into the real world while I was looking for an internship.

The time to land an internship was dissipating quickly. I had hand delivered my resume to the majority of the Rhode Island graphic design community during spring break. I was now giving callbacks and within the second week of summer I landed one. A small four-man team, The Martin Design Group, would be paying me a modest $6.50 per hour. In 1995, that was pretty good considering I would be making the money as a 40 hour summer job, add on the work experience, and then tack on the lines to fill out the resume. It was good and it became a venue where I could measure myself with new people. I would have to hope a business would weed someone out if something where drastically wrong with an employee.

Two paths with different challenges had begun to unfold. I would have my friends to pick up on misbehavior in one corner, and I would have the task of interacting with professionals for the first time in the other. I looked at the internship as the more difficult spotlight to be in front of. There was the unknown, which could lead into any number of mistakes leading to the compounding of emotional unease. In contrary, I believe my friends had the easier angle to see that I was acting out of character. At the time, I didn't take this much thought about the emotions that where there. To make it short and sweet, I was looking for few mistakes.

From the time I had accepted the internship my summer was going to go through the same motions. It was more important to successfully fulfill my obligation as a graphic designer at any level. Waking up and heading to work would be the trend and the norm. What happened after that would be a test of my judgment and how I wanted to show up for work the next day. Summers in Rhode Island could almost compete with those at Penn State.

The biggest difference between PSU and my home state was the amount of gambling. There was an Indian Reservation, *Foxwoods Casino*, just over the Rhode Island boarder into Connecticut, when one wanted real wagering. When you didn't have the real money to waste you would end up in the basement of my friend Mark's house. He's the one visitor to PSU, for what may be considered the real gambling. Instead of dollars the chips would be quarters, playing any derivative of poker you could come across; guts, baseball, beat the bitch, five-card stud…etc. Throw anything wild in, from two's, to one-eyed jacks and suicide kings, made it difficult to answer where the better gambling was held. When I saw cards at Happy Valley, it was to play a drinking game or to learn a trick.

    I could predict the gambling and drinking would run almost nightly with the internship. If that didn't seem like enough activity you would find us at one of the states nightclubs. Rhode Island has a beautiful coast with bars and clubs in different towns along the waterfront. These where mostly designated for Thursday through Sunday. The beaches are also a treat for a sunbather with days off, which I would not be one of. The one thing making all this inferior to Penn State is the crowds. They are all college age people. When you go out in Rhode Island, you could possibly see some one's parents. At the Pennsylvania State University, you also had less distance to travel for more activities. The huge events Penn State hosts in which little Rhode Island can't compete are the football weekends the University puts on routinely during the fall.

    We had a good group for that summer. On any given night, you could find gathered in Mark's basement card table; Mark, Wally, Ed, Steve, Matt, Andy and myself. Mark was a good host he knew the games. I consider him to be a smart and intelligent guy. That was a major part of why I liked him. He was the only other person I know that went away, out of state, to college and graduated. If there where anyone who may have experienced what I was troubled with, it may just be him. He was bright, but sometimes lacked social grace. I first met him playing Pop Warner football when we where on the Pee Wee squad. His father was the head coach that season, one in which we won the State Championship.

    Wally was also a member of that Pee Wee Championship team. Wally and Mark also were part of two other football Championship teams in high school. The Pee Wee team wasn't the only place we congregated. Walter and I were classmates in fifth grade. Aside from football and school, Walter was also on the same baseball teams as I, twice. Wally is one of my very best friends. He would be one of the first to let me know if he saw something wrong. I've been close with Wally for a long while.

I may have been around Wally in several different circles, but I grew up with my friend Ed. He lived down the street, but just far enough down the street that at a younger age we seldom crossed paths. It's hard to say when I met Ed. I don't recall if we became old enough to explore the other end of the street or we met in the same fifth grade class with Wally in it. The girls like Ed. I guess he is a pretty good-looking guy. It's what the girls seem to have thought very early in my dealings with Ed. He is unique in the fact I've had little to do with him in athletics. To his credit he was smart enough to play through the second Championship football season in High School. That was the only time we where on the same squad for as full season. I've done a lot of bullshitting with him through the years. Ed would also question any odd behavior if detected.

Steve, I have no clue when we met. He went to a private school through high school. From what I know of him he was a good pitcher and had a scholarship to a Florida College, but at this point was attending the University of Rhode Island. He was at the table to play cards. He had little if any chance of confronting me in any way. I didn't know him well and to me he was in that seat to play cards.

Last but not least, I have two brothers and you couldn't ask for two more different family members. The thing they had in common is they where there to play cards. Matt was the older of the two leaving Andy the younger. Matt was out spoken and Andy said little. My brother coached them in wrestling. Something they where involved in for a long time. I really don't know if I would have known them with out the gambling element. They where nice enough, I had an easy road past them.

On any given night, you could find another basement gambler. People you wouldn't find at the table where the designers at my internship. Swinging the pendulum to the day job, I was about to meet the employees at my summer internship. I can remember the first morning well. When I came in Phil, the owner of the studio, was elbows deep into the color printer. He was back and forth searching for the correct formula to get the printer going. After some time Phil, remedied the problem and then introduced me to his three employees. I remember the name of one of them for sure and that was also Phil, who I will call Philip to separate the two. The two remaining names I recall being Paul and Kevin, but couldn't be held to that at this point and time.

It was a blue jean outfit, which suited my style. I found my role for that summer quickly. I wasn't there more than an hour before I was on a run for coffee and other beverages. I'd also be dropping off work at spots around the state. I was fine with the duties. I was the low man on the pole. I just wondered if I would get any actual design work? After a day or two, Phil passed some comp work to put together. A comp is an unfinished piece at its most current stage. They were as easy as taping seams together and it made me feel somewhat productive. I was given some small jobs at first and then building. My summer was being mostly occupied in this scenario.

The only other place to find me would be at home, though I mostly only slept and ate there. I lived with my parents as well as an older brother and younger sister. They had a chance of noticing something out of the norm, but I didn't feel I spent enough time with them that they could question me. My father, Joe, worked two jobs to put me through college. During the day, he worked at a "mom and pop" electrical appliance shop as the stores manager. Nights, weekends, or any other free time he found was dedicated to working as a Realtor. He's also good with his hands. My mother, Adele, has been working for a large bank for more years than I can remember. The woman is very family oriented and is an excellent cook. At the time my older brother, Mark, was teaching and studying for his Masters in History at Rhode Island College. If you took a poll of the people that know him they would say he was a bit hyper and loved to talk. My younger sister, Lisa, was working at a department store and attending the University of Rhode Island while carrying around the challenge of a hearing aid her entire life. She was pursuing a degree in Psychology. She's a sweetheart and a very caring person.

My family, my friends and the designers at my internship all would fall short of seeing anything peculiar in me. Although, I still had to deal with it. As time went on the feelings of discomfort became more tolerable. I'll explain it as a squeaky wheel that as you hear it for the first time your startled, but once you've heard it and grow to know it it's not as bad. I gave no one any hint to a problem, but the problem was there.

While at my internship, between the runs for summer drinks, preparing comps, and dropping off work and packages I had lots of free time. I'm not sure when and how it started, but my mind began creating a scenario where there where drugs in some of the deliveries I was making. I guess this began by being the odd man out and wanting to be in the inner circle. If I where doing the job and prepared to hear my role, maybe I would be able to take this into working there after college. That's what I was doing preparing myself for what could be. My entire time there I never witnessed a single narcotic. This all played out in my mind. Although no one could, as of yet, see something wrong me my reality had begun to slip again.

This mental story ended up with me believing if I kept pursuing this line of play my car would end up sabotaged in some way. This was toward the end of the summer. I asked for the internship to end two weeks early so I could enjoy part of the summer. That was it. I put myself at ease and got ready for the up and coming semester.

I attended a Party at my friend Mark's after I left the internship. I got to see my friends there before I left. It was the usual good time we have together. Some would be missed more than others, but it was a nice finally to the summer.

I was anticipating the next stay at Penn State. I was headed into my Super Senior year, which meant I was taking an extra year. I knew the system well by now, better than most of the students. I looked forward to this up and coming year.

CHAPTER 4

When I arrived back in State College, at our townhouse, Keefe was already getting moved in. Keefe had been my Epsilon, pledge educator, a position I would hold a couple of pledge classes later. He had also been an Alpha for the house, or president. I met him warmly. I had the best bond with him out of the three. Brad and Andy would show up later, but exactly when I'm not sure. We where entering into our Super-senior years, we all had that in common. The three of my housemates where knit tighter than I was to any of them. For one they where all from New Jersey, and second they had pledged together. There was also the false impression that I was the youngest having pledged later then they had. If I had gone directly to the University Park Campus, I would have been in their pledge class.

Truth is, I started my Penn State experience at a branch campus, Behrend in Erie, Pennsylvania. I ended up in Erie because Penn State gave me only that avenue into the school. I was coming from a small state and being seventeen I didn't judge the time and distance from Erie to Happy Valley. I thought of it as a school of study, such as the School of Architecture or School of Engineering. I also believed I would be able to pursue the Nittiny Lions Football team from Behrend. I would later find out the distance was too great to try out for the football team. I spent one year in Erie, that one year, I find led to my Super-senior year at University Park, which was my forth year at State College, but fifth in the PSU system.

With three years in State College, I was ready to tackle my final year of school. The classes I recall being registered for that semester where English, Theatre, and Graphic Design, one other escapes my mind. The most important of the classes was the graphic design class, labeled Time and Sequence. A professor with a reputation as being difficult and opinionated conducted the class. This would be a new challenge. Lanny had been in a *History of Graphic Design* book and published in a host of magazines. I viewed him as the most successful person I would have an acquaintance with. While in class, I would try to pay attention with double effort. When this approach was used combined with my unsteady mindset, I left class at the end with headaches. These were not you're regular headaches, these where throbbing, splitting headaches. Intense headaches where when looking into a mirror I perceived the image looked distorted. These came about almost every class. I was still following the idea this was part of my development into an older person.

It would take time alone in my room for the aches to pass. My room was the smallest of the four. I got last draw for joining last. My room was tiny in comparison to the others and close to one of the very small outside walk through rooms one gets in his first semester at the Fraternity. I did do all my studying in there be it the very little I did that semester. Other than sleeping and the other mentioned activities, I spent almost no time in the box. I spent all my time in the living room playing video games with my housemates.

The game of choice was EA Sports Hockey. I was always competitive and video games came no different. I always select my hometown Boston Bruins. The other combatants would select a team the computer gave an edge to because they were a superior team in reality. I did well in the competitions, but I had staked some belief I was losing because my housemates would mentally manipulate the chip to their favor. This seemed like something that was done on a psychological level and not openly. This gave me stronger belief that I was developing and could unlock a higher level of intelligence.

Another spot I was attempting to unlock a higher logic was my Theater class. This was interesting from day one. On the first day of class I took an isle seat. As class was waiting to begin, a hostile male came down the isle and started with, "My girlfriend...this, you and my girlfriend ...that...!" He then proceeded to attack him. This took place two seats from me, so I began to get up to break it up. As I did, they both ran from the auditorium. The professor, an old woman, then took command of the class and made it clear that had been an act of theater not violence. She polled the audience to see how many students it fooled. I was one of many. The class was filled with roughly 300 students. 70-80% were fooled.

AN AMERICAN MESSIAH

One rainy day after an early semester Theatre class I had an interview as a waiter at Spats Speak Easy Café restaurant. The food was Cajun. I met with an Uncle Dave for the first portion of the interview. After I filled out the application, I was introduced to a man, Duke for further questions. I got the job that day. I would start as a busboy and work into the waiters' role. After the semester off from work, I knew how much a job helps to support a student. If one lives just off saved summer money, toward the end of the second semester one begins to run out of cash. This would be another stage for me to test my bounds or my perceived growth. It felt good to land a job and lift that burden.

To add the final venue of my maturation struggle, English fills the slot. This English class was orientated for business majors. Being an art major, I had my choice of four English classes, so I scheduled what I considered to be the easiest. The syllabus curriculum listed such things as a cover letter and resume, a short persuasive paper, and a group project.

Before I get to involved, I'd like to share a personal belief. "If it doesn't kill you it only makes you stronger." This is the approach I took when I had those headaches and the unease up and down my left side. I was in this for the long hall, with a craving to know what was the cause of my malady. I also didn't want to appear week by mentioning it, certainly if it where only a growing phase. Again, no one had said anything as of yet. I had begun to cope with the whole thing internally.

Returning to the house where I was living with Keefe, Andy, and Brad. I used the living room when I could, because my room was small. Though I found myself lying on my bed raising my left arm up and down analyzing my left hand. At the end of my sophomore year in high school, my left hand, specifically the ring and middle fingers tips, were shaven to the bone in a lawn mower accident.

What had happened was: I was changing the height of the wheels on the mar. I was facing the lawn mar when I reached across the top on the machine. I then placed my hand on the four to five inch side that extends to the lawn to pull the mar upward on a tilt. The way one pushes a box at the top to tip it on its side. I was successful at changing the height of the wheel, feeling none of the blade cutting through my tips. My fingers must have just snuck under the side. I first recognized the injury after getting behind the lawn mower. I thought I felt my hand was sweating profusely and was startled to see the wounds.

    Raising my arm back and forth years later. Back and forth – at the time to repair the damage the doctor stitched (grafted) the two severed tips into the left palm. He did this to grow new fingertips from the palm, so my fingertips would then be from my palm. I had to go under the knife twice for this operation, once to stitch the tips to the palm and again to take the fingers and their new tips from the palm. This was delicate work, so I must have been out pretty deep. The question I was developing was what exactly goes on in your mind when I was out? Could this be a lagging side effect from this operation? I thought for a long while moving my arm around, sometimes gliding, sometimes mechanically. What happens when you're knocked out for hours? Only because I had never heard of a side effect coming from being put under for an operation, did I dismiss it as a cause. Strengthening my belief that it was part of maturation to an adult.

    After attending Theatre for a week or so, I could see how the class would be conducted. The senior theatre majors would act out plays. They did a good job of it. They would act out a scene or two for the audience of over 300 students from the readings of the class. This was so nice in the middle of the day to have a play to enjoy that I assumed, in my mind, the role of a critic. I also never bought a book for the class. Feeling if I paid close enough attention to the plays I'd get by. I truly was judging the actors more than focusing in on the class, but that's what I was choosing to do as my change in behavior was continuing.

    When walking around campus I had something asking for my last judgment going into the year 2000, which was 4 years away. My answer came out quickly. "There is a system of government where anyone has the opportunity to become a leader." This happened quickly almost like it was a reaction. I had no doom and gloom in my judgment, but hope for any one who wanted to per sew a political career. I was alluding to the United States government. I'll always remember this, but I had to return to thinking about school.

    Choosing to integrate graphic design concept to the English classroom was something I pursued. My true and final resume would end up in design form. The professor understood, but wanted the business format to show I understood the concept. I also understood and would give in. A cover letter would accompany the resume. For this class I did purchase the book.

A class that did not require a book was my time and space graphic design class. Although, I got a headache for almost each class, there was a lot of time outside the class. This needed attention. I recall on one project I was to come up with a poster. I did the work up at the studio one night. Each senior was given a cube with a nice little desk. As I was putting the concept together I received a question or command from a higher power. "Take me to your leader!"

I had answered questions like these my whole life. When I was in my teens, I used to get questions on how to get rid of the national deficit among others. I went right to work on this mental exercise. As I worked on my poster for class, I came up with a way to borrow time. I never took time to think about it until then, but what I did was take the greatest basketball champion, who is known all over the globe, Michael Jordan, face to face with Bill Clinton. The poster was to look like a boxing tail of the tape. I was never enamored with Bill Clinton and needed someone else that could be thought of as a leader… a leader by example, Michael Jordan. I'm one who believes the athlete makes the best man. I feel they are slighted mentally because of their physical dominants.

It had to be my distain for Bill Clinton that asked for my leader. The poster I was really working on for class was a political statement on Bill. The assignment was to create a poster with slogan "Save the…something" My posters slogan was "Save the Government." I put the capitol building on the center of a mock protest poster. I had "Save the" along the top of the poster and the word "Government" with the Capital pointing downward at the "Government". The capital building was used as a barometer, pointing down when there is time of political doubt. This was pre-Monica, though I still perceived Mr. Clinton as a weak leader.

Putting that aside. I still had my job at the Speak Easy Restaurant. I began working my way into the waiters' position little by little. I always found the menu difficult to remember and the different combinations even more difficult. A new computer ordering system made for more confusion. With this you'll have to remember Duke.

DAVID MICHAEL

He was the boss of the kitchen and maybe the owner of the restaurant. So I came up with a mental game, hoping others would receive it. I would send the message "Duke has it on me". In other words, Duke knows a way to keep me down or keep me humble. I was beginning to believe this mental connectivity worked.

I also found myself slipping into another 'game'. I found myself routinely saying, "I believe so" to the costumers as they ordered. Was I showing my belief system and more specifically my belief in Jesus Christ? I was now processing information internally and did contemplate my belief every time I said, "I believe". This was, in my mind, another way to a higher maturity.

Along with the new computer Uncle Dave and Duke brought in a new waitress and waiter. I was unhappy, so I took the opportunity to use the new people to throw rocks at the establishment. I would tell them how mismanaged they where. I was not getting many hours mostly weekends, but I did get weekend days. They were busy on football weekends, but not enough to make money to live on. I had already begun to dip into some of my summer money.

Where I was living was a different story. With work, classes, and projects I really didn't see them much, equally with all the activities they also had. We did have chances to hang out, but not like at the beginning of the semester. We still played the hokey video game on occasion and I swear they had gained the ability to manipulate the computer chip, but part of me knew some of the players and teams in the game where better than the rest. I still went with the Bruins. The only thing that was out of the norm, was when we hung out I gave up smoking marijuana. It was difficult to quit, but I started in the summer. I stop smoking to eliminate something that may be causing the effect. I tried to feel normal, but I was always indifferent and uneasy.

When there wasn't anyone around at the townhouse, I tried something to make myself feel better or right. One football Saturday when I was alone in the house, I brought out an old high school football tape. No one was home so I could view the tape without interruption or comment. This was the first time I did this in this house. I was hoping the look back would help. Instead, I received shivering and trembling, as if I was going through withdrawal. I didn't finish the tape and I think that's a good thing. This was another strange new feeling I didn't want.

There became a time where living in this house with Andy, Brad, and Keefe just wasn't worth my money. I was staying in a room the size of some closets. I also would enjoy more privacy, being forced into the living room at almost all times. My mind was also being filled with classes and work. It's at this point I decided to move out to live on my own. This decision held little to nothing against my three roommates. I needed more space and guaranteed time to myself.

It didn't take long to find an apartment of my own. After checking a few Real Estate companies for rentals, I found an off campus apartment in the Collegiate, the Penn State student paper. I found it in Bellefonte, a small town ten miles off the University Park Campus. It had two rooms, a living room and bedroom. The kitchen was open to the living room. It also had a garage. The apartment was around the same price as "my hole in the wall". It was unfurnished, but I know I could get furniture from the Fraternity. The only thing I would have to do would be finding some one to replace me in the townhouse. I didn't think it would be that difficult.

Later that autumn, I found myself seated in theatre class waiting for the usual performance in front of the 300 plus students attending class. Before the start of the class, the professor strangely acknowledged the game I was playing. It wasn't done verbally in front of the audience, but on a nonverbal level as she went through the daily schedule for the class. This is the level I was trying to break through to, mental connectivity and messaging. She was telling me I was failing the class. It was a definite possibility. I didn't use the book and didn't even have one to follow with. It made me think all I was using was the Nittiny Notes. Nittiny Notes are notes for a class one can purchase for a particular class for extra help if you wanted it. Nittiny Notes buys the notes from Honor Students, and then copied them onto red paper so as not to be copied again, and then sell them. The big break was the fact someone had given me a direct mental message. I never checked my grades for the class, so it was possible I was failing without knowing and needed a heads up. I had never failed a class at any level of schooling. I didn't really care; I wanted to see the whole thing acted out to the end. I did have questions if I was not making the grade, but an old woman broke through to me. Her age is important due to the fact she had to have seen and learned many tricks through her experiences. Remember, I felt I was maturing and to have an older professor affirm what I was working on was big. This raised my confidence that I was going in the right direction. If there are people who know the games people play they are the older people.

I wasn't even close to dropping the class, though I had drop credits left. There is the chance I could actually pass the class. As far along as I was in my Major, there wasn't time to drop classes. I planned to have just one class next semester and it was Lanny's class, a design class. I believe the headaches where coming from attempts to mentally connect with him, but being denied the whole time.

Lanny's class became a headache. He was one of the most challenging people, I had known, to read. I respected his stature in the design community. He wasn't as bad as people made him out to be. He seemed more fun loving if you paid close enough attention. I did pay close attention and was taking his class next semester in an attempt to get his reference. I also wanted the magazine each student would create in next semester's class. An example of how Lanny was fun loving is the softball game he put on every year. It matched the juniors against the seniors. He was tough in the classroom, but I could see it was in an effort to get more from his students. I could give project after project, which was put together through the semester, but they wouldn't be linked in the direction I'm now traveling. All I can say is more times than not, I would have a splitting headache.

As the Thanksgiving Holiday approached, it marked the end of the semester. After the brief interruption, there would only be two weeks remaining in the semester. Like most students, I'd be making the journey home to see friends and family. My Hyundai Excel would take me back to West Warwick. I had only one final exam to worry about, and it could determine whether I pass or fail Theatre. I think Lanny had given us a project to work on over the break, but nothing too difficult. My English class also had started a group project to be finished with the remaining days of the semester. Finally, the restaurant I worked for was giving me the time for Thanksgiving because I lived so far from State College. I also had begun wrapping things up for the end of the semester. Keefe, Brad, and Andy found a roommate to replace me. A Brothers cousin needed some place to live for that semester, so I was out of that with no problem.

My trek home was uneventful, almost routine. I spent my time at home, but had the Holiday at my aunt and uncles' house, which was customary for my Thanksgiving dinner. It went off with nothing out of the ordinary. Dinner followed by football. My friends made business like appearances, with nothing long lasting to speak of. In fact, I left on Saturday evening to get back early.

Things became interesting when I started my voyage back to Happy Valley. I got as far as a half hour into Connecticut when my Hyundai broke down. The car had problems with the alternator the entire time I owned it. I was going over a bridge and had to coast down it until the car stopped by an exit ramp. When I opened the hood, oil was spilling from all over. This was most likely a different problem than the alternator. On foot, I made it to a bowling alley where I called home for help. After not to long my father arrived and not to far after a police officer cruised in. The officer called in a tow truck. This left me wondering, 'was this the break down I feared while working as a intern?' A foreshadowing of what was to come.

After the car was towed away the officer took use back to my fathers car. We drove back to West Warwick temporarily solving the problem. We determined the Hyundai was non salvageable and left for dead. Next, we needed to commander my brothers' car, a Mitsubishi Precise. This was a same look and make as the Hyundai just made by Mitsubishi. It had no history of problems and after we met with him it would be the car I would take back to State College for the final two weeks.

The next day I left and this time made it back without a hitch. My roommates wondered what happened to the Hyundai and of course I gave the story of the car boiling over and taking my brothers car for the return trip. When I think about it the Hyundai could have left me some place deep in the hills and mountains of Pennsylvania miles and miles from anything. I felt lucky.

Now that I had made it safely I could refocus on the remaining two weeks on school. I had to get my English project done, Lannys' task completed, purchase the Nittiny Notes for Theatre and get to work at the New Orleans style restaurant. I walked to all of these places, but one of those days I was driving in my brothers' car and I got in an accident. All I did was dent in the driver side fender. I was in the right lane and a car attempted to turn right from the center lane, when I saw his blinker pointing left. The other car and I went our separate ways with out reporting the accident. What I did to remedy the problem was go to a body shop and ordered a left fender painted silver, same as the car, which I would put on later.

Again, I only had one final exam. The projects here closed up in a quick fashion leaving time to work if needed or study for the Theatre final. When the final came around I felt good and prepared. When I got to the finals I developed the worst case of the hiccups. I went through a good amount of the test before I asked for a drink. I was granted this wish under supervision. The upper class actors patrolled the test sight. When I was finished, I felt relieved. No more guessing if I where failing or not, I would get my report card in a few short weeks.

I would be making the trip back to Rhode Island shortly. I had to do all my packing because I wasn't coming back to this residence. Once I was packed and ready I said goodbye to everyone in the house. It had snowed from the time I arrived and finals took place, so driving was a little slow. I had to drive home with the fender in the car, because of the cold I didn't get it on. When I got home, I'd tell my brother what had happened

When I returned home the first thing I did was fill my brother Mark in on what had happened to his car. The next thing I did was put the new fender on. Again, I was taken in with no questioning of what I was or what I was doing. The thing that needed to be addressed was finding me a vehicle. We, my parents and I, decided buying a new car should work best. My father knew someone at a dealership, so I went to him. We had picked out a Pontiac Sun Fire from the paper. The next morning I went to see my fathers' friend and I test-drove a black Sun Fire. When my father got home that night I told him how much I liked it. He said the next morning we would go to buy it. We needed to put it on his credit. I had not yet established any and my job was not able to support the car and myself on paper. I realized then I would need to find a second job to take care of the monthly payments. I'd have time with only one class. The next day we went to the dealership and got the car. My parents put down the down payment and told me it would be a birthday, May 6th, and graduation gift. I drove it around for several days to break it in before it would stretch its legs to Pennsylvania.

After a few weeks went by I received my report card in the mail. I opened it a little while after I received it. I was on eggshells to see the results. Just as my Theatre professor was trying to get to me, I had failed the class. This strengthened my belief I was mentally developing on a new plane, but it put me into a spot. After this car, how could I tell my parents I had failed a class and how would I find a class to replace this one. I had failed Theatre. The first class I had ever failed and so close to graduation.

CHAPTER 5

I returned to Penn State with the secret of failing Theatre and thought I had a way out of the mess. I would a) see if I could get the professor to change the grade and b) sign up for a class Penn State offered through the mail, called Correspondence classes. These classes are generally for students who wanted to take classes from different parts of the country or globe, usually over a summer. The classes average around $500.00. Remember I was only taking Lanny's class to get a reference not for credits.

I stumbled across these classes when I looked into taking some summer classes. At the time I didn't take a class, but now the knowledge was an ace in the hole. Now I was working the system.

I arrived in Bellefonte early. I made it to the Fraternity House in a U-Haul truck for some furniture before the house had anyone in it. I took only the furniture that was mine while I was in the house and oddly enough it was in the basement where I could get at it easily. I loaded up and took everything back to my new home. It took a night and a day to get everything placed properly.

The one important thing I was able to take care of, in the first few days, was applying for a job at the MBNA call center - a large bank about ten miles away from campus. I got a job at MBNA and would be working nights 9-12pm. The night shift would be calling the west coast in an attempt to sign individuals up for credit cards. Traveling the 20 or so miles would be easy in my new vehicle. I did have to dress with pants, shirt and tie. I'd needed to shop for theses items. Although I had a new job I was also working at the restaurant. I would be working day hours there.

Once classes started I was the first one to get to the theatre professors office hours. I was hoping what I had in mind would work. I had already sat in on one of the graphic design classes. I went to her to see if she would change my grade. She told me she had never changed a single grade in all her years and she wasn't going to now. I had to except her rationale. I really had no case for her to change the grade other than she was keeping me from graduating and even this wasn't the truth. I would be left with option b).

I already grabbed a Correspondence book before meeting with her. I had also chosen a few classes from the book. The class I had to take was Music, because I was an Art major looking for an art class outside of art, just as theatre was. In this class I would be learning the musical notes and now they where placed on the bar. To do this I would have to drop Lanny's class, which I was taking for one credit. Then I would have Penn State move the money from the graphic design class over to the three credits of Music. The Correspondence classes where all significantly lower in price and my main reason for selecting a class from it. The one credit at Penn State made up just enough to pay for the required three credits of music. Basically I needed to get three credits from the price of one. I knew nothing about musical notes, except I needed it to graduate and to hide the fact I had failed a class.

At some point and at some time my fathers' calls had become annoying. I started to feel his happiness was too dependent upon mine. I'd even begun to think he might just die if he wasn't the only one I was speaking with back home. Further my condition started to put belief he may actually be dieing. I never said anything in any of our conversations, but I never actually watched or witnessed anyone passing away. I also grew to think this could be something slowing my development or maybe it would speed things up.

Going back to MBNA America, I started my training as soon as they got a group to be trained. Basically one sits in front of a computer with a high-speed dial-up headset-calling people to see if they would be interested in getting a credit card that was specific to them. The cards being peddled usually had a photo on the front attached to the college the person being called went to, with some proceeds going to the alumni fund with every purchase. I remember the first day being totally fried with the amount of calls going through that headset. I never got very good at the game of peddling cards, but it was a job paying me an hourly wage and that paid for the Sun Fire.

The music class started as soon as I received the book and material. I needed to stay disciplined and on course to finish well before graduation. I recall having 14 lessons to be mailed and two tests I would need to schedule to take at Penn State. In those 14 lessons, 2 where home tests to mail in. The class came with a book and a cassette. I listened to the tape for 5 minutes and put it aside to see if I'd really need it.

What I did is gave myself 2 lessons a week to stay focused and on target to graduate. It was somewhat a scary proposition keeping yourself on the ball with nothing leading you.

I started the day I got the information and within a few days I got the results mailed back. I received B's, which felt good and really built my confidence. If that were all I'd have to do I would have no problem walking across the stage for my diploma.

Revisiting work. My days where now free to waiter at the restaurant, I didn't have a day class to get in the way. Days where slow, it was myself and someone else just about every day. I didn't much like the job and it probably didn't like me. I didn't make more than $35 in tips on any given shift. I still didn't know the menu completely. The only positive that came from the Café was one day a patron caught my eye. She was reading a children's book. Winnie the Pew from what I recall. I was attracted to her intellectually. Maybe it was the book, but something gave me the idea she was smart. She was in my section so I was able to speak with her. When I asked her what she'd have? She spoke in an accent. I hurried to ask where she was from, followed by her name? She spoke again, "Finland and Mira" She went on to tell me, "Mira meant …look." I love an accent. She then went on to order. I served her as well as I could. Before I brought the bill I asked if she would like to go out somewhere. She accepted and she exchanged her phone number.

I contacted her shortly after we met; I believe it was the next day. We talked for a while. I learned she was staying with her brother who was a student. She was here to see some of the states and just returned from a South American country. We decided to meet at an Italian Restaurant on the edge of campus.

When I arrived she was already there. We had a few drinks and a little to eat. We then elected to go to a Blues Café to catch some entertainment. She was impressed with my car and its newness. The Café was less than a mile away. We sat in a booth and talked above the music. I found out she was five years older than me. I quickly changed the topic to Super Bowl XXX taking place the next day. I attempted to teach Mira how to play the game. I used the most basic formations. I think she may have understood, but she had no care to remember any of it.

We had several beers and after some time I asked if she wanted to go back to my place. She found it to be a good idea and was ready. We got back in the car and shared kisses as we made our way to Bellefonte. We had a drink once we made it back to my apartment. The drink was the last one of the night. We maid our way to the bedroom and with no objections Mira spent the night. By the night I meant the early morning. She had to get back to her place or she thought her brother would be upset. I took her to where she was staying early this Super Bowl morning.

The next morning I stayed in bed longer than usual. I had no plans for the Super Bowl. I knew I had an open invitation at the Fraternity, but I really would have to hear it from the Pittsburgh fans weather they where winning or losing. Though it would be nice to see some of the brothers, I hadn't made a visit to the house in some time. I knew they would also have snacks laid out or possibly pizza.

With that I decided to stay in. While watching I had problems focusing in on the game. All I recall from the game was a Dallas interception for a touchdown and the Cowboys ran away with the game. After the game while I was alone I wanted it to be known the feeling coming from my apartment was coming solely from me. I was making a mental statement to who ever cared. I had a good time by myself and I thought it important. Later I called the house to bust the beans of some of the Pittsburgh natives.

The next day I had to be at the restaurant at 11a.m., come back to Bellefonte to do a music lesson and at 9p.m. make the drive across town to the MBNA. Like anything one does as habit or ritual one forms a system. I had started a schedule were I went to work at 11. After work I would do a music lesson or re-due part of my portfolio. If I had time I would run errands: laundry, grocery shopping. I'd then make dinner followed by cleaning of the dishes. I'd then watch TV until it was time to go to work at night. After putting in three hours with the telemarketing employer I would come home for a brief snack while I watched the Tom Snyder Show, which was on late. If you don't know who Tom Snyder is he is an old media personality, he had to be at least in his 60's when I was watching.

AN AMERICAN MESSIAH

I thought I could see him reaching out to me as a newer and younger viewer. Doing this the same way as my theatre teacher had, with out spoken a word, but with mental hint or physical gesture leading to silent communication. He appeared to attempt to speak to me while still conducting his show. I felt I was the only one he was speaking to, but he still played to his audience. It was an easy task for him to pull off. His show started with call in viewers. After asking a question from the caller I viewed him as doing some double fishing, one with the caller and one with me the viewer. He would wait for two answers. An easy one is, "where are you from?" The other "what's the question?" My perception was he would gather information from both the caller on a conscience level and myself on a sub-conscience level. The second part of his show he would entertain a guest.

I was able to watch him carefully. He was an older, successful man on the stage for all to see. It was quite believable for him to have advanced to this level of non-verbal communication. At the same time I did believe I was developing on this level at 22 going on 23. He was at the least entertaining. His language was advantageous and his humor witty and on target.

As days passed, still early in the spring semester, something came along to alter my scheduling. I was placed in font of Uncle Dave and he let me go from the Speak Easy Café. This had an upside and down side from it. On the down side, I would be making a few less bucks a week. On the upside I could dedicate more of my day to the music class and other activities.

The lead to a new morning found me get lunch and allowed me to glance at the paper before I got to music. The same old system followed and in that I was adapting to my Bellefonte stay. With that I've always been a superstitious person. How can one not be, its talking about mysterious super powers. There was one I was using an awful lot at that time and which was wishing on numbers. I don't know where I got it from, but it's pretty simple. What one would do is make a wish whenever you see the numbers, on a digital clock, registering all the same number. For example: 3:33,or 5:55, or 1:11. I was wishing almost every time to get a good job out of college. It was important to me to get off quickly. I was primarily living where I was to get accommodated to living alone, which more than likely I would be doing if I where successful enough at the start. I was attempting to prove I could take care of myself.

Taking care of myself led to something I thought I could see in Bellefonte. I came to the perception this was a town with a religious backbone. With this I would say a mental "Our Fathers", to show I was a Catholic. As part of my habit I did my laundry in town. While doing my laundry I found I did the most "Our Fathers". First because, the mix of people passing through, but also because the boxes of soap. If you look at the boxes of soap they are either a hard orange red and firry or light blue and soft. I saw these as representatives of Heaven and Hell. I was getting this deep into faith without attending church. Though I did consider going at this point of my experience.

Another part of my events would be attending the same watering hole over the weekend. It was a bar over a restaurant giving a view over the street if that was the place you wanted to sit. Me, I liked sitting at the bar drinking pints. I'd also get the attention of the Brothers when they passed through. One weekend I was surprised by who had found there way there. It was Mira. She came to visit me at the bar telling me she didn't have much time left in the States. She then got her brother to introduce us. He seemed nice enough. I don't recall how the rest of the night went bet she stayed mostly with the group she came with and I stayed at the bar. That would be the last time I saw her, a Finish girl named Mira.

Though that relationship ended the days kept coming and with them came March Madness, the collegians basketball tournament. It's a three-week tournament that invites 64 teams, which crowns the nations basketball champion. I was looking passively to connect with someone during the tournament. I haven't really initiated any none verbal communication, I've pretty much gone with the flow and that's what I intended to do in this instance. I did have a favorite team in the brackets, Kentucky. I liked Rick Patino.

When the first week of games started there was still a lot of snow and I recall going for a walk through the snow. It was a deep fluffy powder. When I returned I focused in on some of the early round games. They were mostly blowouts. I noticed I began to focus even more on the host of the Tournament. Pat O'Brien who was hosting a huge live audience, ranging from office pool know it alls, to Senior Forward on any team in the contest, to the casual watcher, to NBA recruit. This was a competitive crowd. As I watched I believe Mr. O'Brien was borrowing or using the laws of nature that would be awakening and blossoming in the weeks to come. I thought I saw black and white spiral spinning wheels along with an occasional clock or coo-coo clock to stun the masses in an attempt to think clearly and focused. I did nothing but observe. The mental wall Pat had build to allow him to focus seemed to work, he came without a hitch. That was the way I saw him through my troubled eyes.

The whole basketball challenge was very entertaining. Although they where a favorite in the tournament, the team I had chosen prevailed. The Kentucky Wild Cats where crowned National Champions. The end of the exhibition marked the change of season. It was now spring and the end of classes grew nearer.

Shortly after I finished my music class. I got through the whole thing with A's and B's, even the scheduled tests. I finished with plenty of time for Penn State to register the B in music. I would now definitely be graduating at the end of this semester. This was a good feeling. The reward of a great deal of work had finally come to fruition.

The only thing I had to work on from this point was my portfolio. The rest of my day had now diminished in activity, leaving time to enjoy the spring. I still had the credit card telemarketing job to deal with. Though one day they came to me, because I was graduating, and asked if I would like to apply for a job within the company. I accepted the offer. One interview would be held on the sight of the MBNA. This fell on my lap. One never knows if graphic design is going to come up with a proposition with the same ease as this or come around with anything to grab onto. I would be going to the interview in mid-April. They gave me a page to study and set up the interview.

I knew I had a suit to look professional to pull this off. I wanted to be prepared so I studied the page I was given. There wasn't much there to look over so I committed it to memory. I recall a beautiful spring day the day of the interview. They had a scheduled gathering of all the people who had come in for the weekend for one reason or the other. I was invited. First I had to go on the interview. When I arrived I met an older man, 50 or older. We sat and talked for a bit. Then he asked what I knew about the position and I came right back with the information on the page I was given. He was impressed. He pushed me through to the next round of interviews.

After meeting with my manager, I found the next round of interviews would be in Maine. There would be two other employees going with me. This time there was no sheet to prepare me, but I did know the job was for a collection agent.

I recall the three of us flew from Philadelphia after one of the two girls drove us from State College to Philly. I don't remember much more than that. The trip there went with out a hitch. I do remember we had some time at the airport in Maine for a beer before we headed on to Belfast. We would be taking a commuter jet, from whatever airport we where at, to Belfast.

This plain was a little more adventurous. The plain seem to hit all the turbulence on the way. I also recall the person behind me making a lot of fuss. In my mind he appeared to want the plain to go down. I found myself trying to mentally connect with the pilot to help keep the plain in the air. The entire trip was a small roller coaster ride, though it never got out of control. It was just an uneasy ride.

When we arrived it was night. We where picked up at the airport by two older people. I'd guess they where in there 60's or better. They took us and dropped us off at our hotel. They gave us the time to be awake for our day of interviews and then left us to relax. I fished around my room for a while and unpacked. There wasn't much to do so I went to sleep early.

The next morning I was up early and got dressed in my suite. I met the two girls in the foyer. I considered them to be my competition and didn't really warm up to them.

That morning we where picked up by a middle aged women. She took us to the MBNA site where our interviews would be conducted. She invited us into the facility and primed us for our first interview.

My first interview was with someone my age or a little older. He was well dressed and had a habit of opening his eye's wide. From this habit I took he was telling me he was a ware wolf. I mimicked him a bit to show I understood. I had already theories drinking alcohol could change your mental state beyond the buzz on long-term bases. I was trying to show I had also put some back. I felt this was a social visit and my experiences passed him bye. That's all I took from the interview. It was mostly small talk, No nuts or bolts concerning the job.

AN AMERICAN MESSIAH

They called us together for lunch after the first interviews. We all met in the cafeteria where our lunch was paid for. While eating I noticed a single pepper flake in the saltshaker. I've only experienced a mushroom trip once, but in it I had a vision of the most 'holy grain of sand'. This is what the grain of pepper triggered.

The back ground around to the 'holy grain of sand' derives from the Israeli and Palestinian struggle over the Holly Land in the area. In my mushroom hallucination I asked the question on the Holly Land what is the most holly spot, or area to focus or most holly grain of sand. I'd love to see them produce the most holly grain of sand to battle over. That is what this simple grain of pepper had me thinking about.

After lunch I met with a guy who was more casual than the first. He wore casual pants and a colored button up shirt. He took us through the computer and how there where short cuts to the program. He went through it quickly, and didn't appear to want to be there. He shuffled me over to my next interview with no delay.

It's a good thing I was in the chair outside the next interviewer. I had to wait. After this wait I would be questioned for the first time. I'll never forget his name, Chip. I really don't know what happened. I was in his office taking looks around as I answered his questions. At the end of the interview he asked me to, "please get up and leave", but I didn't. I felt the interview was to short. I'll never forget he began slightly bounce up and down in his seat. The second time he asked me to, "get up and leave", I did.

He then came steaming out of his office telling me to follow him, which I did. I followed him to a different office, where I was placed in front of a woman. She appeared to be a higher up than Chip; her office was in a much better location, more private. I recall they sat me right in front of her with no stop in between. When they say you work in a vacuum this must be it. There where very little distractions. She sat for a few minutes not saying much and then left after a call. I sat for at leased ten minutes. In that time my mind wondered around the room to the art on the wall to the best and fastest way to get to a restroom. As I sat the phone rang constantly. I thought to pick it up at points. A few times I almost sat at her desk, but didn't. I also saw the tree or bush she had in her office, as a possible place to relieve myself, but didn't.

DAVID MICHAEL

When the time had expired, a stretcher and a wheel chair greeted me. I guess I had been waiting for an ambulance. This was the first time someone questioned my well being. All I know is I had to go to the bathroom and I wasn't ill enough to get on the stretcher or in the wheel chair. As we left the building they allowed me a visit to the bathroom. They also kept the wheel chair close by. I was obviously being taken to an ambulance and then a hospital, but where. I was alone in a strange place hundreds of miles from people I trusted and knew. It wouldn't be a stretch to call MBNA an Evil Empire. The question I had was what was I doing wrong. Outside of not leaving Chips office I don't know what I had done wrong.

When we made it to the hospital, I'll make this as blunt as possible, it was like a circus. Balloons all around on patients' beds and the name of the hospital was Waldo Hospital. They gave me the typical tests, but when it came time to giving blood I had fair. I was in a hospital reminding me of a circus and they wanted blood. There could be anything on that needle. I was most afraid of a needle with the HIV virus on it. I fought them on the blood for a good while, but after a while where I could watch the whole procedure I gave in.

They did ask me what had happened? The only answer I could give is I was light headed. They had nothing if they where looking for drugs in my system. I had quit drugs two semesters ago, but they where the first to question my behavior.

The next thing I knew two men where going to be taking me home by car, from Maine to Rhode Island. I'm one that likes to play things to the end to see how awful a situation can get. Then you play it back to the beginning attempting to stop what was slowing you down in the scenario. For example: When I was sitting in the back of the car my mind went as far fetched as possible. My mind imagined the small possibility of the two men taking me into the wilderness of Maine and ending my life with a shotgun. With this scenario you can see the possibility of ending my life. This is an act I'd like to stay away from. What calmed me was the fact I was linked to the days events so I couldn't have just disappeared. Traveling distance heightened my trust I was traveling miles to West Warwick and I could trust a great deal more.

After sometime I turned my thoughts to; 'what was I going to tell my parents?' I was about to be dropped off at their doorstep. I was more than likely going to tell them the same I had told everyone else, 'I felt light headed.' I still can't tell you what had happen there in Belfast, Maine or where exactly the Waldo Hospital is, but someone had called my bluff. They knew something was wrong, but I still continued to deny it.

For sometime I was waiting to see who would be the one to question my behavior. Never would I have guessed MBNA. I would have guessed one of my friends. They are a huge bank who probably doesn't have much time for this kind of thing. They likely closed with books on the ordeal, 'someone not feeling well that day.'

The trip took around three hours if I had to guess. When I arrived my parents where waiting. MBNA must have finally contacted my parents to alert them I was coming home. While I was at Waldo Hospital they were unable to get connected with my parents. They where concerned and curious, but they didn't pry, they had time to sort out the mess. As I planned, I told them 'I had felt light headed', as I told everyone else.

They seemed to be quieted by the excuse. That turned us to the second issue. I had been dropped of at home and not Bellefonte where my car was. I had to find a way back to State College. The three scenarios would be: bus, train, and rental car. Renting a car seemed like the most cost efficient method of transportation. I would be able to drop the car off at the airport near campus.

The next day I obtained a rental car to take me back to Happy Valley. It was the usual ride, Highway 95 south, to Highway 287 west, to Highway 80 west. The voyage took the usual 400 miles and 8-9 hours. After dropping of the car at the airport I called the Fraternity house to see if I could get a ride from the airport. I got a brother with a car on the line and he said he would help me out. With in no time I was back to my Bellefonte dueling.

My remaining time in State College was spent preparing to leave after commencement. I also spent a lot of time redoing some portfolio pieces and working at MBNA. When I returned to work at MBNA, I was hit with the same battery of questions. I answered them the same way as normal, 'I felt light headed.' I only had roughly two weeks until graduation. Then I would be headed back home to Rhode Island.

When graduation weekend finally came to fruition my parents arrived on the Friday before the Saturday graduation. I gave them the tour of campus that Friday. My parents had visited Penn State once before at the Fraternities parents weekend. I was excited to graduate. This was the big one, no more school. This was far different than any scholastic hurdle. I was at the end of my schooling, which took 18 years.

On graduation day I could see in my mother the questioning of my wellness. My father stuck by me. Before commencement the Art and Architecture graduates to be, waited under a tent in front of the Visual Arts Building. It was then the a question rang through my thoughts, "Was I thinking or was I drinking? It was at that time I seriously considered putting an end to my drinking. While there my father questioned me for the first time. I was excited to be graduating, but he asked why I wasn't more animated? All I could reply was that I was animated.

As we all walked down to the Eisenhower Auditorium I was spinning and jumping an imaginary self just in case he wanted to see some of that animation. I was truly excited and always had a quiet side to me. While in the lobby of the building we, the graduating students, where placed in the order our diplomas would be passed out. At the time I thought there was a chance the diplomas would be passed out to anyone excepting the diploma. Then a game of who had the others diploma would commence and how would one get it from the other? I watched carefully, because I didn't want someone else's diploma. Once we had been placed in the proper order, we made our way into the auditorium.

One by one students crossed the stage to become graduates. This precession started with the architecture class then made its way to the art class. I recall watching what seemed a long line on architecture graduates. That was followed by the list of other art majors not in graphic design, such as sculpture or photography. When it finally became my turn to graduate I felt a great deal of accomplishment. I proudly walked across the stage grabbing my diploma then officially ending my stay at Penn State. What a strange trip it had been. I was slightly disappointed to see the diploma said Art on it instead of Graphic Design. I guess the school you graduate from takes precedence. On the contrary, it was nice to see my name on the diploma.

It was mission accomplished I left the building as a Penn State graduate. My parents and I returned to my apartment to get them ready for their trip back to Rhode Island. I agreed to let them take my diploma back with them. They left that afternoon. They had their question and doubles, but they got what they where looking for. They still where unaware I had failed Theatre and at this point it wasn't very important.

Now that I had graduated the following weekend the Graduate students would graduate. Their guest speaker would be Bill Clinton. With a student ID a student could get in the brand new Brice Jordan Center to see the then President for free. I had another few weeks on my apartment, so I obtained one of the tickets mid-week.

I went to the Fraternity before leaving to see if anyone else was going to the Graduate Ceremony. I ran into a brother nicknamed "T" who would be attending. We made our way there with some small talk. T still had some time before he graduated, but wanted to see Bill Clinton just the same. We got descent seats, a side view. The graduates where of course front and center.

As Mr. Clinton spoke I couldn't help but ask myself what was so special about this guy. The message of his speech didn't hold my attention. I did find myself gazing at him in an attempt to see how he the man made it to such a lofty position. I didn't see much, but I've already stated I believe sports figures would be better at running things than the people we had now.

T and I left as the diplomas where being handed out. As we left we approached the athletic complex. I suggested to T we go and see Gino Cappelletti's Heisman Trophy. I knew it was in the Penn State Football Hall of Fame. I had seen it once my first year at University Park. T was game so we went to see the Trophy up close and personal. After seeing Bill Clinton it was nice to balance the day with some athletic hardware. In this day I found the Heisman Trophy to hold more important than the President. It's hard for anyone to say, in a time span of 15 minutes they witnessed two such powerful items as the President and the Heisman Trophy. Where else, but Penn State? These events would be something I miss about Happy Valley.

With this experience in my pocket I began preparing to go back home to West Warwick. I spent a few days organizing and putting items in boxes. Then one day I got everything that I owned into my car and headed back to Rhode Island. I was leaving a Penn State grad.

CHAPTER 6

When I arrived at home there were two priorities. My Brother would be getting married to his fiancée Stephanie. They would be getting married the second month I was back, which was June. The second item of importance would be me finding a job. Finding work would rest on my shoulders, while the wedding would be taken care of by the families. It would be my first wedding and I was the Best Man, so I was thrown right into the mix. Locating employment was my top priority.

To help reach as many businesses as possible, I chose the phone book as my guide. I called every design studio in Rhode Island asking if, 'there was any need for help or if there were any plans for hiring.' There was a page and a half of businesses. From this list I got one genuinely interested outfit. They where located in down town Providence, the capital of Rhode Island. I made an appointment to meet with them the next day.

The next day, I got my portfolio and headed down town. I met with someone named Jon. He really liked my portfolio especially the cutting in some of the pieces. He liked things enough to get his boss Constance. She also liked what she saw. She wanted Jon to leave the room so we could talk business. She offered me a job. I asked for $20,000 and she accepted. It took me less than a week to find a job, hopefully this was the one I was wishing for in Bellefonte. I would be starting the next day.

Within my first week of hiring I would create a wave. One day during lunch I went to the main office of Fleet bank, which was in walking distance from where I was working. I was engaging the bank to even up the debacle at MBNA. I went to Fleet for piece of mind. MBNA was a huge bank and now I was pitting Fleet against them. I hoped they would balance one another out and I wouldn't have to think about the MBNA mess. All I really did was go there to open an account. While in the bank I flooded the building with thoughts of my visit to MBNA, almost like a mental confessional. I was attempting to get Fleet to pick up the pieces and avenge my bad experience. I took my sweet time in the Fleet bank main office, which produced a lateness to work.

The problem occurred when I didn't show up for the second half of work. This somewhat mirrored the way I was sent back home by MBNA. The next day they didn't have much to say. They told me to let them know if I would be taking time, although they didn't look favorably upon my disappearance.

Now for my brothers' wedding. It was a big wedding, 300 people. He was marrying a girl named Stephanie. They met at a local grocery store where they both held jobs. They had been dating several years before they decided to tie the knot. The wedding would be held at the church she attended, St. Josephs'. The reception would be held at the Quidnessett country club.

Leading up to the wedding I was engaging in a game of sorts. What I was doing was putting people in the family on a chessboard. I do know how to play chess, but I'm not the greatest. I also feel chess is the most widely known game there is, and every male and female should know how to move the pieces. I had the board structured in this manner: Left rook: my Uncle Tony, Left Knight: my Uncle Ricky, left Bishop: My father Joseph, my brother Mark and his wife to be Stephanie the King and Queen as they where the focus of the event. The other Bishop: Father Joe, Right Knight: Yours truly, Right Rook: Little Ricky my cousin. The pawns run left to right: Isabel, Tony's wife to be, my aunty TT, My sister Lisa, in front of my brother our mother, in front of Stephanie her father, my Grandmother Garcia to the right of center, my cousin John followed and finally my cousin Orlando.

The day of the wedding started with a round of golf for the guys in the wedding party. It was a good time. I was afraid we where cutting it to close to the wedding, but every thing timed out. The limo picked up Mark and I last. We then headed to St. Josephs' church. We arrived on time. This was all new to me I'd never attended a wedding up until now.

The ceremony took off with out a hitch. The Priest took control of the event. He rambled on for some time. One of the priests was a family member. Father Joe, a relative on my grandmothers' side. I had a priest right in front of me and attempted to channel the energy from the people attending the ceremony to the priests. At least that's how I got through the wedding.

After the priests had their doings it was time for Mark and Stephanie to exchange their vows. They both completed their vows with love, exchanging their rings with a final kiss for the bride. They then made their way out, Mr. And Mrs. Mark Garcia. They would be headed out to the Quidnessett country club for the reception. The reception was filled with people I knew, people I should know and people I didn't know. Half the crowd was from Stephanie's family, which I had limited exposure to. I did know her immediate family as well as a few aunts and uncles, but the majority was unknown to me. To make it worse I didn't know some of the people on my side. I knew most of them but there were a few I didn't recognize. As things began to kick off two of my uncles, on separate occasions, told me to, " keep playing". I took this with both a positive and negative connotation. I did consider myself to be playing, not trying to harm anyone. I was a young man, but they made it seem like there was something wrong with my behavior.

The food was good and so was the event. After eating there was a lot of dancing. I even danced and I usually don't. The bride and groom cut the cake. More dancing followed. I opted out of dancing for the rest of the night.

Following the celebration we headed to Stephanie's mothers' house. We had some drinks by the pool, which turned into throwing one another into the pool. Everyone made it into the pool, tux or no tux. It was only water they had to clean the tuxes somehow. I got home not to long after we got wet.

Now that the wedding had passed I could take a better look at the job I had landed. To tell the truth I wasn't employed there for more than a month. I had several reasons for my firing. First off I had flashes of someone in the past jumping from the roof, though no indications or stories of such where brought to my attention. This is something I had visions of from an early stage, but that wasn't why I was fired.

The strange scenario that had me terminated is as follows. One night I was watching the show Dateline and they had an episode on

Celtic culture. As the program progressed I envisioned Jon, the manager, being part of the society. This is most likely false, but my mind was working this way and I didn't question it. I also didn't respect the fact he had no college degree. He was also the only one working in the graphics department other than Constance, which in my eyes appeared to be a sinking ship. They were also behind in technology.

One of the few days I was employed there I confronted Jon. I forget the exact dialog, but I was trying to get more head room by getting above Jon's. Constance was out, so it was just the two of us. All I remember is being Fired and Jon saying "Keep on walking".

That night I had to face my family. My mother was the first one home and I could see the disappointment. If there was anyone starting to build a case to show I had something wrong it was she. My father was still holding out. He had put a lot of belief in me during my younger more successful years. This was the division I could see begin. In fact there started to be such a division in my mind it seemed my parents may be considering divorce.

This belief caused some trouble. One day my mother wanted to know if I wanted to go to a movie with her and my father. She was pulling some free admission tickets from her pocket book, but I thought she was giving me a look at divorce papers in her bag. This instigated me to tell her to, "Go f#%* yourself". My father responded by flying in the room and striking me twice to the jaw. I responded by shoving him to the wall.

I then left the house and got into my car. My father and mother took to the front yard. My father jumping behind my car to stop me, it was a good thing he got out from the rear of the car because I would have run him over. Once I left I just drove around. I thought to keep driving to where ever my car took me. Instead I decided to call the police. Ten minutes later I made my way home. The cops were there and looking for me because I had made the call. In the end I didn't press charges against my dad and the police left. That night my family tried to tell me I had a problem, but I shrugged it off and went my merry way. I ignored what they had to say.

There was tension in the house the week to follow, although it got much better when I got another job. The 1996 Olympics where on and that helped. Michael Johnson's gold shoes are a lasting memory. This memory turned into a mental game for me. Growing up in the land of the Wizards, our high school teams' mascot, I felt the responsibility to play *The Wizard of Oz* with golden shoes instead of ruby red. Obviously Michael was Dorothy. I would use other famous people to finish the script. For example I used Jack Nichols as the Tin Man for his nice ax work in the *Shining*. I could use Joe Paterno as the Cowardly Lion being the Nittiny Lions long ten eared Head Coach and last but not least perhaps Bill Walton as the brainless Scare Crow. The very best Wizard I could come up with is Ozzy Osborne. This was a fun practice one I would do again in the future. I wasn't yet totally consumed by these plays in fantasy; I was still searching for work.

I found employment hap heartedly. I applied at a local newspaper for work as a photographer, but my resume told them graphic design was my area of focus. They must have also needed a designer, that's how the call was made to me. My interview was with a girl named Julie. She liked my work and gave me an idea of what the job entailed. I'd be working on an insert for another newspaper out of Narragansett, but working out of the local West Warwick paper office. It was only part-time and would only pay $6.50 an hour, still I took the job because I had just lost the other one and it was more experience. I could always look for other employment in the other part of my day.

This pacified my parents somewhat. Though there was still decisiveness between them. My mother was pushing for a problem while my father thought I could right the ship. I began to alienate myself from my friends, as well. I felt there where larger things to be dealt with.

For example I found it more important to use an NFL version of the *Wizard of Oz* making Paul Tagliubeau the Wizard, Tim Brown from the Raiders the Tin Man, Barry Sanders of the Lions as the Cowardly Lion, Bill Walsh as the Scare Crow, and the Owner of the Rams, a female, as Dorothy. This was what I came up with for the NFL version.

Returning to my new job. It was easy work. I was basically revising past ads for the insert. There was also a column I was key boarding in every few weeks. Something very annoying in the office was the clicking of the computer mouse. The click, click, click...from Julies mouse was disturbing. I would respond by pointing my curser at an open spot and then just click away, until I was finished. Julie commented on more than one occasion and I couldn't have cared less.

The job was easy and the afternoons had plenty of time to unwind and play mental games. Those afternoons where occupied with memories and thoughts of how I began spiraling downward while others where meant to prevent the current trend. For example I would sit in front of a mirror in our dinning area staring not directly at the mirror, rather out of the corner of my eye. This activity led me to believe the animal I was most akin to was the buffalo. I did this several times a week.

I believe you could also see this animal in my football running style. A kind of trampling herd of a runner and the others joined the herd mentality. With that, I've mentioned a few times I played football and now I'll share some. I began playing organized football when I was nine. In my first year I joined late, and had to play with the older, bigger squad. I took my licks and only played the mandatory four plays for each player. The team wasn't very good either. The next year the league placed me at the same level. I played a little more, but the team still was no good. The third year was much different. I was now a third year captain. I started at running back. In the round robin, opening scrimmage, I ran for a 60-yard touchdown on the first play. This was my very first touchdown. The very next practice I was made a lineman, right Guard to be exact. I never said anything about the move and I think it helped us the rest of the year. That season we won all of our games won the championship and we were invited to travel to play in New England and won! We where then invited to play a Bowl Game in Alabama for what could be argued was a National Championship! Having to travel so far at that young age left us wide eyed. We got creamed, but it was still an experience I wont forget.

The next season at the next level didn't bear fruit. We had an average record and I was still a guard. I did convince the coach to let me run. It was mostly bull work; one or two yards when we where pinned deep in our own end did I get carries. The year was a wash.

The next year I was moved up to the next and final youth level. Our year was up and down until one faithful game in Newport. We where down a touchdown, there wasn't much time left and the other team was kicking off. I was on the sidelines, as I was supposed to be. We didn't have enough players on the field and I was the closest person to the coach. He grabbed me and told me to get out there. I did and wouldn't you know it the ball came right to me. I caught the ball and ran as fast as I could. I was coming out the end of the pill when I was tacked. The game ended shortly after and we lost.

I mention this play because the next practice I was moved to running back. As a team we won a few games getting us into the playoffs. We didn't make it to the championship that year, but it was the most significant change in my life up until that point.

In the off-season I was undecided where to play, with the Jr. High or Pop Warner. My decision was made easier when the head coaches wife from Pop Warner call to get me to play for her husband. It was this call leading me back to the Steelers, the name of the Pop Warner team. It turned out to be one of the best things I've done.

I was one of the two-featured backs in the offense. The other back was Jason, someone I had played a lot of football with. I got more carries than I would have got in Jr. High and I learned how to run. That year Jason and I ran for lots of yards and touchdowns. We won the championship! After our championship we where invited to a bowl game in Connecticut. We went to that game and won handedly and I won the MVP of the game!

I can't begin to speak of or give proper recognition to the impact Coach Gough had on me. If it weren't for him I would have been toiling as a lineman, which I was very undersized to play. I may or may not have played High School football without the move he had made. I also give credit to those years as a lineman, which I believe, made me a better back. It gave me a quick first step and got me used to hitting the lineman.

The next year I went on to play High School football for the West Warwick Wizards. My first year was a learning experience. I was the starting fullback for what I thought was a terrific halfback. He was strong and fast and by far the best player on the team, his name was Matt. I also played linebacker along with Matt. Matt was a senior and saw the best way for him to win was through the new young players. There was also a lineman Pat who could see the same thing. They both took a liking to us, the younger players, early on.

That season we started off 6-0 before we lost to Warwick. We lost a few games after that making us 6-3 or close to that mark. Things kind of came unglued at the end. This lead up to the Thanksgiving game against Coventry, our rival. With our shaky finish we where favored to lose against a team we dominate on Thanksgiving annually.

I can't help but say I'm sometimes in the right position, but the opening kick-off fell into my arms my first Thanksgiving game and I took it for a touchdown! It was a blow Coventry never recovered from. Although the final score eludes me we ruined them. When the time came to pass around post-season honors we grabbed a few as a team. Instead of trying to name all the honors I'll let you know I was named 2nd team all Division Fullback, while Matt was named 1st team All State Halfback.

The following season was my junior year. This was a Team of destiny, but not from the start. We where filled with juniors' with some seniors. We would miss Matt, but Pat was back for another season. The season started by loosing to Johnston. It was in a game that didn't count, the Round Robin. The next game we went to Burrillville and escaped with a win. We then began winning one game after another. The team lost a game to Narragansett deep in the season, but finished with that one blemish and we where on our way to the Super Bowl.

Toward the end of the season I assumed the starting halfback position. We found ourselves heavy underdogs in the championship game verse Bristol. They where said to have a runner, Manny, who couldn't be stopped. When the game was finished we held them to negative yards on offense and I had scored two touchdowns for the win. I was named MVP of the Super Bowl with a thundering herd mentality! At the ends of this season their where many being honored. I can't name them all, but I was named 2nd team All State Linebacker in that 1989 season.

The 1990 season had a lot riding on it. All those juniors where back for more, now as seniors, not many spots needed to be filled. This team would be a Team of dominance. We would be the targets of the league and that didn't help our opponents. He destroyed every team they put in front of us, but one, the Johnston Panthers, again, sort of. They tied us 6-6. That small blemish wouldn't derail us. We went steaming through the rest of the season, blowing Narragansett out in the Super Bowl. I often look at this season as a more perfect season due to the tie. When post season honors where past out I was named 1st team All State halfback. I had also finished my career with a few school records.

AN AMERICAN MESSIAH

Football gave me my proudest moments. I was all about football coming out of High School, but never played in college. In fact I tried out for the Penn State football squad three times before becoming discouraged and deciding to change my focus to the Fraternity and my major. Though in 1994 Penn State was the #1 football team in the country half way through the season and finished with no loses and no ties only to fall to second behind Nebraska at years end. If you where to ask me Penn State finished second because I wasn't on the team. They had a good football player walking all around campus and neglected to have him as part of the team. I believe this in 'my own little world'. It was after seeing this season I stopped trying out for the football team. This was also the only year I had purchased season tickets. It never entered my mind at that time I would be struggling as much as I would be in the future.

This is an example of how my days would go. Work in the morning followed by reviews of the past or games occupying my thoughts. It's now still late early autumn in 1996. I recall the baseball playoffs where now in full swing. As a youth I was one of the better players in my baseball league.

In my first year I was nine and the very last player selected in the Bambino League. Warren Oil chose me, which was the team sponsor. The coach lived down the street from me selected me because he knew me. The team was filled with 12 year olds and I was the youngest and least talented play, sitting the bench most of the games. I didn't play much of a role on the team due to the older players. They had me wide eyed at how good they where. That year Warren Oil won the championship! This was my first taste as a Champion. Be it modest and humbling. I'd like to point out that like football, my introduction to baseball was the same. I played with the big boys to start, although they had different out comes to start.

The next season the majority of the older players moved up to Babe Ruth baseball. I was left behind. That year we lost our coach and our sponsor changed to Rogers Auto Body. We were terrible, and finished up with no wins. Not a single one. Not even one game that went the wrong way for the other team at that level.

The year after our team was a little better and won a few games. I was getting better at baseball as I had more experience with the game and I grew physically, as well as, mentally. That year my dad coached and he made a move with me. He made me the catcher on the team. A move impacted me in baseball almost as much as my move from lineman to running back in football. That season I was named to the All-Star Team as a catcher.

My final season on Rogers Auto Body, we were good enough to make the play-offs. We did very little with that birth. I emerged as one of a handful of plays thought to be the best. At catcher I had no rivals and at the end of the year I had a .600 batting average with two homeruns! Again I was named an All Star, but this time one of the team captains. This group of All-Stars was good. We took the Bambino State Title and were invited to Massachusetts for the New England Playoffs. I believe we won one game and then where ousted.

When the next level of play came along it was a 13-year-old league. A middle ground between the lower levels and Babe Ruth, only payers aged 13. The Expos, a powder blue uniform, drafted me in the first round, the same colors I had played on in the Bambino League. My good friend Wally was also on this team, strengthening our relationship. There were only four teams in the league, so everyone made the playoffs.

I recall loosing in the first round, but once again I was chosen as an All-Star catcher. We played another team from Warwick and where eliminated.

After 13's we where drafted again, to Babe Ruth. This time I was the first player selected overall. The team I was drafted by was the Blue Jays. Once again a powder blue uniform, Wally was also drafted by this team. My first season with the team they made improvements from their former season. I had a good rookie season, but nothing like I had in the past. I hit one home run that season, something not many can say they've achieved at that level or in that sized field. The All-Star team selected me. We hosted the All-Star playoffs that year. We didn't make much hay and were eliminated quickly.

My final season of Babe Ruth baseball was disappointing and also rewarding. That team, the Blue Jays, finished in first place only to be beat in the championship round of the playoffs. I was proud to say I was someone the team built on, but at the same time my arm hurt the whole season and my play had begun to erode. I wasn't that same hitter and my skills were diminished quickly.

I moved up to the High school team where I was in and out of the lineup as a catcher. I couldn't even hit batting practice at one point. My high School highlight came as a JV player. The coach of the JV team, John, let us have fun. One time I was on third base and was given the go to steal home on the pitch and I did. I beat the pitch home. If you understand baseball you can appreciate the play. This would be my last year of organized baseball. I would join the track team in the spring of my last two years of High School.

As I mentioned the major league baseball playoffs had come around. As I watched I grew in distain for my father. I would thump my thumb on the armrest in an attempt to time it to his heart and then stop it suddenly trying to get his heart to do the same. I believe one of the reasons these thoughts of hate toward him immerged from a conversation with an old man I was working with as a courier in the past. I don't remember how the topic came up, but I had made the comment, "The only thing I felt unprepared for was the death of my father." From that point on I may have been on the decline. I felt I was beginning to suffer, because he may be dieing and I wasn't ready for it. So I began to play games that could put him to rest.

While I sat in the chair next to my father, watching the ball games I would watch as the Yankees tip their hats. It appeared to me they where tipping their hats to me. I believed they where doing this to let me know I was doing the right thing.

As I've stated I'm only playing. I do believe life is a game and I was involved in, a death game. One day that fall I was sitting trying to keep everything together, when I spotted in the middle of the floor a dead fly. It had me wondering how the fly got to the middle of the floor and just dieing. Was it crawling and just expired or was it flying and just gave up. After a few minutes I began to weep. The fly became a symbol of the thoughts I had for my father. I took the fly and buried it in the side yard next to the woodpile. I tied two sticks together in the shape of a cross and stuck it on top of the fly.

Something else I would struggle with was my father's workday. I knew when he came home at approximately 6pm. I would sit in my room hoping he wouldn't come home. I would be on the verge of tears knowing the time he would be showing up and wishing something had happened. I would struggle with the knowledge he would come home like he did, day in day out.

Not only was I breaking up emotionally, I found myself suffering from sleep deprivation. The nights would eat away at my sleep. I found myself out of bed visiting the kitchen on several occasions. I would also stare at the stars out my bedroom window. I would become so mesmerized at them I had belief they where moving from time to time. To explain that condition: I felt like I was on a drug, but strung out even more, because I never came down, unless I crashed and cried.

One night that I couldn't sleep, I repeated a message in that 1996 political season: ' Bob Dole is a historic President, Bob Dole is a historic President....' I repeated this in my mind the whole night, for whomever could get the message. I partly did this to get the pressure off of me and on some one in public office. I was feeling like I was being watched through the television, through the radio and people around me.

One night after seeing Christopher Reeves at the Democratic convention, I couldn't sleep. I attempt to help him in his paralyzed state. I focused on my tailbone and lower back, which I believed was the part of the body he needed the most reconnecting. I sent the message with the mental and physical portion of; your planting seeds to grow roses up and down your spine, so cultivate them. I believed this would be help full to him. I also sent the message to use the leg press when exercising. Hire the right people for the spots and try and hang on to the leg press with your legs and feet, this motion may help in reconnecting the body.

I was extremely upset when Bill Clinton won the election. When I was younger, and not struggling, it was under the Republicans of Regan and Bush. I felt the change from Democrat to Republican in this election could have righted my ship back to when things where a lot easier.

I was doing as much, as I call helpful work, as possible, while the work I had at the Times was easy. When at work, if I wasn't making up ads for the Spectator I would be writing obituaries or political ads. Although we finally came to the reason they hired me, which was the work coming from the Christmas Spectator insert. The Christmas insert was too much for one person to handle. It wasn't really that bad, I don't recall any hang-ups or delays being missed. After the Christmas insert the workload went back to normal, with the exception of the political adds, which went away all together with the political season. Each day I'd leave around noon and come back around one o'clock and leave for home around two o'clock.

The holidays went by quickly. That Christmas I had very little to spend with the income I was generating, but I made ends meet. Our family had a typical fish dinner at my Aunt TT's house for Christmas Eve and Christmas dinner at my mothers. It had become a tradition to have the meals in that order. The year changed from 1996 to 1997 with very little excitement for me. I had been isolating myself for quite some time and that New Years I continued the trend. I stayed home and made sure there was one sober person home for New Year.

With the New Year I had decided to ask for more hours at the Times. It took about a month, but that February I went to the top floor to see the owner of the paper Mr. Homburg. I asked just what I wanted, "Would it be possible to get more hours?", I asked. He told me it would be up to the girl, Julie; I was working with to decide. I didn't bother asking her and within the same weeks time I was laid-off.

CHAPTER 7

Getting laid-off wasn't much of a surprise, but it was also somewhat of a blind side. I went right to work looking for a new job. If nothing else working with the Spectator gave me more work experience for the resume. There wasn't much in the papers classifieds, but I sent my resume to all the ads I came across. One quickly responded to my resume, Nova Graphics. I immediately lined up an interview.

On the interview, I noticed right off most of the staff was close to my age. I also noticed they where working with some high-end technology and equipment. This was the job that could get me back on my feet. I wanted this. I waited about a week and a half with no response. I waited so long I paid an unexpected visit to them. It was then they told me I didn't get the job and a letter had just gone out to inform me. Two days later I received the letter. This hit me hard; I thought this was the perfect next step for me.

Now I was faced with my parents. Yes both my parents, my father was now urging me to seek help. He had also begun to find my behavior troubling. I then gave in a little. I met a psychiatrist with my father. I didn't fill in any of the forms they had given me at the front desk and when it came time to meet with the doctor I sat calm and quietly, saying next to nothing. The thing I remember vividly is the doctor saying I needed to be respected, which sounded good to me. Shortly after the shrink let me leave with my father left behind. I took my own car that day and drove back home. That was the last time I met with the doctor.

With out any job I had more time to myself. I found the weights in my basement gym bothersome. These weights where used to train for football. At any particular time you could find John, Wally, Ed, my brother Mark or myself pushing those Olympic weights. The equipment was the corner stone to our advantage in sports. We would compete with one another to see who could lift the most. After some years we all made it out to gyms, but those weights created our strong base. In one gym I was able to Bench 315 lbs and Squat 500 lbs, which never could have been achieved without those basement weights. At this point I wasn't able to lift that much. I was taking myself slowly apart and I did so with the gym equipment in my basement. I took apart the bench and the lat machine. I put everything, even the weights, in a storage area. By taking apart the equipment I felt I was also taking apart some of the friendships and relationships I had forged through the strength and sweet of the past.

To further disconnect with everyone, I went after my old High School works of Art. My father had hung them on the walls in the down stairs living area. I looked at them as amateurish and thought they where holding me back as a professional, being displayed so prominently. Therefore I took them all down and through them into the trash. When my father got home he couldn't understand why I would do such a thing. This just built more of a case with him, showing me as unstable. He rushed to the trash and retrieved any pieces he could salvage. He saved a few, but the bulk of the works where headed to the dump.

Mean while, I hadn't been employed for a month or two and my money was beginning to run low. I had already missed a car payment and was on the verge of number two. I really thought I was going to get into collections at the rate I was going, but my father came home one day and told me he had paid of the car. I wonder to myself how he could have such timing as to pay off the vehicle just as the payments where not being made. I chalked this up as a mental save or my father receiving my problem, which was making payments and since he was also on the payments he would solve the problem for he and I. This strengthened my belief people could communicate mentally on some level.

On some level I was still attempting to solve problems or get a deeper understanding of how things worked. For example I had focused in on the dollar bill. I was narrowing my scope to the pyramid on the back of a one. I saw this as a generational devise. I found my current standing in society to be linked directly to the bottom of the Baby Boomer Generation. I felt they where fighting for the same entry level jobs my Gen. X people and I where trying to land. If you look at the pyramids, because there are two, you have one generation disconnecting in the higher pyramid with the eye on it. The eye is to look after the next pyramid. I suggest the upper pyramid also is flat on top, but is to high to see this. I also suggest the larger grounded pyramid extends deeper beneath the earth cultivating the generation to come and would give it the look of a more pointed object when that pyramid grows from its foundation. I find myself on top of the grounded pyramid left to help the next generation and scrutinized by the Boomer pyramid.

Something else I worked on is the tax system in the United States. Currently in most States the sales tax is 7%. I would change this to a different spenders economy. The first thing I would do is have the IRS tax businesses only. I think people would spend extra money if it were always there, which would keep businesses afloat. Going back to the 7% tax. I would remedy this with a tax the rich and not the poor philosophy. I would have no sales tax on items $9.99 or less. There would be a nickel on every $10.00-$99.99, that would be followed with a dime for every $100.00-$999.99, which is followed with 15 cents every dollar in the range of $1000.00-$9999.99, which is followed by 20 cents for every dollar from $10,000.00-$99,999.99 which would finish up with a quarter for every dollar in the rage from $100,000.00-and any thing over. I put this together with no idea if it would work or not, but I was attempting to do better and good things. Knowing I was trying to do good things made it hard for me to believe something was wrong.

I also find something wrong with the minimum wage. What this basically says is one would give an employee less if we could. I've come up with a living wage, nothing terribly new. A wage many people in the country could make a good living with. To pay all those high school kids working after school a business owner may have to give them a salary and there would always be the commission for those sales people.

When I was much younger and imagined being president, the question of how to pay-off the National debt of Trillions of dollars entered my boyhood thoughts. At that age, early teen, I thought it would be a good idea to force the debt onto a small country and then blow that country up! Now that I've had years to think about this question I've come up with a few different ideas. For one: the government could ask the million and billionaires, or anyone else, to donate money to the deficit for awards, like military honors. They could also will the money. They would be called the Men who Knocked Down the Deficit and a monument would be erected in their honor. Second: In an act of necessity, the Federal government would garnish all the wages for a single week. The week would be the 4th of July to put a dent in the deficit. People in this country have suffered much more than this in the great depression and wars. Third: Working off the 4th of July week, I recommend a possible weeklong sale, where the 75% or more of everything purchased would be handed over to the government. Yes, I believe wiping out the deficit will take some sacrifice.

My mind was occupied by these things as I sat around the house with nothing better to do. In fact I found myself absorbed in such play. That's when something came in the mail. That piece of mail was a recruiting card for the Rhode Island Air National Guard. It didn't take long for me to see this as a possible oasis in a desert of despair. The military can make something out of almost any sad story, straightening out the most confused person or complement the brightest person.

I was old, 23, for the military, but not close to the cut-off. It took only the next few days to make the call to the recruiter. I made an appointment to meet with the recruiter in the first telephone call. The next week I met with *her*. I'm somewhat of a male chauvinist, but I made the adjustment to a female superior. Her name and rank eludes me, but this would be my first introduction into the Air Guard. She informed me I would meet once a month and two weeks a year as a member of the Guard, paying around $200 each meeting for four years. At least that's how I remember it. After signing some papers the meeting was over, though I made the next appointment for a physical. The check up would be about a month into the future.

I wanted to keep this to myself. I had grown frustrated with my family's accusations of the need for help. The way I looked at it, I would be getting help from the most lethal fighting force the globe has ever known. I also wanted to keep this private because it was the first decision I had ever made affecting my life to such a degree. All my other decisions where made with the help of my parents or would have their involvement. I would be doing this for me.

I thought this to be a good avenue to continue my development. If

AN AMERICAN MESSIAH

there was one thing holding me back from seeking help, it was my development. I did feel I was changing and I didn't want anything to interrupt my mental and physical development.

As was the norm, at this point, I sat around looking for topics to occupy my thoughts. I used my most resent endeavor. I asked myself, "What did I want or what was the limits with the National Guard?" At first I just wanted something to be proud of. Then my mind opened to possibly flying a plane, it was the Air Guard after all and I did consider myself to be a good physical specimen.

I thought higher and higher. I wondered what obstacles I would face to travel into space. As I sat there I developed a plan for a manned space landing on Mars. To get there I knew it would take months, so I came up with a vessel to travel in space from one fuel tank to the next. Imagine fuel tanks with stored food fixed in space. Each being a predetermined measured distance from one to another. The tanks would form a loop from earth to Mars, with the craft safely hopping from one point to the next.

One topic I would like to cover at this time is my prediction of fossils existing on other planets. I don't find this far fetched by any stretch of the imagination. Dinosaur like existences on these other planets may shock people and show a Universe filled with life before man. I was preparing for such a find. With our focus on Mars it is bound to turn up a fossil.

As my mind drifted through space it formulated other possible crafts, known to man or not. I due believe in intelligent life in space other than ours. The first such craft was the flying soars a. Never confirmed as a spacecraft, but there are so many sightings I had to address it. I would guess the being operating the craft is just who one would expect at the controls. This would be the ant head with large eyes with a slender build, void of hair. Trust me I tried to make this work, but a flying disk baffled me. A UFO has too much technology for me to understand.

On to a deep space vessel my mind configured to cut through space. Basically this craft is a tube with a pointed head and propellers at its sides and end the propellers are fixed at the center of the tube and are a quarter the length of the ship. The propellers are attached at their ends by cables or other material to pull the propellers back. After the propellers have fully spun through their cycle the propellers are pulled tightly to the side of the craft to retract to the end of the vessel like a squid or butterfly swimmer cutting through the water with a sleek dynamic form. Unlike the known pilot of the flying soars a, this traveler was the opposite in type. I imagined a large muscular, Viking like being, covered with hair. I saw this vessel being run manually, like the rowing system the Vikings had, push and pull.

I placed further believe these two voyagers where on a race to earth. I imagined them as God and the other the Devil. To make it more interesting I chose one to be a women and the other a male who where coming to mate once they got here, too save their species. I came up with the theory all three of our beings, the hairy being, the ant headed being and we human beings, had evolved in one way or another, but may still be able to procreate. We may be the same ancestries and are just from different parts of the vast Universe and each of us had taken a different evolutionary path.

I viewed this as the battle of the sexes, a not if you where the last one on earth contest. Therefore, each was attempting to reproduce with out the other. God, the slim hairless female, would try to fertilize her eggs with her own waste and the scientific advantage of invetro fertilization. She would then scatter the eggs around the Universe, on different planets hoping they would live, the creator of life. She would pray, "Please live". This is one possible explanation on how *we* got here.

The Devil, the muscular physical being, is attempting the more natural route of turning his waste into an egg he could fertilize with his seaman. His direction takes a little more focus, only conceiving one offspring at one time. He would then sit on his egg until it hatched. Slow and steady like his vessel.

This is when I put the Devil in Hell, his own Hell. The image I received was of the Devil alone on a high ledge sitting on his egg on a planet that was erupting all around him. If his egg didn't come out in time the whole planet would explode. As if this wasn't enough, God hovered around the planet wondering if she should come down to save this filthy beast and procreate. The Devil would make funny faces at her sours a to buy more time and to confuse God.

These images lead to a much different game. The Devil put me in a chamber with a lock on the inside. The dial went 0-10. I would spin the dial hitting all the numbers. When I hit the correct number to the lock the door would open to the next chamber and so on. The problem was when one uses the number six three times one was confronted with the Devil. It could be three straight sixes, or spaced out for long periods without a six to build your confidence only to crush it when only the third six remained. I found myself playing this game endlessly. I would put the dial on all the numbers but six at times and at other times I would go straight for the number. My adrenaline would heighten when I was down to that third number six on the dial, knowing he was on the other side of the door.

This practice got me more relaxed to deal with the Devil. At first I didn't know what he was after, but it appeared to be the truth. When I was lying to him he would pace back and forth with big red eyes bulging out of his head and his arms in the air. He would through a mini tirade. He was also covered from head to toe with light bluish gray hair. There was a table to stand at while the Devil mostly sat on his thrown. In my mind I was then dealing with the Devil.

I told him about my football and baseball years. I also informed him of my weight training and track and field. Though he came back to football, because he couldn't believe someone with my talents didn't play in college. I agreed and made note it was a sore spot to me. I also believed I should have played at the next level and felt some didn't remember my High School play for what it was. This is when we started to make a deal. We took all my football numbers, because the Devil likes working with numbers, his sign is 666. My numbers where: 27, 62, 99, 34, and 32. We came up with the solution of living through those numbers. Every time one of those numbers came up in years, such as the year on the calendar or my age, my performance and success in that time would be dictated by the play I had in those jerseys. I had a request. If I where ever inducted into my High Schools Hall of Fame, I wanted my number 32 retired before the Hall. That was my deal with the Devil.

Getting back to earth. My parents where still trying to make a deal with me to see a psychiatrist again I wanted none of this. In fact it was dividing us as a family. On one occasion I asked my father to help me find a Savings Bond I believed they had stored away for me. I brought him the metal box they stored documents in. When I presented him with the box he refused to look. I was irate. I was calling him names, "Joe blow, average Joe, sloppy Joe ", and any other derogatory remark

I could come up with using his name. I was so maddened with this event I locked myself in my room and would only leave when may family members where not home. This was the most divisive moment I experienced with my family.

    I had now cut off communication with my family. I was in my room watching TV from a small black and white, about four by three inches. I was doing this because I felt I was being watched by the television and having such a small screen would make it more difficult to watch me. I watched the Chicago Bulls in the playoffs nightly. Once Michael Jordan and company won one of there several Championships I took the small black and white and through it out. I felt any one who was following me through the small TV would be trapped.

    After I went back to my regular sized color TV in my room. I have to tell you I'm a huge Oakland Raider fan. One day watching the tube I saw an interview with Al Davis, the Raiders Owner and General Manager. At one point he was talking about the O.J. Simpson murder and suggested Marcus Allen had something to do with the murders. Marcus was a former Raider who left for the Kansas City Chiefs. I took what he was saying to heart. Have you ever heard the theory: that you're following someone up. To give a better example, when there's a good established player the other players look to him to lead the way. Well O.J went to college at USC and years later so did Marcus. In my opinion Marcus was following O.J. up. They also both won the Heisman Trophy at Southern Cal. They both wore number 32 as a Pro. I'm assuming the detectives and lawyers obtain information the same way I've been doing it, through mental messaging or clues. I have a theory they stopped gathering or waiting for the information to come. If the clues where, the murderer went to USC, won the Heisman Trophy, and wore number 32 it would surely point to O.J. The piece they didn't get right was the murderer was a Super Bowl MVP. There was an O.J who was a Super Bowl MVP, but it was O.J. Anderson of the Giants. Though Marcus Allen was a Super Bowl MVP. I even used Ron Goldman, at times, as one of the murders. I had Ron kill O.J.'s wife and then Marcus killing Ron. I realize now these theories are false and the work of an over imaginative mind. I apologize to the Goldman's and Marcus.

    I shifted from topic to topic rather quickly at this point. I recall

AN AMERICAN MESSIAH

July 1, 1997 as one of the more memorable days in my development. This was the exchange of power of Hong Kong from England to China. Prince Charles was there for the hand over. I watched as the sky's opened and rain's came poring down. I watched as the Prince stood in the weather coming down in sheets to deliver his exchange speech. The flag of England came down and the flag of China went up.

After the ceremony the Prince was put in a limo. It was a perfect situation for the Chinese to do the Prince harm. I could see the cars rolling down the street with little to no protection. It was the perfect situation for Charles to be shanghaied. I felt my watching helped Charles survive. I am a second son and second child. I came to the realization I was also a second in time. My second was the Hong Kong turn over. If things didn't go correctly there may have been a war. I formed the opinion if someone was thinking or paying attention to an event they are involved with was good enough to thwart a mishap. It only takes one person out of place for something to go wrong.

The delirium was starting to take hold of me. It turned my attention to Prince Charles. If I could connect with others, why couldn't I connect with Charles? When an image of him came to mind he was on a white stead galloping away from me, but their backside would come closer only to move away again. The connection led to a test.

The contest we agreed upon would have the earth go two full rotations, or two full days, without taking a drink of any kind. I could still eat. The toughest part of the challenge was eating breads mostly. I kept my regular diet into the two days. At the end of the bet I went three extra hours before downing an ice-cold glass of water.

He then revealed a book he held. The book told the future if one got everything into place at the correct time, with a fairy tale ending. I recalled his marriage to Diana with the horse draw carriage and he attempting to play the part of Prince Charming. He made it clear he was waiting for a great President, one that could win a national championship ring and a Heisman trophy. I always considered myself to be Presidential, but I was not the one he was looking for. This was my first conversation with Charles.

As I thought more of the position the Royals held, I came up with a role for them to fill. If by chance aliens did visit earth, they would speak with the Queen and Charles. Now they are only figureheads and I would make them a sacrificial goat if the visitors acted violently. This would prove to be a failed test for the voyagers and earth would retaliate. This only works if there are heirs to the throne, which there are.

To show we are only playing I derived a game we could play. We would put our King, Prince Charles, and Queen, Queen Elizabeth II on a chessboard along with politicians around the globe to fill the positions of pawn, knight, rook, and bishop. The Pope would make a perfect bishop. The presidents of the U.S. and Russia would make good knights and others could be located if needed. Positions could be called upon to speak with another opponents to clear matters.

This brought me to think of how long and far this game could be played. I thought of space, after all we did enter the space race in the 1960's. I believe it was at this point we have had to awaken intelligent life in the far reaches of space. I asked myself what the alternate Universe would look like? My theory is we are in black darkness through our Universe; therefore the opposite would be bright and white. After this I guessed at a world of black and white forming a checker boarded deep space. If the game was to work here on earth we could play our way through space sending one position or another through space to work out conflict, to a black or white part of the world.

After a few days of thought, my troubled mind shifted back to the Nation of China. I would sit and think of their closed society and troubled human rights and viewed the Nation as a threat. I would go to War with them over and over for days at a time. I felt my most successful strategy was using Stealth Bombers coming off the coast of Alaska to bomb precise places in the Peoples Republic of China. The Bombers would then be picked up by an aircraft carrier in the southern Pacific. My idea was to knock out their buildings and to keep their death toll down. I played a game. I had an aircraft carrier in the middle of the Pacific almost daring the Chinese to bomb it, but on the contrary. It was part of a war game. I told them not to hit the ship. Hitting the vessel would show they had no value for human life. Unlike the surgical approach I was taking to only bomb building and not attach civilians. They do have a reputation for human rights mistreatment. If they hit that ship I would retaliate, unleashing nuclear weapons.

I brought this war to my National Guard physical. It was time for my physical. As I sat waiting I played out the scenario over and over. The physical took all day and all day I ran through my war. During the examination they did find I had had a knee operation years ago. They made it a problem only in the sense I wouldn't have to perform all the exercises at training camp. The rest was fine, I past the physical.

When I returned home my focus was right to my war. I kept the Stealth Bombers bombing and directed my attention to the aircraft carrier in the center of the Pacific. It was at this time the aircraft carrier was hit, several times. I watched as the ship began to sink and shipmates began jumping ship, for their lives. The massive carrier was going down and quickly. It split in two and I could hear the twisting metal. The solders jumping ship where being sucked under from the current the ship created. I had everyone on the ship perish. Later there would be a monument in their honor.

This gave me the clearance to hit the Chinese with a nuclear bomb. My question was, "What is the largest nuke I could send at them?" I estimated a weapon with the circumference of about the city of Denver. I waited two days before unleashing the bomb. I wanted to get as accurate with the timing as possible.

On the first day I watched as the weapon turned itself on and left the site onto puncturing the heavens, making its way through space. It then straightened itself out gliding through the darkness. On the second day, early in the morning the head of the bomb began to take it back down to earth. Some time around noon that day the head of the nuclear weapon began taking the weapon to its decent. It picked up more and more speed until there was impact. I played the song *War Pigs* by Black Sabbath in my head over and over again as the bomb hurled to earth.

I imagined the ground cracking to the earth's core. People died instantly, but others at the edge of the blast where hurled though the air for miles. I envisioned some of the citizens of China just feeling a warm breeze, only to learn of the devastation later. I estimated the destruction covered at leased one third of the Nation. I could only sympathize with the survivors who would have to deal with the tragedy. Their way of life would be changed for years. I believe the water system would be contaminated for decades.

I realized this was a game of fantasy, but three days later the Emperor of China died. When I saw this I put belief in my war. I thought this exercise took him out. My confidence in connecting mentally with others grew.

I thought of other ways to stop unscrupulous characters. I thought back to my second in time. The way just thinking or giving attention to something or someone could stop them from lashing out. I thought of terrorist groups. My first group was the IRA in Ireland. I paid a lot of attention to them and came to the conclusion they also did things by numbers, at least some of their bombs had to have timers on them. It was this thinking bringing me to the Millennium, year 2000, celebration. I thought this to be a date for terrorist activity. I also saw 1999 as a high-risk date. I have to explain that part of the charge of using numbers is the excitement when numbers line-up. One of these numbers, 2000, has three zeros and the other has three nines, 1999, but this got me thinking deeper. It was now 1997, pre 9-11, and one year away from 1998. As a safe guard I looked at this year with more scrutiny. What I came up with, after some playing, is if one takes the birth of our nation, 1776, and subtract it from 1998 one gets the 222 anniversary of the United States, three hidden twos. I put belief that any attacks in this year would now be covered because someone was thinking of or paying attention to these terrorists.

In my mind I believe we are civilized enough to turn from war to sports. I believe, in most instances, we have terrorism and wars because a country wants respect or attention for their country or the in equity in the standard of life there is. As there are war games, I don't see why we can't solve conflict with games. If one looks at the Olympics, the countries dominating the games are usually the super powers. I'd love to see a sports contest played for a piece of land or to settle dispute. Who ever win's the contest gets that piece of land. There could be High School games to take a little bit of their cross-town rivals city or town. Colleges could change state borders when playing their rival. A pro star team would take land from other countries. It seems to me like most wars involve a dispute over territory.

It doesn't really mater which sports are played. For instance the

AN AMERICAN MESSIAH

U.S. would have advantage in almost all sports, but when it comes down to soccer they are week. The rest of the globe has embraces soccer and could defeat America. As a former football player I have to say football is the closest thing to a war. Your fighting over territory, there are large lineman fighting in the trenches, dynamic running backs, and the quarterback as the field general. They are all attempting to invade the other teams territory. Then there is the lawless defense, which mirrors the offence, trying it's best to keep the offense from moving the ball down the field. The problem with football is its not played by other countries. It is for this reason I would spread the blue prints or plays at a fundamental level so other countries could learn the game. I'd give Russia most of the attention and time. How big a game would it be if the U.S. played Russia in a game for land? On the contrary I gave no attention to China. I would like to close with the fact sports are a new phenomenon to earth. They've only been around for a couple of hundred years if one dates back to soccer, but football, baseball, and basketball are basically a little over a century old if one dates back to baseball. I do believe these new contests can be a diversion to war in the future.

After occupying my mind with sporting games I made the decision to play a game with myself. I had very little money at this point, so I made the decision to get rid of all the money I had. I had the opportunity to go down to zero and start all over again. It was an easy task. I closed my bank accounts. I didn't have much to spend so it went quickly. I even made sure there were no coins in my cars ashtray. I was officially broke.

The madness was bearing down on my thoughts. I was on a high and wouldn't come down. I was beginning to enjoy it. There was an instance the Jerry Lewis Telethon for MS was on. I watched the show, but had no money to send them. This was so amusing I couldn't compose myself. I was cracking up. I thought, how can I feel guilty about watching and not sending money when I had none to send?

My mind shifted from thought to thought, topic to topic. The next images I conjured up where of Death, the Grim Reaper. He came to me looking for a death in the family. I immediately pled my case as someone with a long life ahead of him or her. In my fantasy with Death, I convinced him by killing myself over and over again, attempting to cover and show I was not about to try any of these methods. Though if I did get stuck on something it may be my time. I was now turning the light on others.

My Grandfather and Grandmother on my mother's side where old, but in good health and had a good family history of long life spans. My Grandmother on my father's side was still living, but also was in good health. The person I felt was in the worst shape and primed was my father. He didn't eat right and never exercised. He had a family history of males on his father's side with heart problems. In fact my Grandfather died of a heart attack and my fathers brother had to heart attacks or operations he survived.

I could see the Grim Reaper's long bony arm and finger out stretched in my father's direction. Just to hit the nail on the head I put my living Grandparents and my father in the order I projected them to pass. I had my father first, with my Grandfather second, followed by my Grandmother on my father's side, ending up with my Grand mother on my mother's side. Death was amused and was pacified by me.

That's when Death gave a tragic blow. August 31, 1997 Princess Diana was killed in a car crash in a London tunnel. The thing giving me even more confidence in what I was doing, was I had tried to direct my father to take his own life by driving down a tunnel the wrong way in Providence. The problem was Diana took the hit instead of him.

I watched Diana's funeral with the entire Royal Family marching with the casket it was the first time I had seen them all together. The royal I took interest in was the young Prince Harry. I could see he could grow into a powerful King.

In the days to follow all the TV networks covered Diana's short life. They showed her in a humanitarian roll, visiting the suffering and needy. This went on day after day. It got to the point where I felt they where making too much of her kindness and their where others who did more for the needy. The coverage became maddening and I belted out a mental outburst of someone more worthy of the coverage. Someone worth noting as a real champion of giving kindness ripped through my mind, "Who's Mother Teresa?" The next day Mother Teresa died. This twisted my mind even more. I felt I had taken out the caregiver.

I was consumed by the deaths of these two women so much I attempted to take out Fidel Castro. I could see him laying down to rest. He was particular on how he would die. He wanted a machete to cut his throat. The knife would need to be held gently by the handle putting only the wait of the machete to cut through the neck. He woke up startled if the machete was handled the wrong way. Trying to take his life I added a game to take him out. I would use my football plaques and Chi Phi memorabilia hanging on the walls to play chess. I would move one plaque across the room to signify a move. A Rook here a pawn there. After a few days of this game I received a call from my Uncle Tony.

This was my father's brother, the one who had two heart operations. He was a quite man and kept to himself through the years. I knew of him, but I didn't really know him. The thing I did know is he had become wealthy through the years and I had to respect that. He called wondering if I wanted to do lunch. I accepted.

We met at an Italian restaurant for lunch and we sat at the bar. I talked most of the time. I talked about my relationships with my family and things interesting me. The food was good, but my uncle was not there for my conversation. My parents must have sent him, because he was giving a pitch for me to see his psychiatrist. He was trying to talk me into it by saying; "There is nothing wrong with it." The same way I thought the TV was watching me or sending me messages was what I turned to for answers. He had made a tempting offer, but when I turned to the TVs at the bar, they said, "NO!" We had another lunch date after that one, but it had the same results. I didn't give in.

I had been waiting for over a month now for the National Guard to follow up, but they kept me waiting. This was my ticket out of this mess, but as I waited my thoughts and images kept flooding my mind. What I decided to do to occupy my mind was make a movie. I call it the *Fantasyland Killings*. The film begins at the Gingerbread House of the witch in the story of *Hansel and Gretel*. Hansel and Gretel are seated with a visitor. The visitor is a home alarm salesperson and has one of those blue or yellow dots over his head on the screen to conceal his identity. Hansel and Gretel are making improvements to the Gingerbread House and comment on how they want to keep the old witch out of the house. As they show the bathroom of the house the salesperson pulls out a gun with a silencer and shoots them both down.

The next seen begins with two detectives looking over the crime seen. They have been working together for a long time and one of the two is retiring at the end of the day. The detective wearing all black including a hat is the retiree, while the other is in white from head to toe. They review the seen and find a card that states, " The number of the house is your key." They make note of the 456 numbers on the house and continue searching. One of the bullets went right through one of them, which they determined to be a silver bullet. They both agree Hansel and Gretel were killed in the bathroom so it wouldn't be so messy. As they leave the crime seem the detective in white says' "I guess I'll be playing this one solo," and wishes the retiree the best.

The action now turns to the home of Adam and Eve who are sitting with the same alarm salesperson, this time with a smile face over his head to conceal his identity. Adam comments on the beautiful garden in the back. When they give the grand tour of their house they are also murdered in the bathroom with silver bullets and the same calling card, "The number of the house is your key." This time the detective in white makes note of the 11 on the house.

The next seen starts like the others, but this time it's just one man, Davie Joan's fortifying his condo. This time the killer's head is blurred over. Same M.O. the killer guns him down in the bathroom so as not to be sloppy. The white dressed detective is on the seen once again. He finds the calling card and makes note of the 666 as Mr. Joan's condo. He also makes note the murderer is gaining access to the homes without a struggle.

At this time he is growing frustrated and calls his old partner for some help. The white clothed detective feeds all the information to the retired detective. The best he can come up with is, "For the silver bullets, it must have been the Lone Ranger."

The next house to be *secured* is the castle of Dracula. Same scenario, Dracula sitting with the murderer who has a black bar across his face this time. They make it around the castle and when they get to the bathroom the murderer makes his move, but Dracula comes at him in defense. The killer shoots him in the chest with his silver bullets and feels lucky to make his way out. The detective goes over the murder seen with all the same clues, but this time he was messy and the numbers on the house where 874. This made no sense. Could the number of the house mean something else? He quickly turned to the telephone, could he mean that number?

AN AMERICAN MESSIAH

He then pulled all the phone records of the victims. What he found was a telephone number they had all called. They had all called the same small alarm company. What they planned to do was call the number and get the salesperson over to a house for a sting operation. They called the number and put a young detective, who replaced the man in black, in a house as the owner. They where ready to get this murderer.

The alarm salesperson found his way to the house with a dark shadow hiding his existence. It didn't take long for the young detective to make his way to the bathroom, but nothing happened, confusing everyone. They then made their way upstairs and over to another bathroom where the murderer takes out his weapon and shoots the young detective in the chest. The police force then comes in catching the murderer red handed. When the detective got to the killer he was in shock. It was his old partner, dressed in black from head to toe. As they took him away he yelled out, "I was only playing!" The young detective died from the gunshots, but he would always be remembered as a hero.

This movie was created in the time I was waiting for the National Guard to call. It was now growing late in the summer and entering autumn. While I was waiting for them I try to put myself in the worst shape possible. I did nothing all-day and changed the way I looked. I grew my nails and hair long.

While I tried to make myself a project for the Guard to take care of, I watched football on TV. The season was now reaching the meat of the schedule. I watched and watched and became more and more disturbed with the games. I began to turn on football because I felt it had abandoned me in college. I would never know how good I could have been and felt betrayed. The madness reared its head and I cursed the game of football to mishaps and poor play.

Once I was through with football I assessed my position and realized I finally would have to do something to get some money for gas and a hair cut. I changed my mind about growing my hair long. I didn't want to be considered a troublemaker as my first impression with the Air National Guard. The only thing I had that was worth anything I could depart with was my CD player and CD's. I took the CD player and CD's to a music store and sold the lot for around $50. I then filled up the gas tank and got a hair cut. I had some extra money, but didn't really need it for anything.

This brings me to Columbus Day 1997. As I gave in with my haircut I made the choice to leave my room and start patching things up with my family. I left my room for the first time while they where home and went downstairs to the living room. I recall diner starting and my mother calling me for the meal. I didn't feel like eating with them, so I stayed downstairs. After another call my mother came to confront me. She came down with the strangest question. She asked, "Do you want us to die, do you want us to die?" My reply in a twisted mindset was, "We're all going to die! ...We're all going to die!" I was yelling this over and over, which got my father involved. He came down and called 9-11 for an emergence. I then took my father, for calling the police, and tried to through a punch at him. The best I could do was to push him over a chair.

In minutes the police arrived and they disarmed the situation. They put me in cuffs and dragged me out of the house. That's when I noticing one of the officers as someone I had played baseball with on Warren Oil. I commented, "I knew you Cory we played ball together." They then took me to the back of the cruiser. I waited in the back of the police vehicle for some time as they got statements from my parents. I was hoping this would be a temporary position with my parents dropping the whole thing. That didn't happen.

The next thing I knew they rushed me to a cell in the West Warwick police station. I didn't know how long I'd be held and with no window it made it hard to judge time. After some time I knew I was in for the long hall. I occupied my mind with Loony Tune characters. During what I judged to be night, I went Loony tunes and couldn't get my mind away from Daffy Duck.

In what I thought to be morning, I was fed some toast. I was hungry so it was good. They then opened the cell and put the cuffs back on. They where getting ready to transport me to court. The Kent County Court House was only a few miles from the station. They rushed me there and to the holding tank in the courthouse. I stayed quiet in the cell. After about an hour in the tank they called me out. I was brought to the courtroom and seated on a bench to wait for my case to come up. While I waited there quietly I remember wanting to state 'my freedom of speech right was being infringed upon'. I never hit my father and all I was doing was yelling. I wanted to break my silence and yell this out as I waited, but never did.

Before I knew it I was called and was appointed a lawyer. Even then I didn't mention my freedom of speech rights, but it was time for my case so I had to pay attention. The judge had all the statements from my parents and gave me two choices. One was 40 days in jail and the other was to go to a psychiatric hospital until they saw fit. My lawyer pled with me to go to the hospital, but I was in no mind to make the decision. They didn't have time to see which I should do, so they put me back in the holding tank to weigh things over.

When I got to the holding tank I was anything but silent. I shared my dilemma with the other jailbirds. It was humorous to most of them, but very few gave input. I realized which would be easier and decided to go to the hospital. Now I waited until the days docket was finished and they called me back up. When they did I gave them my verdict. I was then taken, by police car to the hospital. I again remembered one of the police in the passenger seat. Scott was a pitcher and I was his catcher for the baseball Blue Jays in Babe Ruth, but I didn't say anything to him. We drove quite a way, by Rhode Island standers, to get there.

CHAPTER 8

There I was checking into the place I was trying to avoid for so long. The facility was Butler Hospital located in East Providence. I was un-cuffed upon entry. After signing in at the front desk I was placed in a waiting room. The room was half full with people. There was a TV in the room and the nightly news was on. Seeing this I estimated the time to be some where between 6:30 and 7:00pm.

After some time I was called in to be evaluated. I was sat down with a young girl for questioning. The questions and answers I recall are as followed. I was asked, "Do you share thoughts?" My reply was, "If I say something, like apple, you and I will both get a image of an apple, they may not be the same but it's a shared thought." The next question was, "Do you hear voices?" Again I wasn't going to give in without a fight, I commented, "When one reads a book they make voices for the characters in the story." The last question from this young lady was, "Do you feel as if the world revolves around you?" My reply was, "as a football stand out I have been the focus of a lot of attention."

I was left to wait in her office as she called upon someone else. She brought in what I find was a doctor. I have no idea if this was normal pros edger or something unique to my test. This was a male and he seemed very serious about the whole thing. I spoke with him for a few minutes, but can't recall anything other than he was worked up about something. Maybe he was trying to get the answers out of me with a serious demeanor. I thought I had a chance to talk my way out of the mess, but that didn't seem to work.

After my evaluation, a nurse came for me and took me to the unit I would be staying in. The first thing they did when I got up to the unit was the taking of my vital signs. They took my blood pressure and temperature. The second thing was to sit me down and asked if I was hungry. I hadn't eaten since the breakfast toast in the West Warwick cell, so I was hungry and stated so. They got me a burrito. At that time almost anything would have been good and the food was enjoyable. It was dark and quiet, looking at the darkness of night out the window, it had to be 9:00pm or later. I was then shown to my room. There was already someone in the room so I was careful not to awake him. No matter what time it was I then went to sleep, I didn't sleep the night before in the West Warwick cell, and so this was a welcome rest.

In the morning I was awaken by a dietitian who asked what I wanted for my daily meals. I had choices between a few different meals at each meal of the day. This would go on every morning. My vitals where taken again after that. This also would be something routine for every morning. I then met my doctor. Doctor Furman and his Assistant where on my case. I would meet with them every morning, as well, with the exception of weekends where there would be a substitute. The other constant was Group Therapy. This would meet two times a day everyday, even weekends. I remember a young thin guy ran Group. If you didn't go to Group they wouldn't allow one to go out for walks outside.

There where always two male nurses in the unit, watching our every move. I guess they where there to stop problems between patients or to react to any patients in need of help. The showers where not in each room and one would have to ask one of those nurses if they could take a shower. All the showers where located on the other side of the unit. A washer and dryer were provided to do ones laundry during their stay. A pay phone was a fixture, to make calls to who ever one wished. I never really counted but I estimate 6 to 8 rooms where occupied by patients. A smoking both or chamber was located in a corner directly after the kitchen, for smokers who needed a puff. One would also find game tables for checkers, chess, and backgammon. We would meet our doctors at said tables. Magazines and books where left hanging around the facility. A book cart would come around at night. There were also plenty of puzzles. A TV was mounted on the wall, but no one really paid any attention to it.

The first few days of my stay at Butler I moved around the unit getting familiar with the area. I would do a bit more than that. I would make squat thrust moves to gain the attention of the staff. I was attempting to tell them I was special and unique and could prove it to them. The documents and tapes, I had at home, of my high school football carrier and my college Fraternity memorabilia would serve to be proof.

Nightly the World Series between the Cleveland Indians and the Florida Marlins was on, but I paid no attention to the games. Instead one night I found myself looking out the window noticing a glow from a lamppost. The light from the post was the same shape as the table I was sitting at. Each shape was a trapezoid with a long top and small bottom. The sides ran equally from top to bottom. These shapes got my mind sending notes of my findings. I thought this could be a configuration lending itself to teleportation. The alignment of the person in this room sent through the window and into the light of the post. That night I played this over and over.

While I played a name came to mind in the form of a question, "Who is Michael Irvin?" I knew the name, but couldn't figure out how I knew it. I automatically thought sports, but couldn't come up with it. That's when I made him someone in the future of great importance. I made him the first person to be teleported. I also made him a great general in a war between North and South America to unite the two continents. He would then become a President. Perhaps the first Black President. On another level I made him the first man to make it into the alternate Universe. Maybe he was destined to come up with an Aids vaccine. I felt I had to look over him and guide him through whatever scenario he had to go through.

It then came to me that Michael Irvin was a receiver for the Dallas Cowboys. The first thing that came to mind is there could be a more famous Michael Irvin in the future. Maybe he would be an ancestor of the football star. All I knew is a Michael Irvin would be in a position to achieve great things.

As I've mentioned, group was held everyday to help with coping. It happened so often I don't remember much about it. The session standing out in my mind was one were we had to name a song from the 80's. My first choice was to answer Van Halen's song *"Jump"*, but I changed my mind. I had heard the song had messages of jumping off buildings to commit suicide. I then changed the Song to Bobby McPheron's song *"Don't Worry be Happy."* I felt this was a good change for many reasons.

Speaking of jump. I had a great leap at a football in our second Championship game. It was a two-point conversion in the forth quarter where the points didn't really mean much. That's when, I'll swear, I took a jump at a ball and my mind and body traveled further than I new possible. I'm stating I flew for a all be it brief fractional second. I wanted to tell the doctors or nurses, but thought they would think I was just being delusional, so I kept it to myself as I had for several years.

Other times you could find me looking out the window from the entrance doors. I would look into the unit across the hall to see what they where doing. They did most of the same stuff we did. While looking through the window I noticed the doors opened out and would remain open if the stoppers where pushed to the down position. I noticed the stopper would drag on the ground as the door swung open only to stop the door wide open before it closed shut. I tested my theory. That night I acted like I was looking through the doors, only to push the stopper down. I waited for the book cart to come and when it did the door opened and the cart came in without anyone noticing. I walked to the door, where I could have walked out, and lifted the stopper to close the door. I don't believe this would work with the meal truck.

The meal truck came in on time every day. After several days it was one of the things I looked forward to most. During one lunch, a nurse with some medication approached me. I took a look at it in its little cup. It was half of a little pink pill. At first I resisted, but was persuaded to take it. After taking it down I was monitoring myself through the next several hours, but felt nothing. From this point on the dos of medication increased slowly.

Although I was humbled and embarrassed at the position I was in, I had visitors. My parents visited the most, but I had other visitors who where unexpected. My Uncle Tony, whom I had lunches with, and his new wife Isabel visited me. My Aunty T.T. visited with my Aunt Jerry. My uncle Johnny took my Grandparents to visit. It was nice to have visitors, but as I said earlier it was a humbling and embracing spot I was in. It was being proved I didn't think correctly and that's not something one wants to think about.

As my roommates kept leaving for home or different rooms, a visitor of a different kind joined me. Outside my window was a ledge and whom do you think showed up on that ledge. No one but the Devil I had seen on a high perch in hell. I could see this was becoming my Hell and he was there with me. These dilutions didn't last long as the med's increased almost daily.

I have to say other than lunch the walks outside where the only source of enjoyment. It was the middle of autumn and all the leaves had changed. The *Butler* campus was on a nice location where the leaves really came to life with firry yellow, oranges and reds. It's only because of these walks around the buildings I went to group.

Something I began to do out of habit and because my medication was making me hungry was eating cereal and toast in the kitchen. I visited every night. Other patients could also be found in the kitchen eating. I didn't really talk to anyone the whole time I was there. I was concerned with myself. This is when I noticed one of the patients just slept through day after day. I then decided to do the same thing, in bed morning noon and night.

I had now been at Butler for nearly 30 days. It was at this time I was told by Dr. Furman's Assistant that I was "psychotic". I immediately snapped back at her, "Where, where am I psychotic!" She left me there, but my snap back at her was almost enough proof of psychosis. That's when I began sleeping right through group, loosing my walking privileges.

Shortly after Dr. Furman diagnosed me with Schizophrenia. This really sent me reeling. Just to think I didn't think right was a massive weight. The next time I saw my father I told him I was tired of this place. I also confided in him. I told him, "I have lost everything in the past few years. I lost my girlfriend Michele and I lost football, I lost my friends. The next day I was released. I was there for around 40 days. I never really was keeping track. I was released on Halloween.

I arrived at home that afternoon. My father picked me up and brought me home. I remember him lighting a fire in the woodstove downstairs. Later in the afternoon my Uncle Tony stopped by. He stayed for an hour or so and then left. It was nice to be home and away from *Butler*. My mother came home to greet me after she finished work in the very early evening. Trick or treaters where already on the streets going door to door for candy and my house was like all the rest. Sometimes I would answer the door to give the costume wearers some candy. It felt good to be doing something other than sit there feeling sorry. It was a positive experience and helped me on my first day out. It made me feel like I was part of the community.

Although Halloween was a treat, it was still hard to cope with the fact I had a disorder, which affected my thinking. It's quite a blow to the ego to go from that mental high to wondering how to speak with others correctly on a topic or hold a conversation where someone wouldn't see I had mental illness. I had a long way to go to build my confidence from this point. This is the lowest I had ever felt. This had to be my personal hell. Everyone I knew would know I had stayed at Butler Hospital. This is the reason I had after care.

My after care program was at *Gateway* in Johnston. On my first visit, my father took me to the therapy. The first day was to register me at the facility. The next trip I took myself. That was my first time attending group. I would have to be there one or two times a week. This was a little different from the group in Butler. They gave us the opportunity to talk about what was going on with each of us. They wanted to know what strives we where making to get well. There was a lot of listening. When it was my turn I always asked if I could stop taking the meds and they would always respond with a no. I would follow up by tell them I would be going to the Nation Guard. They also encouraged exercise, so I told them I would do my best to put my old weight lifting equipment back together to train. I tried, but couldn't get it assembled. Therapy was nice to get me out of the house, but didn't really help.

The next part of my coping and maintenance was seeing a psychiatrist or doctor. The doctor taking on my case was at the Summit building and his name was Dr. Demby. He was there to make sure I was taking my medication, as well as correctly, and give prescriptions for them. He would also take an interest in what I was up to and if I had any questions. I was also assigned a nurse named Brian. I would see him sparingly. One consistent thing with all my help, they asked if I was working or planning to work? My parents echoed this question

After a week or so of looking in the paper I found a design studio near by which was hiring. I got my portfolio and zipped right over there. After the owner saw my work he gave me the job on a temporary bases to see if I was right for his studio. Other than the owner there was one other worker and he was leaving in two weeks. The first day I didn't do much of anything. The only thing to speak of was a book the other designer was working on. He showed me some of what he was doing so I could take over once he was gone. We where the only two working, the owner was rarely there. On the second day I was given an easy assignment, but it took me all day. This task gave me a panic attack like I had never felt before. The following day the owner and I agreed I wasn't the right fit for the job. At this time I was totally unprepared to hold this job or any other for that matter. The only up side was I had worked for a couple of days and had some money, be it a small amount, coming to me.

It was in the middle of this difficult time I received a strange piece of mail. I was chosen for Jury Duty. I wondered if they had made a mistake, I was just in court as a defendant a short time ago. My mother was jealous. She always wanted to sit in on a case. Jury duty was to be held later that winter.

It was now late November and I had met with my doctor and therapy at Gateway was finished, but there was one more item needing to be taken care of. I had a court date with the Judge who had heard my case. He wanted to follow up to see if I was complying with my treatment. It was an early court date and I was called quickly. I guess he had gotten reports from Butler and Gateway, because he had reports on what I was up to. I knew I was complying and he recognized that I was. He was satisfied, so off I went. A small piece of this disaster was completed.

Having satisfied Butler, Gateway, Dr. Demby and the court system, I turned my attention to the Air National Guard to see if they attempted to contact me while I was in the hospital. I contacted my recruiter and she had not tried to locate me in the time period. That was a relief, but I had to make another call to see if the medication I was taken was O.K. with them. It took them about a week to get back to me, but they gave me the bad news, the medication I was taking would prevent me from joining the Air Guard.

By this time my thoughts where drowned out, I was tired, sluggish and mind num. I found myself asleep on the couch nightly, but awaken by my mother to move so she could occupy the couch. I would move to another seat just to fall asleep again. The medication, Risperdal, was turning me into a zombie, but I was in a position were I couldn't do any thing about it. I was also slowly putting on weight. The only thoughts I had where distant, but there seemed to be something or someone checking on me. They seem to be checking to see if I was still there and a reminder I may be needed. These thoughts or messages where distant and didn't happen to often.

    I was still being pushed to find work by my parents and doctor. That's when I answered to an Inventory job in the paper. I got the job and asked for a curtain schedule, which didn't seem to be a problem for them. The only thing I was asked to do was wear a pair of black pants. I had a pair at home. The other thing worth noting was the travel time the crew took to a job was unpaid. Here I was a Penn State graduate working a menial job, but I took it anyhow.

    The first day I worked we where at *Home Depot* somewhere in Massachusetts. It involved getting close to the ground and made my pants filthy. I found it difficult to work the keypad and I assumed it would get easier the more I used it. The next time I went out it was at a pharmaceutical company who wanted their drugs counted. The capsules where packaged in packets, so it wasn't so hard to count them. That was an easy day. Though the managers had, disappointingly, failed to put me down on days I wanted off. The next day was at a retail store. I was kicked of the crew and told to wait outside in the cold of winter this job. I was so out of it at this point I had no idea why I was cast aside. The next and final day working for this inventory company was at a *Job Lot*. I did work that day and the keypad never got any easier. I never showed up to see what the next job would be. I had quit!

    It was after this bad experience, my father wanted to know what I was going to do with myself. He extended an offer to work with him at *D and B Antenna*. I thought it over for a short time and accepted the offer. I would start as a party time employee. I had worked there before during summers and some weekends when help was needed. I was going to be working with Denis, who I had already worked with on those past experiences. This would be different; he would be showing me how to put up antenna and satellite dishes. I would assist him at the beginning of my experience. He would mount the dishes and I would help find the right angles to point it. It was fairly easy. I started during the winter and it was quite an ordeal to strip and fit cable, never mind going up on rooftops with bolts, screws and nuts.

While working on only a few days of the week, I went back into the classifieds. I located a job opening as a photo finisher rather quickly. I thought this would be categorized as a job within the graphic design circle. I called the Massachusetts based company for an interview and we agreed on a time and day to meet when I was not working.

It took some time to get there, but I arrived ready for the interview. The first think I noticed is they had *Kodak* all around the building. I had to wait a little while for someone to meet with me, but I took it in stride. Someone finally came to give me some direction. They sat me down in a room and asked me to fill out an application, though I had a resume with me. There were also some office policies with the paper work. Once I was finish, someone to conduct the interview greeted me. We touched on a few different topics before the interviewer divulged he was also a Penn State graduate. He continued to let me know this was a second shift position, which I had reservations due to my medically induced slumbers. He also let me know there was a drug test. I then told him I was on prescription meds, which he commented, 'wouldn't be a problem'. They were testing for illegal drugs. It was nice to hear I had someone on my side. We talk about similar places around the campus for a few minutes. He then proceeded to give me a tour of the facilities. Stations for every portion of the films processing was established, from opening the bags the film arrived in and sorting them, to putting them in the developing machines. After the tour he offered me the position and I accepted. I would begin working after the drug test had been conducted, usually two weeks.

I took the drug test at the designated post on a day off. Before the test I was asked if I took any prescription drugs. I answered, "Yes." And the nurse inquired, "What do you take them for?" I was embarrassed and afraid it would get back to the employer to say, "Schizophrenia." Though I had prepared for the question and replied, "Racing thoughts." I would then begin the waiting to hear from this company.

While I was waiting I had something to occupy my time. The date for my Jury Duty had come up on the calendar. The duty was at the Kent County Court House, which wasn't even two miles from my house. I got there early as the green card I had received in the mail directed. I found myself amongst what had to be 30 or more potential jurors. They held us all in a room in the courthouse for, as I remember it, three days or more days. Most of those days we would be dismissed before two o'clock.

Once the waiting was over we were escorted to the courtroom each of us given a number. I was hoping we would be excused all together, so I could get to the job as a photo finisher. My drug test had come in free and clear and I was now delaying the job because of the Jury Duty. If I were called as a juror, I would have to ask for more time before I started.

As we all sat waiting the lawyers would select potential jurors, put them in the jurors box and one by one would question them. Many people were dismissed after their questioning. They where sent home for being unsatisfying for one lawyer or the other. I was hoping I would be sent home after my turn and my turn did finally come up. I was sat in the box with some other jurors to be and questioned. The lawyers asked such questions as, "Are you sometimes swayed from one opinion to another?" "Do you listen to details carefully?" Then one of the lawyers asked, "Give me an instance where you have changed someone's mind?" On the spot the only thing I could think of was being at work and I answered, "I work putting up satellite dishes and sometimes we debate on where the dish should be put on the roof." I guess they both liked what I had to say, because I was selected. That evening I contacted the people at the photo-finishing job and told them I would need more time because I was selected as a juror. They informed me they would need to find someone else who could start at that time. I was disappointed.

Now that the jury had been established the trial was ready to begin. It was a rape case. In a nut shell: one Friday night there where people drinking and a girl got to drunk and passed out, so her boyfriend took her home to bed. While passed out in her and her boyfriends' bed, the boyfriend's half brother got into the bed and raped her as she was passed out. The case lasted about a week and we the jury came back in a couple of days with a Guilty verdict. We where then released and sent home. I never did hear the sentencing for this trial.

It was then back to the job at *D and B*. When I got back I was now working full time. It's at this time Denis started giving me the task of going up on the roofs to put up the satellites and antenna. He had also started working at *Fed Ex* on his day off. Some days the weather was miserable and I still had to go out there, but the days passed and it was the end of winter. It was also the end of Denis.

He had been looking to get out of there as soon as he could and had landed a full time position at *Fed Ex*. He always would comment how bad it was do work there and there was no future. That's when they hired a new employee to take Denis's position. I work with a man named Joe, up until spring. What I do recall is allergies. Not only did I have allergies, I was gaining more weight. Not only that, I sometimes found myself gazing over the edge of rooftops with thoughts of jumping. I was still in a terrible spot headed no were.

I decided to do something about it. I joined the old gym, *Power House*. It was a difficult task getting back into the gym in the shape I was. I would look at the other people in the gym and wishing I were them. I made some progress in strength, but never lost any weight. Though, I made going to the gym part of what I did and stuck with it.

I was still seeing Dr. Demby every other month. I would meet with him for about a half hour. From time to time I was still seeing Brian, my nurse. Dr. Demby would take an interest in my life, but he was there to write prescriptions for me to fill. It was very non-therapeutic. I wish I could have met more often for a longer time, but he wasn't conducting a private practice.

At the beginning of the summer I would find my next employer. Another ad in the classifieds pointed me in the direction of assessor's assistant. The job entailed walking around neighborhoods measuring homes with a six-foot stick one length after another. I then would map out the houses dimensions on the information page I was given. The work was long and monotones. I worked there for a long three months through summer and the beginning of fall. With that said I turned in my stick and started looking elsewhere.

The next job in the parade of non-enjoyable work places was at a Mortgage lender, *New England Mortgage*. They where located in Foxboro, Massachusetts, not the worst commute. I was hired as a loan originator, which meant I wore headphones with a microphone hooked up to a telephone and computer. The computer automatically dialed over and over again so one could contact more and more people. Once one got some one on the phone they would see if they had any interest in a mortgage. If they were I would type their info into the computer.

DAVID MICHAEL

I was never good at it and was doing this for $7 an hour, more if I got people to sign up for mortgages.

While there I met Everett who also worked there. I had played one year of baseball and one year of football with him in High school. He was a loan officer, where the info went after one types it in to the computer. It was nice to see a familiar face. He also got me to thinking maybe I could get out of this position and into a loan officer position. I inquired but they said they wouldn't be considering anyone until the spring.

One thing I distinctly remember about this job is the Boston Red Sox in the play-offs. During my lunch break and during my fifteen minutes break, I would turn them on the radio in my car and listen with my seat back. As happens every year they where eliminated before the World Series. I wished I were home to watch them.

One thing about this company, they gave away a lot of gifts to there employees. On one occasion they gave everyone a down jacket. It had the logo on they chest, but it was a nice jacket. The people there were fun, though the work was not the best. Like I said I enjoyed the people, but I found myself leaving early faking sick. The next day I drove all the way there, only to turn back. I went to *Foxwoods* instead, a casino just over the Connecticut line. It was a good trip. I won about $200. The next day I did the same thing. I never told them I quit. I just stopped going to work. They did send me my last check in the mail.

After this stint I was frustrated. I knew I wanted a job in graphic design, so I went to the phone book and called every design studio in the book. A firm *Accu-graphics* showed interest and we set up an interview. The interview was in East Providence with the owner Walter and art director Sue. They where impressed enough to call in the rest of the staff to see what they thought. They all liked what they saw and had some questions for me to answer. One of which was from Walter, "Have you ever used drugs?" I replied, "Not since college." Which was the truth. The owner wanted to hire me on a preliminary bases and I jumped. This is what I needed, a chance to show what I could do. I landed the job just before Thanksgiving and would have something to be thankful for on this holiday. It had been a long time since I could say that.

CHAPTER 9

After almost a week I was ready for my first day at *Accu-Graphics*. When I walked in through the back door Walter had mistaken me for a delivery person. I told him I was there to work and it jogged his memory. I was then introduced to everyone. There was Jason, Molly and Erik who where designers. I had met Sue and Walter earlier. Denise found work for the studio, while Janice was the office manager. The final person in the office was Dick who headed *Accu-Com*, a company he and Walter where partners in. After the introductions I was led to the print room.

I was given a white-faced art desk to work on. I was instructed to put together Christmas cards for the office. Erik had already laid out the cards. The cards where assembled in two pieces. One piece had a sleeve for the other. The other part was a card sliding out of the first sleeve. In the center of the card was a window where season's greeting where written and when the card was slid out a Christmas tree could be seen through the window.

There were a lot of straight cuts with an e-xacto knife. I made a template I could trace to make both parts of the card more easily. The first day I grew tired from the repetitive nature of the task. I asked for a break from the work and was given a small cleaning job. I was able to cut and assemble all the cards after that day, without a break. In all I believe there where 250 cards when I was finished. Once I finished the task Walter wanted to meet with me.

It was a quick meeting but very important to my future. Once the cards where finished he had to make a decision on what to do with me. He told me, "They would like to take me on." He then asked, " What kind of money I was asking for?" I follow his question with, "I'd like $20,000 per year." He said, "$18,000." I bought. I was now employed in a good situation. The money wasn't great, but I lacked computer experience and he knew that, because I had mentioned it on my first interview.

DAVID MICHAEL

As you may have noticed from the Christmas cards, Christmas was upon us. I was lucky, I wasn't even there for a month and I was going on the office Christmas celebration. I say celebration, because of the unique day taken to notice the Christmas Holiday. In the morning a limo picked us up and took us to breakfast at the Biltmore. The limo then made its way to Thanial Hall in Boston, Massachusetts, where we did some browsing and light shopping and had a few drinks. From there we traveled to the I-max theatre in Boston. The movie we saw took us on an adventure through the Amazon. To finish the day we stopped in at an Italian restaurant for dinner and more drinks. While we were there eating we met a group of gentlemen who picked up our tab and this was no cheap restaurant. Walter got their names and numbers, so he could do something for them. Once we finished our meal and thanked, who I believe to be Frank and his friends, we made our way back to the office.

Back to work, I was assigned to go through the PhotoShop and Illustrator tutorial programs. They gave an over view of the programs, but didn't really train a person to be ready for the work place. I also made deliveries to *Hasbro, Lightolier,* and *Allied Signal*. I didn't mind the trips. They got me out of the office for a little while. Although the first piece of work I was directed to work on was a toy. I was to us the Illustrator program too Illustrate a small *Star Wars* space vessel. It was awkward at first, but I think I picked it up pretty quickly. Walter helped me modify the illustration. My skill as an illustrator improved as I finished more and more illustrations.

Having landed a job I felt more comfortable and I started to reconnect with my friends and make new friends. New Years Eve, entering the New Year of 1999, I met up with my old friends, my friend Wally's younger brother, Jason along with Eddy and his roommate Steve. I was also introduced to a guy named Ray. He came with Jason and was close to Jason's age. We gathered at Ed's apartment. We drank a little before going out. Some of them took some ecstasy, but I passed on the drug.

We where headed to a club named *Club Hell*. This would be my first time there. We would be meeting my friend Wally and I would be meeting his girlfriend there. Once we got into the club, the first thing I noticed was the amount of black being worn. It was somewhat dark; I mention this because the flashing spinning lights on the dance floor lightened up the place. It was still dark enough for glow sticks to be part of the dance moves. I don't dance so there was little for me to do, other than drink and people watch.

Wally and his girl Shannon showed up after some waiting. Most of the night I hung out with them at the corner of one of the bars. I don't remember the New Years festivities being anything special, though it was a good night for me. I hadn't been out in public for some time.

After the New Year it was time to return to work. Part of my duties at work included collecting the work of each artist on a Jazz disc, then putting the work into a computer. I would then burn the work on to disk as a back up and turned into a history of past information.

Every other Friday half the staff would have half the Friday off. This was good for me. It gave me the opportunity to schedule appointments with Dr. Demby and make other errands. I would also go to gamble at *Foxwoods* when I had no appointments. I was still seeing Dr. Demby and mentioned I had been to *Club Hell* with my friends. He laughed a little and asked where it was? I gave him the closest landmark, "Behind the court house in Providence". I was still asking to get off my med's which he again denied.

Though I was meeting with a doctor every month or so, I didn't tell him everything. There was something bothering me and I hadn't told anyone else. I started to develop panic attacks that would last a full day. I would have them at work, specifically on Mondays. It was tough to focus on my work. It was such an uneasy feeling; it was sucking the confidence I had built up, right out of me. When driving home during one of these episodes, I would concentrate on the license plates in front of me as a guide to get home.

A positive thing I had started was dieting. My weight must have been close to 250 lbs and I'm only about 5'9" on a good day. My diet consisted of a glass of orange juice to start my morning with a regular sandwich for lunch, and dinner would be some kind of fruit, mostly bananas. I would have no snacks. The diet worked well and I gradually began taking off weight.

On Martin Luther King's birthday I had one of these attacks. That day we where all supposed to go home early. I was working on something needing to be finished that day. All I had to do was align some measurements. My lack of focus led me to measure incorrectly on the piece. When Walter saw this he assigned Molly to help me. She did and we got out of there close enough to lunch.

Away from work I was reuniting with my buddies. Again we met at Ed's apartment before going out to *Club Hell*. It was the usual suspects: Ray, Wally, Jason, Steve and Ed. Again there was some drinking and partying. This night pot was being smoked and I decided to join in. It had been a long time since I partook and it felt good. I missed it. It was the best I had felt in a while. We all went to *Club Hell* after we where finished. Again I don't dance so I stayed close to the bar and admired one of the female bar tenders.

The next weekend we met at the same place with the same people. This time I would be introduced to a girl named Jill, who was Ed's girlfriend's friend. She sat and smoked marijuana with us and drank a little. Later in the evening the ecstasy or as it's call "E" was busted out once again. Mostly everyone did the drug and I caved in and tried it. I didn't know what to expect, but I felt fine while at Eddy's. Later that night at the club I took a seat and never left it. I could barely stay awake. That night driving home from Ed's was quite a task, but I made it.

The partying had expanded from the weekend into the week. After I came home from working out I would head over to Ray and Wally's apartment. It was run down, but it was a good place to hang out. Wally had to work nights so he wasn't there until around 10:00pm, so he missed out a little. Ray and I would smoke pot and drink a little. Jill would come over on occasion with her friend Tosha. I was finally enjoying myself again.

Work was also enjoyable. The more illustrations I did the better I got. I would work on any thing from a *Star Wars* toy from *Hasbro* to a light fixture mounting for *Lightolier*. The artwork was all black and white line drawings, mostly for a direction or instruction sheet. I had become a Jr. Illustrator for *Accu-Graphics*.

The people working there were nice and helpful. If I had a problem with something they where glad to lend a hand. The only thing not there that would have been nice was someone who liked sports. They where all art people, but one day Janice the office manager was talking to me and mentioned a friend of hers went to a round of the NCAA tournament the past weekend at the Fleet Center.

AN AMERICAN MESSIAH

I had to tell her see surprised me, "I had no idea the Fleet Center was hosting part of the tournament." She may not have surprised me with her knowing a friend had gone to the games, she surprised me in I didn't know the regional was held at the Fleet. That was about the extent of my sports conversations at *Accu-Graphics*.

Walter brought his son Michael into the studio for his spring break. He wasn't really there to learn anything; he already had experience in the design programs at home from Walter exposing them to him. He was a good kid. He was a senior at Hendricken High school and was looking to put his portfolio together to send to the colleges he hoped would accept him. By the end of the week he got the thing together with a little help.

By this time I had worked enough I could indulge in something I wanted. I had saved up enough to get my own computer. It would have to be an Apple, because that's what we used at work. I decided on an I-Mac. I also bought a printer and scanner. Since the I-Mac only comes with a CD drive I had to purchase a Zip drive to store work. It was the biggest purchase I had made up until that point.

When I got my I-Mac back home I had to get all the peripherals loaded into the computer. It was easy. I also had to load the PhotoShop and Illustrator programs I had bought. The same programs I used at work. That was also easy. The only thing I didn't have was the inter-net, but I rarely used it at work and had no desire to use it. Above I was mentioning I liked sport. The first thing I put into the computer was a football formation, the "T" formation.

At work I was working on an R2D2 illustration for *Hasbro*. It was to be an instruction sheet. Upon finishing the artwork I was flustered and didn't know how to correlate the stickers to the art. That's when, I'm embarrassed to say, I faked sick for two days hoping someone else would finish the work. As I had at *New England Mortgage*, I took the days off and went to gamble at *Foxwoods*. This time it was different in the fact I returned to work at *Accu-Graphics*. When I came back, Sue had finished the instruction page with the decals.

Outside of the design world I was partying enough I quit lifting weight, but I was still dieting successfully. I was loosing slowly but surly, but again I was still having fun smoking dope and drinking with Ray and who ever stopped by. I was enjoying this so much I started to hate my job. I had to get up early and couldn't stay out late, but when at work I was enjoying the challenging nature of the job. The only unenjoyable things at this point where the panic attacks, so I mentioned them to my parents.

My next doctor visit I told Dr. Demby about the attacks. I asked if it could be the medication I was on, because I never had them before the meds. He said the Risperdal wouldn't do that to me. He gave me anti-anxiety meds to take when I felt the attacks coming on. That week an attack came to me at work and I took the drugs, but it had no effect. He also had me visit another doctor at Butler. She gave me a physical and scheduled an EEG for me at Rhode Island Hospital. I also took this test with no results. In the back of my mind I thought it could be cancer.

The light partying at Mill St., Ray and Wally's place, was about to get a little bigger. A tattoo artist named Don was about to occupy one of the rooms. He moved all his stuff into the third room of the apartment. Right from the beginning it seemed like Don was ready to party. He not only partied with us, he also liked going to *Club Hell*, but no one liked *Club Hell* like Ray did. Myself I didn't enjoy the club that much after going a few weekends in arrow. It was at this time I went out on my own to a club called *The Fish Company*.

I like the club much more than *Hell*. The people seemed to be having more fun and they weren't all dressed in black. I enjoyed the crowd a lot more, because it wasn't all dark. I still didn't dance, but they had a lot of dancers on their floor. The girls also looked better at the *Fish Co*. This would be my new place and I would be coming back often. It's not to say I was breaking with my friends, I still saw them during the week.

June 11, 1999, my brother and his wife Stephanie had their first child. It was a big deal for my family. Zachary Garcia was the firstborn child in the next generation of Garcia. Zack would be more than my nephew. My brother and his wife asked me to be his Godfather and of course I said, "Yes." His Godmother would be Stephanie's sister Denise. It was nice they asked me and showed they still viewed me as a part of the family and not some cast off.

By now I had lost a considerable amount of weight. My clothes no longer fit, they where baggy and loose and I would have to pull up my pants to keep them up. My dieting had paid off. I felt my slimmer self represented me much better than the heavy one. I was always slim and athletic and I had another thing to feel good about. People from the office and some of my friends would comment on how they noticed I had drop a lot of weight. It was good feeling when they noticed.

Now, through out this book I have stated, "I'm only playing." If one were to ask me what the rules where I would have to point to the Constitution. It is there one will find the President has to be 35 years old, born in the United States and a U.S. citizen. I also find the "…pursuit of happiness…" is something one can follow and probably does on a subliminal level. How many times has one honestly heard this part in of the Constitution? I believe this has programmed the U.S. to strive further than other countries. This also makes me believe we are a big human experiment.

This led me to a document I began while watching a baseball game on TV. I don't really call it anything, but maybe the Doctrine of Man. In this document I call for the Freedom of all man Black, White, Asian, Hispanic…all Races. This sounds like something we all know already, but I question if it's been made official someplace, maybe it has in the *Bill of Rights*. I also continue to call for the freedom of the Soul, Will, and Spirit. To build off the "Pursuit of Happiness" I call for man not only to pursue happiness, but to mold himself as…strong, intelligent, free, viral, quick, noble…etc. Something anyone would strive to be.

Jill had always wanted to see my design portfolio. One night I brought her over to take a look at my work. We went through my portfolio and she was impressed. I also had some black and white photos I had taken in college I showed her. While looking through my things I came across a pamphlet on Risperdal, the medication I was taking for my schizophrenia. I showed it to Jill before I started looking at some of the possible side effects. As I went through a number of the side effects I came across 'anxiety' as one of the side effects. I was upset and disappointed Dr. Demby hadn't made the connection with my meds and the attacks I was experiencing. The next day I made an appointment to see him.

When meeting with him, I told him, "I was disappointed he said the meds didn't cause the panic attacks. It was then when I asked, "Do I have to take my meds?" He replied, "You don't have to take them if I don't want to." I wanted to get off the meds for so long I almost couldn't believe it. I didn't let my parents know, I knew they wanted me to take the meds.

DAVID MICHAEL

Two weeks after stopping my meds, on the way to work I was getting hot flashes. That morning we had a team meeting in the office, the hot flashes persisted and I almost asked to go home. I stayed at work trying to fight through these flashes of white. They lasted all day. I made it all the way until a half hour of work was left, when Sue gave me a pieces needing to be looked up on one of the CD which where burned. I back logged to a few disks and couldn't find the work I needed. It was a combination of frustration, not finding what I was looking for and the flashes having me leave the office 15 minutes early without telling anyone.

On the way home I was experiencing some hot flashes at a more rapid rate, but I made it home. When I got home I laid down hoping these flashes on white would subside, but they didn't. When my mother got home I couldn't control myself and began crying. When she saw me I said, "I can't handle it any more." The first thing she asked was if I was taking my medication and I told her I wasn't and Dr.Demby said I didn't have to. I had some of my Risperdal left so I took some. After I started to feel better. That night I even felt good enough to go visit my friends. They knew I hadn't been taking my meds and I told them what had happened. While there I had some minor flashes. I left early and went home to relax.

The next day I had to answer Walter. He asked me what happened to me. I couldn't bring up the schizophrenia during my early drug test and I couldn't get it out off me at this time either. I told him I had a fussy feeling on the left side of my head and was being tested by doctors. He just told me to tell someone when I was leaving and we left it at that. That day at work I scheduled another appointment to meet with Dr. Demby as soon as possible.

When I met with Dr. Demby I told him what had happened. He told me I had flashes because I didn't get off the drug gradually and my body was going through withdrawal. That's when he gave me a new medication to take, Seroquel. He gave me a schedule to follow slowly increase the medication, until I was on a full dose. I asked if there was weight gain with the Seroquel and he said, "It doesn't." It was at that instance I started eating again and I didn't gain a lot of weight.

Back at work, we had a big *Bostonian Shoe* project. My job wouldn't be designing, but mounting the art work to black board.

AN AMERICAN MESSIAH

There was a lot to mount and a lot of the pieces where posters. I used the spray adhesive Super 77 to mount the work. *Accu-Graphics* has a spray booth, but the amount of work going through this day and spray I was taking in I almost passed out. Everything was getting dark at one point, so I went outside for some air. Once I got myself back on my feet I finished the assignment. I wanted to finish this so as not to look like I was having more problems.

The 4th of July holiday gave a day off from work and I enjoyed the day. I had a few people over to my house. Don, Jill and Tosha stopped by for some drinks and to smoke some weed. We sat around for a few hours, but then went to a party at Tiogue Lake in Coventry. We drank a lot more while there. Don was the one who knew about the party, so when we got there he ran into a lot of his friends. The thing I liked most about the party was they played "God Bless America", every 15 minutes. This became one of my favorite holidays.

The new medication didn't have weight gain, but it also didn't have the effects I needed. Slowly I began having psychotic thoughts even though I didn't notice them slowly make there way into my thinking.

These thoughts started to distort my thinking while at work. Another big job was coming to *Accu-Graphics, Safety First*. Walter took me on the meeting to nail down what products we would be illustrating for Safety First. Walter asked me to take notes, but I didn't. My mind was elsewhere. Some how my thought had me thinking I was the Messiah during the meeting. This revelation almost put me to tears, but I held them back. When we left Walter was mildly upset I hadn't taken notes. I knew from sitting there we would be illustrating baby monitors and seats.

Although I considered being the Messiah a very serious distinction, it didn't really occupy my thoughts as I was back to business as usual. Two new employees where hired during this job with *Safety First*. I thought I had finally got some people under me and was no longer the low man on the pole. For one of them to get started the needed for another computer was evident. They gave one new employee my desk and computer to work with and gave me the computer at the desk where the scanner is. At the desk there was a note pad and I started drawing. I put a hooded executioner with an ax.

I had also begun eating out for lunch, alone. I was isolating myself again. Another thought that was out of the norm was to get my name out mentally. The radio was always on in the studio and again I felt the radio and TV were watching me, so I was trying to get my name out to be recognized. I would think of my first name, then last name and middle initial as the messiah, thinking the radio was recording it.

One morning I decided to go through all six New England states to see if I could. I used no map just the East, West, North and South directions on the road signs. When I got to it I decided to stop in each state to get something, like a memento. In Massachusetts I stopped to have lunch. In Maine I picked up a bottle of wine. In New Hampshire I bought a pocket watch. In Vermont I had a glass off wine at a bar. Finally in Connecticut I bought gas. The whole trip took about 12 hours, but could probably be completed in eight hours if it where mapped out and one didn't stop.

Along with strange behavior and thoughts, the hatred for my father had returned. This was so intense I was thinking of killing him. I was planning to follow him and take an ax to him when he wasn't paying attention. I had bought the ax to do it with. I also wanted to do this in a purple suit. I had about $1500 in my bank account and figured I could have one tailored. To show how loose my thoughts where, I had to find a day to do this because I worked. I asked Walter if I could have the two days after Christmas and he said no. In my mind, because I couldn't get those days off I had no time to go through with his murder. I really thought I could get away with it. My mind didn't register I would ever get caught. In reality I would mostly likely be the first person they turned to. I could have simply blown the days off, but that wasn't in my thought process. This would be the end of my plot. An example of how twisted my soul had become is; I mailed the ax to the Bill Clinton, because I thought he was where the buck stops. I have to explain. Early on while befriending the Grim Reaper, I felt I was killing hundreds of thousand of people a day just thinking about it. It had become one of my chores. I felt I had become the last doorway for thousands of people who passed away each day. I imagined this was something powerful people had to do in their daily routine. I assumed the president had the same thought process. I was trying to get the President to specifically, mentally kill off my father; this would be conveyed through the receiving of the ax. If I was ever questioned by anyone, perhaps CIA, why I had sent Bill an ax, I came up with the line. 'I mailed this gift to the President so he could chop down this year's Christmas tree.' I did mail it to him with the attached label reading 'Christmas gift'.

Something I noticed late that year was a ticket for an event. Upon reading the ticket I noticed the year was 1999. I recognized my deal with the devil had come through in this year '99 one of my old Pop Warner numbers. Looking back at this year it was a good year.

I know I was detaching from the people at work and maybe felt I was on the chopping block with the addition of the two new employees, but it was getting close to Thanksgiving and I didn't think someone would get fired this close to the Holidays.

I was mistaken. One afternoon Walter called me into his office. I thought it was possibly my years review, but it wasn't. Walter said he was sorry, but I was down sized.

I got my coat and left. As I made my way home I wondered what other excuses there where to get rid of someone. I had now been fired, laid-off, and down sized in the design world.

CHAPTER 10

Accu-Graphics was a good experience for me. It was the longest I had held a job, about a year. I also got familiar with the programs used in the field and for that I owe *Accu-Graphics*, specifically Walter for giving me the opportunity. I have to say I had the feeling I was on the fence when the two new employees where hired. The day I was having flashes and the excuse I gave for leaving couldn't have helped my cause.

What really got to me was I had been fired, laid-off and down sized in my discipline. I then began to think to myself I probably shouldn't be working for someone. I should maybe try my hand at starting my own business. I already had a computer and the programs, as well as, the computer background. My biggest hurdle would be finding clients.

The first place I tried was a lottery giant, *G-tech*, whose world head quarters here stationed in Rhode Island. I made a contact at the company and set up an interview. When the interview took place I met with two young ladies. They liked my work, but they where looking for someone to setup and manage their web site. I had no experience with designing and managing web sites, so this was a swing and a miss.

The next corporation I went after was *Coca-Cola*. They had a plant in Providence. I visited to see if I could get someone to talk to. Once I got there I met a man who told me I would have to contact their head quarters in Georgia. I took this information and went to the drawing board. I designed an annual report for Coke, hoping they would like it and see promise in my work. I explained the layout in a letter and sent it off to Georgia.

The final potential client I went after was *Citizens Bank*. Citizens supplied the trophy when I was name the MVP in our first Super Bowl. The state of my mind thought they would like to help me because of the prior connection with them. While poking my head around there offices in Providence, I met with someone on the top floor. I gave her my information on a card to relay to the proper person.

Turning to Christmas I gave a CD to every member of my family and if they didn't have a CD player I bought them one. I covered all the CD's with either a green or red label. All the CD's where linked to one another through the words in songs off each CD. Some of them where linked through the musician and others through the title of a song. I was testing the people in my family to see if anyone was playing the game I had given out. I had no reply, with the exception of my little sister Lisa who gave me a, "thanks a lot..." Like I was a jerk. I guess she was offended because she wears a hearing aid and may not be able to enjoy the music as well. After Christmas I spent New Years Night lying on my roof looking at the stars and watching plains come in and out of Warwick.

Though I was canned by *Accu-Graphics*, I was still hanging with my friends, but something happened I disapproved in. One night my friends and I were leaving a local watering hole, when one of them punched a cars headlight out. I was disappointed and had no room for such behavior. This caused me to leave my friends and disconnect with them. I was now again isolating.

I may have severed ties with my friends, but I was still going out. I had been going to the *Fish Company* alone and frequenting the club. That's when the strangest thing began to happen. On two or more occasions the Bouncer kicked me out of the bar. I still don't know what kind of behavior I was demonstrating for such treatment. Maybe my mind was occupied by overwhelming thoughts and didn't notice my behavior as out of the norm.

For instance, when they played the song "Dancing Queen" at the club, I would imagine dancing with the current Queen, Elizabeth II. We would waltz around the floor with no one else there. I believe I was connecting with her and gaining favor for showing her a good time. Even if it where in fantasy.

In reality there was a blonde girl I talked to at the club. I noticed she had been to the *Fish Company* a few times, before I talked to her. She was very attractive and I thought about her outside the bar. It made me wonder what kind of life we could have together. Right down to the house I had been designing before I met her, to a dog. The dog would be a boxer, name Marcciano. I also imagined sharing all my football experiences. I saw her there a few times more before I could no longer find her in the sea of people as weekends passed. Nothing would come from my fondness for this female.

I know my mind was occupied when I was there. I also thought of the *Fish Co.* as a think tank and everyone was sharing my thoughts. On a few occasions I played a game with the crowd. It had different levels showing a persons' logic and thought process. On the first level one would meet up with the traditional monsters: Dracula, Frankenstein, the Wolf man, the Headless Horseman and the Mummy. One met Dracula first. One would have to sympathize with his loneliness and thirst for a companion. Frankenstein was afraid of fire, so one would have to steer clear of using fire in front of him; those who did would go back to the beginning. The Wolf man is an animal and is affected by the moon; similar to the way the moon affects ocean tides. Not only this he has flies to contend with and needs to be scratched. If one provokes the Wolf man they go back down to Dracula. The Headless Horseman needs a head; so one needs to give him a playful Humpty Dumpy head. Finally the Mummy is just looking for the treasures stolen from him, so leave his things to him.

Once you pass through this level you would graduate to a cauldron where one needs to perform white magic. One has to put something that is good into the stew. I'll give the example of pelican wings, or a dolphins tooth. Once passing this simple level, one progresses to a level where the power of levitation is given. Ones conduct is watch to see how the power is used with others. It's supposed to be something fun not something to fight with. After using the power one makes it to the top level, where there are a bunch of women reading to the individual to test the understanding one has of language. Forces and powers would be read aloud to see if they could be sparked sole by an individual's knowledge and strength. It is designed to have one sit there while the power is channeled through them to fight evil.

I would play this while at the *Fish Company* and thought there where many people trying to work their way through. At the same time I would play another game. I felt I was being born again or given new life. I would play in my head the line, "It's alive!" from the movie "Young Frankenstein". My mother tells me she went into labor watching the comedy. She says she was laughing so much she went into delivery.

Now I was free from a job and would look for things to do. One day I went to Block Island, an island just of the Rhode Island coast. A ferry brings people back and forth to the island and I bought a $10 ticket. When I was in High School my friends' and I would go to the Bluffs on the backside of the island to ride the waves. This trip was being made in the dead of winter. I was taking the trip basically because I could. I didn't know they ran the ferry in the winter, but I guess one has to make it back and forth somehow. When I got there I found somewhere to have lunch. After lunch I made my way back on the ferry.

I would also delve into such topics as time travel, which I didn't think would ever exist, but then I thought to myself one of the phrases I kept close, "any thing is possible." Logically I thought scientists would create the teleporter while attempting to solve time travel and still do, having considered time travel a little more. That's when I came up with a theory. The future is looking to connect with us in the passed, but we haven't built the receiver to except the future. It's like not having a car radio, the stations are still broadcasting, but there is no radio there to except it. I also believe if the correct person didn't go through the time portal all kinds of hell would take advantage of this mistake. All I saw was the first time traveler was a military man. I also suggest the first thing to go through time should be a diamond, and the first mammal should be a lion. These may also be the directions to teleportation.

Although I had isolated myself from my friends I was still sociable with my family. In fact one night I believed my mother was mentally communicating with me. She was pointing me to the *Foxy Lady*. As one could have guessed the *Foxy Lady* is a strip club. I had never been there and was a little nervous to go. I had heard it was one of the best gentlemen's clubs on the east coast. I planned to go the next evening and made a plan. I was going to go in like I was wired on some kind of drug. I would also stock up on dollar bills.

When I arrived at the *Foxy Lady* the next night, I went right to the runway and took out my ones. After I sat down I bought a beer. I went through quiet a few ones before they had their two for one. That's two lap dances for the price of one; it also came with a free tee

AN AMERICAN MESSIAH

shirt. It wasn't long before one of the girls asked if I wanted a lap dance. I was there for some fun, so I got up and followed her to the back room. The dances where well worth the $35 at the time. After the dances I went back to the runway. I stayed about another half hour before I made my way home.

Though I didn't stay long I had a good time and decided to go back the next day. On Fridays they're open during the day, as well as night. Again I loaded up on ones. This time the place was almost empty and I got a good look around before I sat down at the runway. I wasn't there long before one of the girls came to me and asked if I would like to go into the Champagne room. I said, "Why not?" I thought I would put it on my credit card. The girl led me into the Champagne room, where you got what else, but a bottle of champagne. One also received a platter of fruits. When we first got in there a waitress was there to serve us. The thing is it was a $500 expense, which I thought my credit card would handle, but it didn't. The manager came back to asked if I had any other way to pay, but I didn't. He then called my credit card company and asked for an extension to pay the bill. They obliged and I was good to go. I have to admit this was a big waist of money. I did talk with the stripper for some time. She asked me where I went out and I told her the *Fish Company*. She then told me she wanted to meet me out at the *Hot Club*, which was next door to the *Fish Co.*, that night. Needless to say I went to the *Hot Club*, but she never showed up.

I learned two things that day. The Champagne room was a waste of time and one shouldn't believe too much into what a stripper says.

Getting back to the business and the business I was hoping to get off the ground. I received a response to the annual report layout I had sent *Coca-Cola*. They sent me a letter telling me they didn't except work from anyone other than the people working for them in Georgia. It was nice to hear back, but it was a bummer. I think I would have rather had no response and had it fade away.

I didn't let it get to me I just kept doing what I was doing. I went to the *Fish Co.* as I usually did, but on one of my visits things went wrong. On this particular night I was drinking soda. Then the bars manager confronted me, he said I had to leave, which ticked me off. When I got outside I saw a cop across the street and called for his help. He came over and I told him, "I wasn't doing anything wrong, in fact I was drinking Coke's. The bars manager William, as he told the officer, began pointing fingers. That's when I pointed mine. As soon as I did the cop grabbed me by the throat and put me up against the wall. The next thing you know I was in the cop car headed for the station. He had my wallet and I kept medication in it incase I didn't make it home one night. This would be such a night. I was printed and put into a cell, but never given my meds. I stayed up all night. The next morning they brought me in front of a judge. They let me go on my own recognizance, which was everything in my wallet. That would be the last time I went to the *Fish Company*.

I found another bar quickly. I had noticed a bar called *Challengers* in downtown Providence. It took me a while to actually locate it, but I tracked it down one Saturday afternoon for some football. I liked it a lot they had three big screen TV's and a bunch of other screens with all sports. It was nice to watch three different games at the same time. There was also a waitress that appealed to me. Almost immediately my imagination made her a wife in a past life. I was then asking myself what went wrong in that life. I never approached her, but would have liked to. I was caught up in so much fantasy I never tried to talk to her.

The distain I had for my father caused me to sell my Sun Fire. I felt the car was a link to one another and wanted to lose all connection with him. I took it to a Pontiac dealership and sold the car for $3500. That left me without a car, so I had to find one fast. I'd use the money from the sale of the Sun Fire to pick one up.

Checking the classified adds, I found an old BMW for sale. I took a cab there and had already made my decision to purchase the vehicle before I got there, baring any major work needed to the car. The owner of the car, Dan, showed me that the only problem with the car was a switch for an alarm, from a past owner. It would short out the electricity if the switch was in the wrong position. All one needed to do if this happened was to take the cables off the battery and then put them back on. Dan wanted to go to his mechanic, so I could get a first hand account of the history of the automobile. The mechanic gave the car his blessing and told me to come by if I had any problems, but it was on the way back I got a leg up.

While taking us back to his residence Dan asked if I knew any graphic designers. I quickly told him I was. He then told me he was trying to put together a catalog for his customers. He was the owner of *Hook-Fast Specialty*, a company making badges, belt buckles, name badges, small flags for lapels and a bunch of other items. This was how my world worked, I got put in the right position and the work fell on my lap. He told me his wife was a designer, but they had just had a baby and she wouldn't be able to produce a catalog. We scheduled a time and day to meet and go over the project. As for the car I bought it for $3000.

Right after buying the BMW I went to the *Foxy Lady*. It was an afternoon so it must have been a Friday. I had a drink or two and talked with a few of the girls. There wasn't much crowd those afternoon hours, but as usual the girls looked great. I believe I did get a two for one that afternoon. It was just a little celebration in honor of the Beamer.

That weekend I made an attempt to leave my house. The first night I went to *Challengers* for a while. Later I followed up with the *Foxy Lady*. I was making overtures, telling the girls I had no place to stay the cold winter night. I was hoping one of them would feel bad and help me out, but I saw the establishment close before I got any offers. It was now two o'clock in the morning and I knew of only one place to go this late at night. The *Foxwoods* casino was open 24 hours a day. This would give me a warm place to hang out. I didn't gamble I just walked around. That's when I took my medication. At night I took more of a dose than in the morning. About an hour later I really felt the Seroquel kicking in. At one point I felt like I was going to pass out. I knew I was in trouble I didn't want to be found at Foxwoods passed on the floor, so I went to the front desk to see if I could get a hotel room. I didn't have the money on me, but I did have my checkbook so I wrote a check. It was for around $135 and I didn't have enough in my checking account, but I was desperate for a place to crash, so I bounced the check. Once in the room I went right to sleep.

The next day I went back home, defeated with no place to go. I paid the debt from the room quickly. I was back home, not where I wanted to be, but I didn't have any choice, because I didn't have the money for an apartment. While at home I began creating art pieces on my red I-Mac. I called the style of work "Free Form." In all, I had about eight pieces.

I met with Dan around that same window of time. I visited him at *Hook-Fast Specialty* and he showed me examples of the items this company produced. He also gave me a look at past catalogs to give me an idea of what he wanted. We agreed that I would work with him and his wife to get a catalog out and he would pay me $800 every other week.

Now the ball was rolling a little. I then began making a move to get some more funds in my pocket to get myself out of the house. First I went to *Bank Boston* for a small business loan. I filled out all the documents they had, but in the end they turned me down. I then turned my attention to a credit union, *Cateway*. They had fewer forms, but denied me just the same. I wasn't going to give in. I finally put my interests in *Sovran Bank* and they came through for me. I was approved for a $5000 loan. I could now search for a place to live.

I looked at an apartment in East Providence, but they didn't have any opening until the spring. I looked at a place in West Warwick, but it was a dump. That's when I found an apartment at *Remington Pond Village* less than two miles from where I was living. All they had where two bed units for $700, but it was available right away, so I took it. Since I was self-employed and had no way of verifying my income, the owner of the complex took two months in advance, which hurt my pocket a bit more than I would have wanted.

The apartment wasn't furnished so I had to by some furniture, which I located at *Gilmore Furniture* on credit. Bought the TV and radio from *Best Buy* on credit. Purchased an upright washer and dryer from *Sears* on credit. *A throw rug at Home Depot* was put on credit. I spent more and more on credit including nights out.

The next item to bleed on my finances was a cell phone. Again I was going to use it in conjunction with my business. I felt I could be reached anywhere I was. It would be through the cell phone my family would locate me. My father, who I was trying to get away from, called me on the cell phone while I was driving. I hung up on him immediately and put the phone up against the speaker in my car his next attempt. It wasn't long after I started getting visits at my apartment. The only two people too visit where my mother and brother. My brother brought his son Zack. I'm just glad my father never tried to show up.

AN AMERICAN MESSIAH

It was nice to see my mother. The distain I had with my father is the opposite of the way I feel about my mother. When I was young my mother would get everyone up, get them ready, cook breakfast and have lunch ready and had all three of us out the door to catch the bus. She would then go to work all day only to come home to have dinner ready at 6:00 pm. She was also famous around the neighborhood for her Saturday lunch, homemade pizza. I had no ill will toward my mother through my whole ordeal.

Having some businesses meant it was time to register my businesses. I went to West Warwick town hall and registered each one, *the Opposite, the Meadow Design Co*, and *My Evil Empire. My Evil Empire* was the parent company of the other two. They where each taken care of for $10. Once in the system, I went to work on the logos. I thought they all came out well and started them on business cards.

My Evil Empire was to be taken tongue and cheek. I've always liked one of the bad guys. It's also *My Evil Empire* no one else's. I have a different image of Hell and Evil and the Devil. If I had to guess I'm more likely headed and preparing to going to Hell, but if I don't Heaven will seem much more glorious. The problem is I've developed some problems with Heaven and God. For example: is heaven filled with old people or does one get a choice of age when one shows up. My problem with the man upstairs is we have so many disabled people, if man is made in his image he has some real problems coming from him. I also have a problem with internal defects. Why do people get cancer, MS, diabetes, mental illness, etc...? I can see if someone breaks a bone or is hurt in an accident, but to have something just fail is wrong in my mind. And if one looks at it there's no good without evil. Like white and black. Somewhere out there the path that's been taken is evil. Don't you believe in Hell? Many people work and pray all there lives, but don't include reincarnation. How else does one expect to appear at the pearly gates? If one adds reincarnation they open the door to multiple lives, which could make an infinitesimal amount of life, were an individual must go to both Heaven and Hell in such future lives.

Going back to the *Foxy Lady*, I received a free ticket for admission for their Super Bowl party. This was enough to get me to go there for the game between the Tennessee Titans and the St. Louis Rams. I got there relatively early for the game. I got a good table with a view of a big screen TV. I was seated alone and two guys asked if they could sit with me. It was crowded, so I let them join me.

At half time of the game they where giving away prizes. One of the questions for a prize was, "Who has the most passing yards, all their games combined, in Super Bowl history?" I thought I had the answer, Terry Bradshaw, and sent one of the guys I was sitting with up with the answer. It was wrong and many other people got it wrong, which got me to think away from the winners and to the losers of the Super Bowl. I came up with Jim Kelly. I went up and was correct. My prize was a Gold Card to the Foxy Lady. This card gave me free admission up stairs and to the all-nude room downstairs. It would save me anywhere from $10 to $20 any given night. Getting in for nothing I would visit more often.

Having my own place I could do as I pleased. I would go out to *Challengers* during the day to play some free pool or have lunch. One of the best things about *Challengers* is they didn't only serve drinks, but they had food. I would stop in one early evenings for a snack, drinks and a sporting event, but I never got to closing time. I would end up at the *Foxy Lady* to end the night.

One day at *Challengers* there was a radio station broadcasting from the bar. It was a sports talk station named the Score. I was playing pool as they did their show, but once I got board with pool I went over to them and gave my best sports fact or paradox. It was something I came up with myself. I told them, "In the 1980's the Raiders and Redskins won five Super Bowls. They both begin with the letter R. In the 80's there was an R for Republican in the Whitehouse. In the 1990's Dallas and Denver won five Super Bowls. Each began with a D. In the 90's there was a D for Democrat in the Oval Office."

When I was finished they told me I had too much time on my hands, which was humorous. As a gift, for such a revelation, they gave me a Score T-shirt and two tickets to the Boston Bruins for that night. My biggest problem with the prize was I had disconnected with everyone and had no one for the other ticket. That's when I thought to ask Dan. Perhaps he would like to go to the game, but he declined. I ended up going alone. They where ski box seats. I forget if they won or not, but it was my first time to the *Fleet Center*. I left early to make it over to the *Foxy Lady*.

I had been to the *Foxy Lady* a few times, but never to the all-nude room downstairs. Now I had the Gold Card and was ready to make my way down stairs. It was something I hadn't seen before so I was a kind of nervous. That night I ventured down there, I passed by the boxing ring where they had shaving cream and hot oil wrestling with customers and girls. I gave my ticket to the doorman and was let in. I didn't make it three feet in the door when a girl had me sit with her. Her name was Carmen; at least that was her stage name. She was very attractive. I enjoyed her company, so we had a two for one. I would talk to her again later on in the night. As for the nude-room there was a bar girls striped down to nothing on. There was a runway toward the back of the room where they also bared all. They had back rooms for the lap dances. I would also drink a lot at the *Foxy Lady*. I would order a shot of Jack and a beer to start. Its about $5 a drink, and would pollute myself with what ever came to mind the rest or the night.

There was a night I got way to intoxicated on merlot. I made it back to the apartment just fine, but was sick as soon as I got there. I was smashed and started crying asking, "Why didn't I make the team?", team being Penn State. That was very rarely like me, but I had too much to drink and I am somewhat conflicted over the topic. Something consoling to me on the topic is I may just have picked up a serious injury if I had played there. Many times I felt I was saved from a broken neck by not playing. This almost makes me believe the correct decisions where made.

One other night I would work on the catalog for Dan without sleeping. After one such night I had to show the work to Dan. One morning I met him and we went over the beginning of the catalog. After going over the layouts Dan surprised me. He asked if I would like to work as the designer for *Hook-Fast* only. He offered me a job and I declined. I didn't want to give up the current freedom I had gained.

It was this freedom that made my visits with Dr. Demby easy to schedule. Yes, even though he had let me down I was still seeing the doctor. When I met with him we just talked about what was going on and with the 15 minutes to a half hour he couldn't really notice the psychosis that had crept in. He was basically there to get my prescription filled. At least that's how I felt.

To get those prescriptions filled I had to find health insurance. I found insurance after several calls to local officials who directed me to *United Health Care* through my business. I would have to pay $200 or so a month to get benefit I also had a $25 co-pay on my meds. That was now taken care of.

I had taken action to keep myself well. I then decide to join a gym to get healthy. I wanted to find a good gym with a low chance to see anyone I would know. The place I decided on was *Gold's Gym* in Warwick, just before the Airport. That cost me $40 a month.

The Illian Gonzalez fiasco was unfolding on my TV screen around then. This was the boy who came over in a make shift raft with his mother from Cuba. His mother died on the trip and Illian was staying with his Uncle in Florida, but his father was back in Cuba wanted him back. If one asked me the boy is in the United States, so we should make an example of how great the country is. I would have guaranteed him all the best schools. In fact I would have given him a free ride through Penn State, if one asked me. Not only that I would put him in the Rose Bowl Parade every year so people could keep tabs, but they raided his Uncles home and sent him back to his father in Cuba. This was terribly handled by the Clinton administration and Janet Reno.

Something else I had to have for my business was a digital camera, which went on the credit card for a good $800. I hoped this would make me more professional and would help the businesses grow. It wasn't something I needed just something I wanted. I found a use for the camera instantly. I had been tinkering with starting a daily log for some time, but never got around to it. With the camera I could take a daily photo and write over it.

Something I did for fun was a self-portrait on the I-Mac. I started with a sketch of myself and scanned it into the computer. I then filled in the drawing with small strips of color. I used the zoom tool for most of the work. It took me about two days, on and off, to complete. It came out better than I expected and added it to my 'Free Form' collection.

I had a meeting with Dan one morning and gave him a card for the *Opposite Design.* I had finished the work we where reviewing the night before. I had procrastinated, he had given me a few days and I waited until the last day. When it came to it he couldn't tell if it was done during the day or at night. Things seemed to be going well.

While in the gym I would wear my free *Foxy Lady* shirts, from all the two for ones I had gotten. No one seemed to make notice at least no one commented. In fact I didn't talk to anyone, but the people who ran the gym. The head games made their way around the gym. Sometimes I would go in for mornings, while other times I would go in during the late afternoon. I saw basically the same people when I went. In the morning I noticed a tall filled out 40-50 something with his wife. They worked out separately. I don't recall how or when it started, but I would think to myself, they where the King and Queen of the gym. Then I progressed into the gentleman being one of the pieces on the chest board. He would be a Rook and I a Knight. My imagination made us positions, which saved kingdoms and wouldn't sit on the Kings thrown. We would try to preserve the thrown with heir apparent. If one couldn't be found we would bring in people from the village to take a temporary seat. I played this game many times. I made us part of a team coming in and cleaned up kingdoms in kayos.

On another occasion I had spent sometime tracing back the origins on thing on earth. I found myself in the gym and I was doing all right, but couldn't figure out where metal originates. I knew that oil came from fossils, but had no idea about metal. The other thing that stumped me was how does electricity work and who invented it. That sent me to the bookstores. The thing I really wanted to find was when and how electricity was produced. I couldn't find a trace of the history of electricity anywhere, but I did find a book covering the history of earth throw the last 2000 years. I bought it. It took my mind off of electricity.

The book was packed with people, invention, wars and achievements. I thumbed through it several times, but what I found on the first fee pages excited me. It showed the game of chess was being played over 2000 years ago. Something else I found interesting in the book was there was a Princess Ann, sister of Charles. It was these two facts combined with the mental game I was playing in the gym, that started me thinking more about having a chess board with actual officials on it to settle disputes.

The position, my position on the board would be a Messiah also known as the Knight. There has been a calling for this position through time. One Messiah would choose the other in the couple. The others I also felt where up to me to choose. I give favor to the larger man and always have through sport. I focused on that position, a man that's like a building, the Rook. I came up with the name of Visroi for this position, which there would be two. I had a rhyme when it came to me, "A Visroi is a big boy, that needs a toy." The final position was already there, the Pope is a replacement for a bishop. The only problem with that position is it never figured out how to set up the board to playfully settle disputes. I also wanted a different religion in the other bishops' spot. I thought long and hard before I came up with the Jew as the match for the Pope. I made the connection with the holocaust of WWII. In my mind Hitler got it very wrong and it warped him. He was in a position of power and chose to attempt to exterminate a people of a religion. Perhaps he was to come up with the one most sought after Jew, not killing all of the Jews. I don't favor a man that reads and finds all his answers from the same book, but in my mind the Visroi may favor the man with a book. For the pawns, I would make them all knights to show the position, which set up the board.

Playing this game put my mind at ease. I was prepared to lead if somehow it all came down to me. I would set up a Kingdom on a checkered board challenging another foe to do the same, so matters could be ironed out in a civilized way. Something else I was trying to prepare for is an Aides vaccine, but there is none at the time and it is a concern of mine. It will be a great day when this disease is gone. A reproductive virus may be the beginning of extinction of man kind if it where not for condoms. This mind set led me to an experiment. I took the black joker, not colored joker, from a deck of cards and taped it over a nail hole in the wall. I thought this to be some kind of vaccine that stuck to white blood cell to make them last longer. I know the virus attacks the white blood cells, but for how long? I made note the card stayed on the wall for three full days then fell on the forth. My experiment was over, but my concern about aids continued.

Over a period of time I had, what I thought, gathered clues in the creating of a vaccine. One of the clues I had come up with was, Penicillin State for Penn State. The school I graduated from could perhaps put a solution to the virus and I was in the mental pool, to help. The second clue I came up with was the 'Birds and the Bee's...' which is a way to explain sex to a young person, and this is a sexually transmitted disease. I then took the Bee from the 'Birds and the bee's...' and combined it with penicillin, which is mold on bread, and came up with honey that was spoiled. My final clue was the pet name lover's have for one another, "Honey". The deduction I had made was Penn State should have a vaccine on the way, which is based on spoiled honey or the mania was suggesting this.

Now it was time to relax. I went to see Carmen at the *Foxy Lady*. I spent lots of time with the women. She was easily my favorite. In fact she remainderd me of a blonde Statue of Liberty.

Though one night this would all come to end. I was there one night when the nude-room wasn't open and was seated up stairs. As I sat there someone at the next table was looking over at me. After a while I was giving looks back and one of the times I flipped the middle finger at him. That bubbled over to a small shouting match. We where then led out through the back door. I remember being pissed off and yelling at him, "...are you my sacrificial lamb..." I shouted it more than once. He was with two other people, who also found the exit. I'm glad the bouncer stuck around until I combed down some. While I was leaving the bouncer who was a big and heavy guy told me 'never to come back'.

From there it was all down hill, my finances where a mess. My credit cards where at the limits and I owed the bank for the loan, and furniture company for getting everything by credit. Not only my only source of income told me to take a hike. Dan told me one morning the colors where all wrong and he had already gone over it with me.

That's when I quickly tried to get myself out of this mess. There was an ad agency RDW I had seen on my drives to Providence. I gave them a call and asked if they could help out a young designer. The gentleman on the phone told me to come in and he would look at my work. We set an appointment for the next day.

I brought my portfolio the next day and he seemed to like it. He gave me some work to do and told me, "Do the work and we'll pay you." What he gave me was a beer bottle to label and create a box and some advertising. The beers' name was *New Port Storm*. I left and went to work on the project.

I work on three different labels for the bottles, as well as boxes and ads. It took me a few days, but I was ready to show what I had. The problem was when tried to get back to the man I had talked to, I was told he left to start his own ad company. Never the less I took my work to them directly at *New Port Storm* and left it for someone to look over. I relayed the message I should have gotten paid, but there was nothing done.

Something began getting in my mind after that. I would hear, "The 27 year old genius who changed the world." I heard it mostly in my apartment as I began making a plan to get out of this mess. I was on the verge of my 27th birthday, so I let it be known to anyone paying attention in the mental pool to put the pressure on and pile it on. Leave me with the things you screwed up. I would hear it over and over and it amused me more and more, because I saw I was going to be 27. That was the number I wore in Pop Warner when the team went to Alabama to play a Bowl Game.

To generate a little bit of money I sold my TV to a pawnshop in Providence, which gave me some spending money. My mother came through for me on my birthday for a few hundred dollars, but she had no idea I was in up to my eyes in debt. That went to bills and didn't go far. I also had enough credit on my CompUSA card to buy another I-Mac. I had no intention of keeping it. I sold it to a computer store in Westerly for a few hundred bucks.

As part of my morning ritual I would watch C-Span on the small television I had hooked up to the living room. At t he time I felt congressmen where helping me get out of the mess. I can remember my mind playing with the officials. I imagined they compared me to a young hawk ready to spread his wings in foreign soil. As I gathered I felt they where feeding me the get away. I knew I had too much debt to tackle and didn't want to go back home, so I came up with a plan to leave the country. I felt I was still strong enough and young enough to take on the abuse of leaving without a place to stay. I was also single and had no children depending on me.

Somehow or somewhere I got into my mind the city Verecruz, maybe it was a topic on C-Span. I had no idea where this place was so I went to the bookstore to buy a map. I was only playing and came up with the rule I couldn't use a map from North America, so I bought one from South America. I looked all over the map but couldn't find the location. I looked and looked again.

At this point I didn't have the money for the rent, so I told my landlord I would be out the first of the month. I made it my job to sell my radio to a pawnshop across the street. My digital camera was bought by a small computer store in East Providence. I called a furniture company to take the washer and dryer, and furniture quickly. I also sold my red I-Mac to the computer store in Westerly who took the first computer. The apartment was void of everything, but the Queen bed and my personal belongings, trophies, plaques, awards as well as clothes. I would pack all these things away in to a trunk (awards and trophies) and a bag for clothes.

I had applied for a passport because I didn't have one. I registered for one at the Coventry post office and put a rush on it because they told me it would take about ten days to come in. I had a P.O. Box in East Greenwich I had. My plan beyond the passport was to go to the Chi Phi chapter at URI to stay until the documents came in. It was now summer break so most rooms had to be vacant. After stopping to see if was O.K for me to stay, which it was, someone showed me a room, but it had no bed. That's when I went back to the apartment to get the bed. I tied it to the beamers' roof and got it into a room at Chi Phi.

The guys at the Fraternity where very inviting. I remember one night we went out to the Coast Guard House, a bar and restaurant on the edge of the Atlantic Coast. When the brothers asked where I was going I told them South America.

I had a few hundred dollars at this point, so I didn't do much. The waiting was tough, the nights where long and the days even longer. Finally after several days the passport came in and I was ready to leave. My plan was to drive the BMW all the way there, but a huge set back took place. While picking a few things up the entire exhaust came off the car and it barley moved. It was in no shape to make the trip.

As I mentioned I had a few hundred dollars. That's when I decided to Go South to South Carolina and south to South America, until I was in the north of South America. I called a cab to take me to the bus station. As I waited the movie "Young Frankenstein" was on and all I could think of was "It's alive." Which made me think of my mother and the birthday that just passed.

When I got to the bus station I paid for a one-way ticket to Greensboro, South Carolina. I was left with very little after paying for the ticket. The ride was long and we had stops on the way. At one stop middle easterners boarded the bus, so I kept a close look at them to make curtain they where not terrorists and up to no good. As stated the ride was long and I didn't sleep at all on the ride. We left in the afternoon and got to Greensboro in the afternoon. When I got to the bus stop I took a taxi to a hotel to get some rest. I didn't have the money for it, but they took a check, which I had a whole book of. That's when I told myself I would only use two checks in the U.S. and two checks in South America. I had decided to bounce a check to get on a plane to South America and was already using one for the hotel.

The next day was a Saturday and I knew banks where closed, so the people at the airport wouldn't be able to run any checks on the check. When I went up to the ticket salesperson, I asked for the next flight to South America. He told me there was Caracas, Venezuela. I wrote the check for $900 and some change to him, he gave me my tickets and off I went. I had a lay over in Miami for a night, so I had some waiting to do before I took the flight.

Sitting there I began to make the passers by people I've had relationships with in past and future lives. I would make someone a father another a brother. At times I played someone as both. I came to the thought that I could play this over and over again because of the advent of the computer. Imagine we are all in a big computer and can be imputed at one place or another at any time. Copied for use in another world. Playing out scenarios infinitesimally.

I played this game all the way to the departure gate to get on the plane. Once on the plane I was more focused on having an even state of mind. That morning I would be leaving Miami and arriving in Venezuela that afternoon.

CHAPTER 11

As the plane made its' descent I was able to make out dwellings along the hill sides. They where scattered for miles. They were small in size and made of stacked cinder blocks. I wondered how so many people could live in such poverty. This sight prepared me for what to expect ahead. They stretched all the way to the surroundings of the airport. As soon as the wheels of the plane touched down I mentally reported, "I'm on the South American continent."

The first thing I noticed where the armed solders at the airports gates. They where well armed with automatic weapons. I spent my first day in Venezuela dragging my trunk and bag around the airport waiting for an opportunity to arise. One thing I did was flush my meds down the toilet. I drank from the bathroom faucets instead of eating for the first couple of days and stayed up nights. I had my clothes to change into to keep a little cleanliness to myself. I also had my raiser to shave.

One of the first few days I met a man, whose name I can't recall, pulled me aside and asked, "What are you doing." He had noticed I was in the airport for the past couple of days dragging my things around. I told him I had left the United States because I didn't like the treatment I was receiving there. I told him, "I may not go back for as many as seven years." I stated to him I was an artist and he told me he would get me some food if I sketched a portrait of him. That was an offer I couldn't refuse. I tipped my trunk to its' end for something stable to draw on and obliged him with a drawing. He thought enough of the illustration to take me back to his apartment.

This kind sole's apartment was maybe one or two miles from the airport. I saw this young man as a grandson, from another life, perfectly placed to help. It was nice getting away from the airstrips and the constant influx of people into the terminal.

DAVID MICHAEL

At his apartment I met his brother, who went right to work to get me something to eat. They served me what was mostly ground meat and saws. It was something like a sloppy Joe without the bun. In the shape I was in at that point, just drinking water from the faucet, this was a well-needed meal. They also gave me a place to lay down for about an hour. Once my trip to this oasis ended it was back to the terminal. That's when I noticed there where two airports side by side.

After returning to the airport I made my way out of the building and on my way to the Airport right next to the other. What they had done was separate the International Airport from the National terminal. I spent time dragging my things back and forth pretending I was a General delivering valuable goods, my bag and trunk. I felt I was connecting with the military ghost of the countries past. I would stop and correct my grip on the cargo to ensure its delivery. Back and forth I went until I grew tired. I spent several days playing this game while still drinking from the faucets in the bathrooms with nothing else to consume.

I waited a few days for something to break, other than me. There came a point I thought I was going to collapse, due to the lack of sleep and nourishment. That's when Jesus R. approached me. He asked if I needed a hotel room and I acknowledged I did. He picked my things and me up into a pick-up truck. I had given up and needed help and help had arrived. This would be where I planned to bounce my first check in South America. I hoped the Innkeeper would take the check and he did. I was in.

The room was small, though I wasn't expecting much out of Caracas. The first thing I wanted to do was take a shower, though I changed my tune quickly after getting a look at the showerhead. The showerhead was like a penis just pissing down. I then turned my attention to the bed. I didn't need anyone to tell me I hadn't had enough sleep, so that's what I did, sleep. I slept a deep sleep.

It was so deep I was awaken by Jesus R. to pick me up from the hotel to take me back to the airports. After returning to the terminal, I spent a lot of time hanging around Jesus R's tourist cube. It was there I met Eduardo. My mind went to work on these two. What it finally spit out was they were two bishops from my kingdom, here to help when it was needed most. I also met the people in the cubes surrounding their cube.

AN AMERICAN MESSIAH

One night Jesus R. took me to a club. It had the music and bright colored light you would expect in a nightclub, but it was stuck in a 70's time warp. We each had one drink before leaving. Are next destination was another airport, which was close to the two main terminals, but drastically smaller. Jesus R. told me he was training to be a helicopter pilot there. He took me there for a place to sleep, but I saw a gun on him and didn't trust sleeping while he was there. I let him retire, but I stay awake outside. I laid on a bench to get some sleep, but the insects had a feeding frenzy on my shoulders and arms. My distorted mind put belief in a man with a machete in the high brush around the small compound as I lay there.

My mind was excited and the games I played intensified and heightened. The people around me took roles in past, present and future lives. They assumed characters from my mother and father to friends and enemy. My fantasy positioned them quickly.

The next day Jesus R. took me to his girl friends apartment. The first time I saw her I had love at first sight. She was very attractive and I found her to have a regal look. They spoke in Spanish and I said nothing. I silently admired the photos of her framed around the living room. If I were a king, in this life, I would make her my wife, a queen. I felt I missed her each time I saw her.

After thinking of myself as a King at Jesus R. girlfriend's apartment I began sitting beside people in each of the large airports when there were only two seated in a row of three to sit. I would then occupy the third empty seat to play three kings. It was a game I played several times. My imagination would come up with the scenario. I would usually have to do leg work to satisfy the other two, usually, older men. Though the sad truth was I was a poor per trying to survive in this third world country. Nights I had found the tables in the international airports pavilion to be a good place to get a little shuteye.

As I spent more time in the airports the gray Devil appeared in my thoughts. He had grown disappointed in the child he had conceived by himself. It was slow and had little motor function. Goes to show, one can't get the whole thing right on the first try.

He then went through the process of creating a second one. He carried this one close to his body rapped in large jungle leaves. He saw this new one was much more attentive and focused than the first.

It made me proud to be a second.

The problem now was what to do with the first child. He decided to have him walk into the water. If he kept walking and the water went over his head he would drown, because he didn't know any better. If he stopped, knowing he was going in to deep, he would live, showing he possessed better judgment and didn't always need to be told what to do. The gray Devils son just kept walking until he drowned.

It's at this time I'm beginning to feel the wear and tear from my trip. I started to look for someone to save me. A girl is what I wanted, to take me away from this old airport. One night I thought Queen Elizabeth II had arrived to save me. This is when I crossed paths with what my mind told me was 'my archenemy'. He was with a girl I thought would be rescuing me if it where not for him, but they whispered sweet nothings to one another. All I could do is watch. They finally left together and I was left stunned and alone.

As the sun rose on the next morning I imagined my trunk I was dragging around was inside the arch rival's head. I then thought the trunk was growing in size and eventually got to big for his head to handle. His head then shattered into pieces. That's when I sat down exhausted. I was seated in the dining area in the International airport. It's the same place I was sleeping nights. As the gallery filled I could hear the conversation of the people surrounding me. It was as if they where in my head instead of out. I could hear and feel the buzz of the crowd and it wore on me. That's when I had had enough. I broke down. The tears began to swell up in my eyes, when they came streaming down I went to the men's room in an attempt to compose myself. I spent a good 15-30 minutes in the men's room. I looked at myself in the mirror as the tears streamed down my cheeks. At one point I cried out to Prince Charles letting him know I deserved better than this and he never had it this tough.

On a neighboring night, Jesus R. took me down to a surrounding town. We went to this small workshop. What the function of this shop was; was a lost on me. It was late at night and I was among two new strangers and Jesus R. They spoke in Spanish, so again I was the odd man out. That's when a gun came into play. One of the men I had just met was sitting with his gun on his lap. The rest of us where standing at arms length. I was anticipating something to happen with the gun, so as soon as the weapon came off of his lap I grabbed his hand and then let it go as his arm went limp. I was in a place and with people I didn't know. It seemed the right thing for me to do at the time. Jesus could have been trying to get rid of me for the check I had bounced at the hotel or perhaps the content of my trunk and bag.

Upon returning to the cube I noticed a disputed territory on one of the maps. The disputed area seamed to be in New French Guiana. My distorted mind came to the idea there was a fallen star in this territory and no one knew what to do with it. My theory grew to include the star as an omen. It was there to choose the next sight of a great war on earth. My thought went to Michael Irvin and the possible roll he could take in a war like this. I imagined him in a fighter plane bombing a countries capital, ending the bloodshed. That's if Michael presently exists.

Something it took me a long time to notice, and that's due to the lack of money I possessed, was the currency in Venezuela was 80 Bee's or Bolivar's to one American dollar. They also put the commas and periods in different places on there money. The money was named after Simone Bolivar, the countries favorite son.

After spending days in the cube without noticing a sign for a trip to an island off the coast named Los Rojas, I found myself enchanted at the possibility of going to the island. That's when I took out my checkbook and bounced another check with Jesus R. I believe the cost to get there was around $200. I didn't care. I told myself I would bounce the same amount of checks in Venezuela as I did in the States, which was two and this was the second one. After writing the check I had to be taken to yet another small airport to catch my flight. The plane I would take was a small commuter plane. At that airport I checked in all my belongings. I was worried they wouldn't take them on such a small plane, but they did. Before I knew it I was on the plane headed to Los Rojas.

Once I had made it to the island I had to get my bearings. I dragged my trunk and bag through the sand as I navigated my way around Los Rojas. My first impression was it wasn't much better than I had seen on the main land. After some time I found a convenient store by the shore. I was thirsty and needed a drink, so I opened up my coin collection. It wasn't much of a collection. I wasn't losing much by spending them. I had enough for a soda and not much else.

This store was right by the shore. I couldn't resist the ocean. I cut the legs from my jeans and made my way into the water. The water was worm and seagulls flocked. I went in very slowly as not to disturb the birds too much; at times it looked like they may attack. It was refreshing to get into the water. I totally submerged myself to get a better sample of their water vs. Rhode Islands' ocean water.

After my dip into the warm Venezuelan water I dried off and started my way more inland. I had mentioned how run down everything was on this island, but as one makes their way, as I did, to the center of the island there are some nicer cleaner options. I came to a nice hotel. I was going to bounce another check even though I said just two. Well I stayed at two because this Inn keep wouldn't take checks, so I took my things and dragged them through the sand. Something worth noting is there weren't any cars on Los Rojas, so one has to travel on foot.

By foot I made it to the other side of the island and then to the backside. It was then getting dark and late and I needed some food. That's when I came across a restaurant which looked appealing. I took a seat and put my luggage beside the table. The dinner for everyone was the same; it was a soap or chowder. As I ate I noticed one of the girls running the restaurant was, in my excited mind, was a real sister in another life and may help me. After finishing the meal I gave them my credit card that was at its limit. I was trying to pretend I had no idea the card was at its limit and then told them I had no money to pay. That's when they called in the cavalry. Men armed with semi-automatic weapons came to take me away. I guess my believed sister was of no help.

I was taken to a small military compound. I was held outside on a bench built into a wall. I lay there for about two hours, at gunpoint, until the mayor of the island came to my rescue. The mayor then took me to a building, either his home or the town hall. He gave me a room to stay in with a bed.

I had a sound night sleep, which where far and few in between, and was waken by the mayor the next morning. He put me on a passenger boat with about six other people to a remote part of the island. The water was crystal clear and the beach was void of beach goers until we got there. I didn't have anything to lay-on, so I spent most of my time in the water. I walked with water up to my waist for about 40 yards before the sea floor hit a decline. And once in the water I made the most of it. I swam and even did hand stands in the water. At lunch we where brought food. I remember it as fish and rice. Any meal was welcome at that point. It was a beautiful day and I had made it to an island paradise. The water was so clear I could see little tiny fish swimming around. When the day ended I felt satisfied with my trip to Los Rojas. At the end of the stay I was given a ticket back to the main land and flew back to my temporary home, the airports.

When I got back to the main land Jesus R. was upset I bounced the check to get to Los Rojas. I went to my bag and gave him my gold necklace my grandparents had given me. That would more than pay for the ticket. He was mildly appeased. I wanted to point out I had all ready given him my brown blazer and one of my championship football jackets, Eduardo had the other championship football jacket as a token of friendship. This is also the first time, but not the last I can recall Jesus R. telling me I was crazy. He had obviously begun to detect my behavior wasn't always normal.

They had slowly taken me in to help them with their cube. On one of my first days I was manning the cube while Jesus R. and Eduardo where attending to a young ladies things. She gave me a hand full of money and I took it, telling Jesus R. and Eduardo nothing. They never asked me about it, so I never said anything. It was the first time I had any kind of money. I remember the first thing I did with the money was buying myself a sandwich and I had some money to spear.

I spent more nights in the terminal than I care to remember. Once I tried sleeping on the outside veranda, but grew afraid someone was going to do me harm. I felt safest on the dining tables of the indoor eatery. I spent most of my nights alone with my head down on the table trying to get a few winks. Getting sleep was difficult. On a random night a couple sat at the table across from mine. They where far enough away that I couldn't hear their conversation, but not to far away for the male to reach over and pull a thought from my mind. He stuck his arm out and grabbed at the air the same time I had a thought pass though my mind. At least that's what my intense thoughts experienced.

Jesus R. was the only person on my voyage thinking I was in need of help. What he did was take me to the embassy. As I was going through the gates to the main building Jesus R. pleaded, he wanted to go to the U.S., specifically Boston. I didn't see how it was possible, but I did keep it in mind as I entered the embassy. After waiting in a room full of people for about 45 minutes it was my turn to give my story. I told them I had no money left, but they where unsympathetic and told me they couldn't help me at this time.

I took my things and left the building, back to Jesus R. We returned to where else, the airports. While in the airports my fantasy took me to Jesus Christ. I do believe in Jesus, maybe not as someone who walked the earth, but as a spiritual ideal who represents good and powerful things. I do believe, but question his mortality on earth. If he did exist on earth he is undoubtedly the star of religion and I do have respect for him as a mythical figure or a star that transcends man. I also believe somewhere out there, there just may have been a Jesus who had to carry the cross, because that is what he was created to do. It's this respect for him, which was me looking at him as a friend instead of an ideal for worshiping.

His story is now infamous, carrying the cross to exhaustion only to be crucified upon the lumber. This is when I intervene. In my mind when Christ begins to lift the cross, I strike him down with a lightning bolt. I do this over and over, to save him from the suffering. I also like to think of what the Roman's would have thought if he was stricken down before they had their precession.

As I stated above this is what Jesus does, that's his mission, to carry the cross. I then became more playful, asking what would happen if it where my turn to carry the cross. Be it now, past and future lives. How would I perform the same task? Well I can tell; if the rules to this game where I carry the cross until I fall three times and then I'll be crucified on the same cross. I think I may just tell the Romans to spear me down to death right there, I'm not carrying any cross. On other occasions I would give the cross a lift, only to through it back at the Romans. I would then take off running in a zigzag pattern to avoid spears. If the time to really carry the cross came about I thought I would carry it in circles or triangles or other shapes. If it really came down to my turn I would sink my feet into the sand on each step and when they crucified me I would try to rip my hands and feet from the spikes to get off the cross. When it was really my turn to go, in my mind, Christ would show up in a UFO to beam me up from this predicament.

After I was beamed up I got into an argument with my friend Christ. He thought it was more natural through the progression of time to get beamed up. I find it more natural to get stricken down by a lightning bolt; it is a phenomenon of nature more than a flying sour sir. This led me to play more. I would now appear in an executioner style uniform, beamed down from the UFO. Sticking down Christ with lightning bolts from my hands, as soon as I witnessed him attempting to carry the cross. It was after this playing with my friend Christ, that I had renewed faith in him and myself.

There where only so many games I could play before I was then consumed by hunger. I had gone without food for a day or two. Most of the time the hunger was dulled by the occupation of my thoughts, but it was time to eat. I still had my credit card at its' limit to play with. I went out to the terrace where they served food during the day. I sat at a table and ordered from the menu. They served me and I ate. I sat for a few minutes to take in the always-tropical air. I knew the card was at its limit, but came up with a solution. What I did was leave the card at the table while leaving. The restaurant could then put two and two together once they found out I wasn't waiting for the over the limit card.

The next time I had to eat I went into a restaurant in the international airport. It was a nice restaurant having a view of the tarmac. Again I ordered from the menu. This time my imagination took over and made, who appeared to be the boss to me, into a boxing champion. I created a relationship with him where we fought together. I never said anything allowed, but every time I looked at him I saw a glorious boxer. I saw him as an undefeated champion and was just happy to make his acquaintance. The food then came and I ate it down with no way of paying. I didn't have enough money, but still had a few dollars from the girl going to Los Rojas. When it came time to pay the piper, I told the champ I had no money and he understood. He didn't do anything. He allowed me a free meal. Though he gave no hint of it, I'll always remember him as a boxer.

Now I was getting greedy. I was eating free meals all around the airports. This time it would be different. I went to the inside restaurant in the international airport, which by the way the two airports had just begun construction to modernize and combine the two, for something to eat. I sat and ordered from the menu as I usually did and was served without a problem. This is where it gets dicey. I have no credit cards to speak of and very little money. That's when I got up and walked away. My bags where left at the travel cube with Jesus R. and Eduardo. I walk away and down the hall, but turned around to see if I got away with it. That is when my waiter tracked me down and called for security. Security came quickly and I was taken away. Where I was headed was unknown to me. What could be the punishment for eating and not paying?

Where they took me was jail. It was filthy. Two cells made up the holding facility, each with about four men in it. The cells stayed open from what I could tell. There was an aisle outside the two cells where I remained. They had girly posters and pictures on the walls. If you had to go to the bathroom they had a bucket. I refrained from going to the bathroom. Everyone in the cells spoke only Spanish, but one. He was a South African named Frank. The prisoners interrogated me the best they could and I got out my Marcus Allen theory for the first time. I also told them I would not go back to the U.S. I would go to Africa next. One of the prisoners showed me a game with cigarettes, something to due with moving a pebble out of the boxing in cigarettes. I spent one night in that jail. That night they slept on cardboard boxes, I stayed awake. The next morning I was released, but if I had to stay there for a stretch I don't know how well I'd come out. I guess it was a good experience for a night.

The day after I got out I was right to it once again, chew and screw. This time I stopped by a restaurant across the street from the national airport. I arrived with a plan. I would order than eat and after I would get up from my chair and run down the street in my best sprinter form. That's exactly what I did. It was an easy meal.

Now that I've given the idea of how I kept myself from starving, I would like to focus on the people who got to know me. Of course there are Jesus R. and Eduardo, but there where the people who where in the surrounding cubes. There was someone named Johnny, who had me write down some lyrics from a musical tape he was listening to. One of the girls in the cube to the right gave me a cheese sandwich and I gave her my high school Honor Roll pin. Toping it all off, the couple in the cube to the left invited me to their daughter's birthday party, which I did attend and had cake.

AN AMERICAN MESSIAH

As I grew weary of the airports I ventured just down the street into a small-impoverished town. The roads where dirt and the market place's where all open air, with flies hovering for there next meal. I saw an old run down ball field. It looked like soccer. I walked down the road for a while only to turn back. I didn't really gain anything from the trip, other than it's tough to imagine the poverty still exciting today on earth.

Again Jesus R. thought it would be a good idea to go back to the embassy. I went to the embassy for a second time and for the second time they told me they couldn't help. We then traveled back to the airports.

When I got back to the airport I stayed outside watching the flights take off. After a while it felt like they had gotten into my head and were using it for a landing strip. Even when I got into the airports my mind was buzzing with planes taking off. I really thought I was going out of my mind at that point. That's we Eduardo ask me to come home with him.

Eduardo took me to his apartment in Caracas. This was the furthest I would travel away from the airports; in fact he took me into the center of the city. As we pasted through the sprawling city I noticed the architecture was dated by the 70's. He drove enough that I had no idea where I was, but Eduardo got me to his apartment. It was a small, one bedroom apartment, with only a kitchen and bathroom.

Eduardo was a much better host than Jesus R. He gave me a place to sleep, all be it a mattress in the kitchen. He also gave me a place to shower and clean up, something I hadn't done in several weeks. He also gave me the O.K. to eat anything I could find. His cupboards and pantry were relatively empty, but I was able to put a few odd combinations together for a bight to eat. For instance I can recall having tuna with olive oil, and pasta with mayonnaise. The one things I didn't due where the dishes and that's due to my stubbornness, demanding a liquid soap to do the dishes instead of the soap in a can Eduardo used. Once he got me the liquid soap I was more than obliged. His apartment was a good place for me to regroup.

He took me to the Mall to look around while he was with his girl friend. It was interesting to see the prices in the thousands of Bee's for a pear of Levis. They priced out about the same as in the U.S., only the currency exchange was out of whack. While in the Mall I spent the rest of my Bee's on a tribal blue beaded ankle bracelet. Nothing else much interested me, for the money I had left.

As Eduardo his girlfriend and I drove around the city I couldn't help but notice they where holding elections in Venezuela. There was one women running for some office reminding me of Carmen the stripper from the *Foxy Lady*. I immediately connected the two as mother and daughter. I also saw almost all of the billboards for the current president had red paint thrown over his picture. I thought this to be a negative threat to the President.

Most of the time I was left alone in Eduardo's small apartment, but it was a far better existence than the airports. I also got a better look at the TV programs. I watched some soap operas, some animal planet and some strange show, which seamed to take place at a resort. There where a lot of bikinis. I found the show to be totally ridiculous in nature and would never be shown in the States. All the shows were in Spanish so I never really got the stories down.

As I spent more time alone my mind occupied the minutes. I came up with a play in this down time. The play begins with a women singing and dancing, in traditional Spanish attire. The following seen moves to a castle with a balcony. In the balcony is a beautiful princess and at the foot of the castle stands her father. The father is trying to find someone worthy to wed his daughter. As men come in one after another the one sister greets them with song and dance for an introduction. Each suitor comes prepared with a gift for the princes, but the King throws the gifts back at the men in disgust. He tells them all 'they fail to see the beauty in his daughter'. Finally a humble man approaches the father and asks for the hand of the singing and dancing maiden. The King then turns and say, "You have seen the beauty in my daughter, I accept you as her suitor."

Eduardo picked me up one day and we drove around the city stopping here and there. On this trip we stopped for gas. I believe I saw the gas price was 35 something a liter. Be it Bee's or dollars that is dirt cheep for gas. I know the Venezuelans are an OPEC nation, but we should be better friends with our neighbors to the south. Something else I noticed was the nations countryman, Simone Bolivar was not only all over the book covers in the airports' bookstore, but he was all over billboards, posters, and statues. He was everywhere. In the U.S. we don't even give Washington and Lincoln this kind of fan fair. The Simone mania that gripes Venezuela is probably their biggest problem, living in the past.

I met some new people this day, they where friends of Eduardo. They where nice enough and they spoke English. Eduardo went there to have his truck looked at. One of them was studying to be a graphic artist, so I had to see some of his work. It was O.K. It was just kind of image manipulation than it was straight creative graphic design. I bit my tongue knowing this was a battle I didn't want to fight, with all his brothers around to defend him and make trouble for me.

The next trip we made was back to the airports. On that visit my delirious mind fantasizes that I was a King and Jesus R.' girlfriend is my Queen – I believe she is only with him because I owed him in another life. As King I pretended to look over the rail of the second floor of the airport down at my subjects. I imagined the sight of me would raise their spirits. Something else filling my mind was in my Kingdom I would allow this Queen to stick me with a knife. She would look into the blade before puncturing the skin in attempt to look into the body. I would go along with this as long as it is not in a vital area, but this is not my Kingdom and these where just thoughts.

I then made my way away from the airports, to the right, to see what was there. It didn't take long before I found a small airport with a small military base or baric almost attached. At this time I was going with the flow and wasn't too worried about anything. I felt I had been in Venezuela long enough to survive. I sat in the front of the buildings watching the military people go by. I also imagined the Devil, with a military helmet, doing his best to leave evidence he had been somewhere. What he was doing was pulling off one of his fingers and then closing the open end with some hair. He would then burry the artifact in the ground for someone to come find and ID. He would also take off one of his arms and stab it into the grown with the hand pointed up, so it was visible from far away. He also would put his army hat on the raised arm.

Sometime during that day I was asked if I wanted a tray of food from the military. Of course I said yes. Whenever I had the opportunity to get some food in my stomach I jumped at the chance. It was good for military food and I was very grateful. It wasn't long after that that I was invited to sleep over in the military baric and I accepted the offer. The military people I was bunked with were young guys and they where well disciplined. All I wanted was a place to sleep, so that's what I did. The next morning I showered and left the baric.

I made my way to the airport right next door. I got into a conversation with the two people running the airports eatery a guy and a girl. Other than the staff and myself there wasn't anyone around. That is when I asked if the two liked music and they said they did. I then asked if they would trade a CD for a sandwich and they gave a yes. I named a few of the CD's I had in my bag until I came across one they liked. They liked Guns 'n' Roses. I had a live CD, but when I looked for the CD's they where missing along with about seven other CD's. The guys in the military baric had stolen my CD's while I was showering, so I went back to get them. I was fuming and asked them in an angered voice, "Where are my CD's?" I had to ask a couple of times before they surfaced. I took them and then went back to the small airport to get my sandwich. They took the two G'n'R CD's and put them into their CD player. The sandwich was as good as almost any food was at this point.

Sitting back where I was when the military people gave me food, I was grabbed by the authorities and brought back to the jail I had once stayed in, so much for going with the flow. All the men from my last stay where still there. They greeted me and they got over my stay quickly. Just as I did in the first trip to this jail I didn't sleep all night and again I was set free in the morning. I still don't know why they took me in that time.

When I got back to the cube where Eduardo and Jesus R. worked I thought Venezuela would be a terrific place for an Olympics. I looked at the people in the country and thought how strong they would be if there where less poverty. I due believe a certain amount of suffering will make one stronger if they are given time to regain there strength. It was with this thinking I came up with 'My Greatest Athlete'. No this is possible, but very unlikely. I imagined a man from Venezuela who would win 11 gold medals in the Olympics. He is a decathlete who wins the decathlon, but is so physically gifted he also wins the 10 events outside of the decathlon, to make eleven. That is 'My Greatest Athlete" be it fantasy or reality.

As far as working with Jesus R. and Eduardo I didn't do too much. In fact Jesus R. hung up a poster of what looked like a pterodactyl. I didn't think it was right for the cube, so I through it away. Jesus R.

was quite upset and told me he had thrown away my bag and trunk. I had nothing to say to him. He told me I was crazy for what had to be the tenth time and that was that.

After the argument with Jesus R I walked to the airport he was getting his helicopter pilots license to talk with the people who owned and ran the travel business to apologize for the poster and to see if I could get into a better spot in the airport. When I arrived I was received by two of the people who worked at this airport. I had previously seen them both, but I was greeted with hostility. One of the men took a few swings at me and when I retreated two more men came out of the woodwork to try and get their licks in. I also recognized this couple, one of who had a pipe with him. There I was confronted by four men in a third world country and not a lot I could do about it, so I took steps backward at a pretty good clip to get away from them and their airport. I made out of there with only the shot to the face by the first man.

My options where now closing. My last day in the terminal Jesus R. left his gun on the desk in the cube. I picked up the gun with a stapler remover, so as not to get my fingerprints messed up with some gun, and put it in a box hidden under the counter.

I spent my last night in the airport that evening. That evening I met twin girls who had a layover. They looked pretty young, but they showed me their passports and they were twenty-one. I talked with them for most of the night, for we where the only ones in the airport that night, other than a women who came to ask us some questions. She didn't speak English so the twins set her straight and she would now wait with us. As she waited I saw her as Princess Ann of the Royals. I imagined her stolen away at a young age by Spain and hidden from the Royal family in all kinds of Spanish speaking countries. I took a seat beside her and told her to go to British Columbia and then Great Britain. I not only did that, but I gave her information about Apple Computers and design programs for it. I gave this information to give to the Royals as a computer and programs to revolutionize the computer world.

That night wasn't that long because I had company to occupy the time. The next morning I took a taxi to downtown Caracas alone and with no money to pay the taxi driver. I told him I had no money and he didn't put up much of a fight, he then drove off. The only thing I had left with me was my blue bag of CD's. I took them with me as I attempted to get a loan from the *Banco de Brazil*. I told them I wanted 2 million Bee's to start a robotics company. They took my application into consideration, but they came back with a no. I also forgot my bag of CD's at the bank.

As darkness fell I made it to a church and sat in on the sermon. I focused most of my attention on Jesus while in the church. After the ceremony I asked the father for some help, maybe a place to stay, but he was of little to no help, but he did ask his parishioners to help me and help they did. A few of them gave me some money, which would go toward my next meal. I left gratefully.

The next day I went to the embassy to see if they could help me, now that I had nothing left but the passport and ID I kept in my back pocket. This the third trip to the embassy, they said they would. They told me there was a law that would send me back to the state I reside in. All I had to do was call home. That was a sour task. I didn't want help from my family, but I did what they wanted. I allowed them to call my house and they contacted my mother. When I talked to her I told her I wanted to go to San Antonio, Texas to continue playing. She said no, so I hung up on her, but the women at the embassy who was helping me called my mother back. On this call we agreed to send me back home.

That night the people at the embassy put me up in a hotel and arranged for me to have a pizza pie for dinner. The hotel was relatively nice considering the country I was in. Again a shower at the hotel was a welcomed lug gory. It was also nice to get into a comfortable bed. I went to sleep quickly and woke up ready to fly back home.

That day I went back to the Airport for the last time. I would be leaving my home away from home. I made it through the necessary check points to board the plane. It was off I go. My flight had a connection in New York I had to make to get home. I was tempted to take off from NY, but I didn't. I took the flights right back to Rhode Island.

CHAPTER 12

Boarding the plain I had nothing but the clothes on my back, my passport and ID, as well as, the plain ticket. After approximately 40 days in Venezuela I was headed back to Rhode Island. I was tacking a flight from Caracas to New York, with a connection in New York carrying me to little Rhode Island. Having no one holding my hand I was tempted to miss my connection in NY and attempt a run from my family. I should be able to survive with less trouble in the States, but I had surrendered and would wait to fight another day. Once I arrived in New York I boarded the commuter plain for home.

When I arrived in Rhode Island I planned on getting a bus to the *Foxwoods Casino* on the Connecticut line. I thought there must be free buses from the airport to the casino. As I stepped off the plain I had no time to follow my plan, my brother was waiting for me. After being greeted by my brother I was taken back to my home. The car ride was very quiet. Back at West Warwick I was greeted by my family and was given something to eat, when around 45 minutes to an hour after arriving the police and a rescue was summonsed to my residence.

I was then placed in the rescue and taken to Kent County Hospital, where I was placed in a room to wait for the next move. I was there all alone waiting to see what was next. After a short wait a woman from Butler Hospital appeared. She asked me some questions, none of which seemed important at the time. It would be her to fill me in on the next move. She was there to take me to Butler. The thing was I didn't trust her to take me. My mental state was still working over time. I could see myself ending up in some part of the hospital they experimented on their patients, at least that was my fear. That's when I noticed the police presence around the unit and I demanded to be taken to Butler by an officer.

They granted my wish. I was placed in handcuffs and brought to the cruiser that would take me to Butler. There was no conversation on the way there; only the sounds of the police radio filled the compartment. We arrived in a speedy fashion and I was taken to a side entrance and dropped off into a waiting room with a desk in it. I remained cuffed for some part of the wait and recall thinking I would soon be out of this mess. Shortly after I was released from the chains bounding me, when a Butler staff member took charge of the situation. He would take me right up to the Kent County unit at Butler.

I didn't want to be there, though no one there wants to be there. I still felt like there was nothing wrong with me. In fact after Venezuela I felt I proved myself as survival ready.

My first morning I was greeted in bed by Dr. Ferman, my doctor from my first hospitalization. That morning I gave him my spoiled honey vaccine to conquer aids. He didn't seem too impressed, in fact my stab at proving myself as well had to have done the opposite. That would be the last time I met or saw him. I would be assigned another doctor. I'll call him Dr. H. I met with him and his assistant a few minutes each day. I would refuse the medication he was prescribing.

The clothes I wore had been on me for several days and needed to be cleaned. I washed them, but as they where being cleaned I was given a Hospital rob to wear around the unit. As my clothes washed my illness thought me to be a kind of King in this simple hospital gown.

Unlike the last time I was hospitalized, I socialized with the other patients and nurses. Early in my stay I met a patient named Paul. I could tell he was heavily sedated; he would almost fall asleep standing up. As a token of friendship Paul gave me a Walkman. Another patient I was introduced to early on was Kevin. He seemed introverted and in a dais. He was an older man most probably in his 50's. As for the nurses, they took advantage of my artistic ability. The male nurses in the unit took a greater role in my stay than did the females. They discovered my artistic ability quickly. A relationship started and two of them sat for portraits. My talent gained favorable reviews and my doctor and his assistant queried if I could get them both on paper. I accepted their request without hesitation, but they would have no time to sit, so I sketched them the best I could from memory. I would like to add all my works where done with a pen and ordinary paper. I gave them the illustrations the next day and they where a good likeness for having nothing to reference. Later in my stay I would sketch Paul and his fiancée from a photo as a gift back for the Walkman.

Drawing wasn't the only method I used to kill time. I did a puzzle of the Eiffel Tower in France. My brother visited, disrupting the puzzles construction. He was the families first representative to see how I was. I attempted to angle my way into his home, but he would have no part of it. This made me angry. My own brother wouldn't take me in my time of need. It was well known I had distain for my father. He left shortly after, leaving some of my clothes behind. Once he left I went back to the puzzle and as I put the finishing pieces into position, the television reported the Concord had exploded. My mind automatically connected my puzzle with the crash. It was a thin connection, but I felt I had a hand in the accident having both the Tower and the Concord coming from France. It was a split second connection thinking my mind blew it up. I kept this internal, but had a strange feeling about the events. Not long after this incident, the Venezuelan Little League team won the Series. I thought this occasion with the third world nation of Venezuela was more than a coincident. I made comment to a couple of the nurses and they enjoyed the irony. I never felt there was anyone out to get me and it wasn't paranoia. I just wanted to be considered as misunderstood and special, not mentally ill. I just believed I was the center of some events. These instances passed and I could be found enjoying my favorite spot in the unit.

I would lie on a couch butting a window. In the afternoon the sunlight would radiate through the window. I would take in the bright light the sun provided. Another feature making this a sweet spot was the nurse at the side desk. I remember her as Lisa, my sister's name. She had long blonde hair and I enjoyed just having her close by, she was easy to look at.

Next to the station was a bookshelf. On the shelf I found a stack of National Geographic magazines. Looking through one of the magazines I found something not to believe. There was a map of Mexico, where on the 22 parallel, on the east coast I found the city of Veracrus. I was satisfied that my journey had been completed. I had found the city I had been searching for through this whole ordeal. That led to an inner piece followed by the decision to listen to my Walkman.

All the songs were new to me I had been away for over a month. Out with the old in with the new music. There was a song I liked. I believe it was *Rock Super Star*, by "Cypress Hill". Not that I played that song any louder than the other songs that came on, I just enjoyed that one most. Like I mentioned I played all the music loud and one of the female nurses took exception to this. She wanted me to turn the radio down. I guess it was loud enough one could hear it without the headphones. She demanded I take off the headphones. I plainly denied her. That's when she attempted to grab the Walkman from me. A split second later the male nurses stepped in to forcibly take my Walkman away. I resisted to a point and I wound up in the rubber room in the hall.

This room was approximately 10' x 7', the walls where a consistent rubber all around. A mirror ran across the back wall, about 2 feet in height and 10 feet in width. The floor was also rubber. I spent my time in this cell whistling until I grew tired. After about 45 minutes to an hour I was released from this box, back into the regular population. That night I tried calling the State Police, to tell them I was being held against my own free will. Remember I was also denying my medication and really wanted nothing to do with this whole stay.

A day or two pasted before a young kid named Vaughn entered the unit. He was asking me why he was there and why this had happened to him. I had no answers. I didn't want to be there myself. After sometime he settled down and I found he like to work with the inter net and putting up websites. I thought he could make a good inter net man if I tried to get my businesses up again.

My parents visited me for the first time. The visit was tenuous. In my mind they were the ones putting me in this position. They where also pushing for me to be court order medication, because I was refusing the meds. They didn't seem to be on the same page as I was and the hospital wanted me to go back home, which at the, time I was trying to avoid. They would make a few visits after this one.

In a strange way I was enjoying my stay at Butler. I had made some friends and I was being fed three times a day plus nightly raids of the kitchen (mostly for toast and cereal). The summer weather was nice, which made the afternoon walks pleasant and fun. I also enjoyed playing the game of chess, having now added the new dimension of using the ancient games pieces for political positions.

I attempted several times to teach Kevin how to play the game. He started by asking if I was the Ameron. He asked a few times which made me come to the conclusion that Ameron was his title for Messiah. This gave me more confidence in my political chessboard.

He could figure out how to move the pieces, but he would quit after the matches would advance. I never really had an advantage when he would quit, so it seemed like he stopped his play with out effort. This is when a new patient asked to play chess. He defeated me in about three to four moves. He beat me soundly each time we played. His name was Richard and he told me he had been a chess champion in the past. I got along well with Richard and we formed a friendship. He was most probably in his 50's and quite thin. He also didn't want to be there. He told me he was worth a million dollars, which he had made in the computer programming business.

As we shared stories, I came up with one of my: you wont believe this story. In the last football game I played in, the 1990 High Super Bowl, I was giving my best effort to catch a pass in the end zone for a two-point conversion. As I leapt for the pass something, some higher power propelled me past my ability and I believe I flew for a fraction of a second. I believe other players have also experienced this feeling. For example Hershel Walker going over the top at the goal line, as well as, Walter Payton and even Marcus Allen. All have taken flight for a fractional second. One has to look at my claim as they would the Wright Brothers. They didn't fly all over the place on their first flight; they made a modest leap in aviation. I do believe this happens to pro athletes more frequently then they realize. I also think it to be obvious, that if man can fly, a representative from the sports world would be the chosen one. Richard didn't challenge the story what so ever.

Patients came and went, but none would make the impact of one patient. Her name was Stephanie. She was younger. I think I remember her as 18. I noticed her right away. She was a good-looking girl who let me now, when we met, she was trying to be a model. She was there for slitting her wrists. She was battling depression. It didn't take her long before she was whispering sweet nothings in my ear.

DAVID MICHAEL

The day my doctor and my parents were waiting for had finally arrived. I had an appointment to court order my meds. I was taken to the campuses gymnasium. I waited for some time seated on the basketball court. This made me laugh. The Court was in the basketball Court. With humor, I wondered if my basketball skills would be judged. The court actually resided in a side chamber of the gym.

When it was my turn to face the judge I did a quick sketch of him as they went over my case. The whole thing was a sham. There was someone there to defend me, but he thought it a good idea for me to get court ordered meds. That's exactly what happened. At the end of the proceedings I was order by the court to take my meds or have them forcibly injected. When it came down to it and they where ready to give me an injection, I caved and began taking the medication prescribed to me.

The days had the same feel and schedule before Stephanie arrived. She occupied most of my time and it wasn't long before we where sneaking kisses around the unit. She appeared at a good time for me. It was nice to have the touch of a woman again.

All the characters I met during this stay at Butler were a motley bunch. They would make a good staff for *My Evil Empire* or maybe they where the people running the Empire the last time around, bringing ourselves together in a most unflattering way. To show what a strange crew we had assembled, we watched "One flew over the Coo Coos Nest" one of the nights, which I thought was smothered with irony.

I always enjoyed getting out of the building and the walks did just that, but the stroll around campus was even sweeter with Stephanie. We had created a strong bond during our stay. She even made activity time more enjoyable and I made a potholder for my mother. Our relationship was built in a strange place and I wondered if we would see one another outside of Butler.

Now having taking my medication and everyone in the unit knew who I was after more than a month of detainment, they allowed me the liberty of running down the unit's schedule to the rest of the patients. No other patient had this honor, at least not during my lengthy stay.

Early one morning my friend Paul and I where watching the TV. We scrambled through the channels before we found an old movie. It was set in a prehistoric time and all the actors would say was, "Akita." What made the film entertaining was the woman in the movie wore little to nothing. We spent that morning echoing the cry, "Akita" here an "Akita" there. It was one of those catch phrases that run for a long while and if others had seen the film, could spread like wild fire.

Finally after about a month and a half, I was given a release day. Though Stephanie would also be getting released a day or two before me. We made curtain to exchange phone numbers, but she said she would call me at one of the unit phones. That she did. The day after she left I received a nice call from her.

It was now the day I would be leaving. I got Richard and Vaughn's numbers. Paul didn't give me his number, but invited me to his bachelor party at a social club I knew. I accepted his invitation happily.

I would be going back to my parent's house, back home. I really had no other choices than that. To be honest, the difference between this stay and my first were night and day, but I was happy to be leaving just the same. I said my good-byes and headed home to see what Stephanie was up to.

When I got home from Butler Hospital, I was surprised by the amount of work my father and brother had done to accommodate me. They finished off the rest of the down stairs, giving me a living room, bedroom and bathroom of my own.

Once I was home the first thing I did was call Stephanie. We got together that night and we went for some Chinese food for diner. She was a very aggressive companion; she let it be known what see wanted. She was a beautiful young girl and I couldn't deny her overtures. After we ate we made it back to my house.. We had started a tryst, one that came from a strange meeting place. She was able to return to her job at *Wal-Mart* were she worked late at night to early mornings. At the end of her work hours she would come over in the early hours to blow of some steam and have a little fun.

On a serious note, I thought the hours' she was keeping at *Wal-Mart* where the primary reason for her depression. In my opinion, it was throwing off her body clock. Stephanie and I had a fling for a few weeks, and then out off the blue she decided she wanted to go her separate way. She never gave an answer of why, but I didn't need a reason. Our relationship wasn't based on a lot of respect it was built on escapism. For a few weeks we thought about each other instead of our problems. She probably just wanted time alone to think things over.

I met with a new doctor after leaving Butler, for my follow up treatment. Her name was Dr. Koyfman. She spoke with an ascent that sounded Slavic. In my first meeting with her she informed me they had now diagnosed me as Bi Polar. I was happy to hear this, it sounded more accurate than schizophrenia.

Finding myself back in the United States I had an issue sticking in my side. Toward the end of my stay in Venezuela, it came to my mind to change my name. This wasn't the first time I had considered such a move. While in Venezuela I never felt my name of Garcia gave me any kind of kindred with the people I encountered. I didn't feel like my name gave me any advantage in the U.S. People would mistake me for Hispanic, which I'm not. I'm half Portuguese and half Italian. I don't speak Spanish, though I do get annoying phone calls from people trying to sell me something in the Spanish dialect. One of the major events that impacted me negatively was my encounter with a small Pennsylvania College named Swarthmore. I was recruited to play football for them as well as attend the school, but when it came down to it, the football department told me I didn't get into the school because I wasn't Hispanic. If I where Hispanic my grades and SAT scores would have gotten me accepted to the school. On the opposite side of the coin, I thought it was all right to change or delete part of my name, because my grandfather had to take part of his last name away when he came over to the States. That's exactly what I would do, take away the Garcia name and use my middle name, Michael, as a last name. This alteration in name would also break me with my family members. It would make me more of my own person and the most unique person in the family. The move was also symbolic. I didn't feel I was the person who scored all those touchdowns, got all those hits, got good grades and made everything look easy. My life had become more difficult and none of that could help me now. There where no more championships to be won or tests to pass. I wanted to break free of what I had been, to create a new chapter in my life. It was like getting a fresh start, shaping a whole new person. I was attempting to abandon my achievements, so I could try to achieve in the game of life. This isn't something that just came to me. I had been thinking about this change since I was a sophomore in college. It wasn't something I had been waiting for years for, but it was something I had considered in those years.

Once I had made the decision to make this change from David Michael Garcia to David Michael, I went ahead full stream. I went to the West Warwick Town Hall and filed out papers to get a court date to have my name changed legally. I told no one about this, not a sole. I didn't want someone to try and talk me out of it. For the record, the official reason I gave for wanting to change my name was: I wanted to sound more English speaking. Now that the wheels where in motion I could turn my attention to a different venue.

It was still summer when I contacted Richard, who I met at Butler. He had told me he could help me with work if I was willing to work around his house. At this time I was again out of money. After a call to Richard he gave me directions to his home. Using those directions I was able to locate him. His house was disheveled to say the least. He had things thrown all over. I don't know how he lived in such conditions. Luckily it wasn't cleaning his house he wanted help with. He wanted me to put a brick patio or walk way in his yard. At that time I needed some money, so I accepted the work.

We agreed I would be paid $10 per hour. I would work a few hours each morning. It was backbreaking work. The summer sun beat down as I placed one brick after the other, bent over on both knees. I wore the Walkman Paul had given me in the hospital. The music helped break up the monotony. Most of the days ended with Richard treating me to lunch. My afternoons were usually free from this endeavor. The one thing I remember most about Richards house where the Buddha figures he had scattered around the yard and the inside of his home. The one I remember was the Happy Buddha. Once I was done with the brickwork I stopped seeing Richard, but I due have to thank him for the work. At that point and time I needed the job.

The money I was able to earn after about two or three weeks made up the difference I needed to buy an I-Mac. The rest of the *Apple* computer would be put on my *Sears* charge card. It was luck I had some credit left on my card and even luckier *Sears* sold Macintosh computers, most computer stores don't carry them. I bought all the rest of the computer necessities at *Best Buy*. The printer, the scanner, zip drive, and the CD burner where all purchased with my *Best Buy* card, which was put to it's limit. These purchases officially gave me no more credit to work with.

Now that I had a computer to do some work on I contacted Vaughn. He had told me at Butler he could put up web sites. I figured I could design the sites and he could get them up on the inter net. Though Vaughn could put up web pages for himself and his friends, he couldn't put them up as individual sites and wasn't much use for me on a business level. What I saw in Vaughn was a lost young man. He was thin and seemed very fragile in his mechanics. I stopped calling him after few weeks. He would call me to see if I could help him with his life, but I had my own problems to work out.

My credit was destroyed and I had no money, it was time for me to find a job. Looking under artist in the classified ads, I saw an ad for an activist. It spikes my interest and I called to find out more. I set up an interview, which went well enough for me to land the position. The topic they where fighting for, at that time, was affordable and universal health care. What we would do was go door-to-door asking for contributions to raise money to lobby the government and raise awareness. We would get paid half the money we were able to accumulate. I wasn't very good at the begging for money, so I quit after about three weeks.

Shortly after this activist job, I received the court date to change my name. After a few weeks my court date came up. The day of my court hearing, I had a short wait before I went before the Judge. The Judged questioned about the domestic dispute between my father and I. I told him we had patched things up and where doing fine. He then decided my name could be changed. All I had to do was file it with the state. That same day I went to Providence to fill out the paper to get my name restructured. They told me after I filled out the proper forms; the legal documents would be ready around January. It was about August when I had everything done, making January seem like an awful long wait. Around that same time I stopped taking the court ordered med, Zyprexa.

As autumn started to change the leaves, I went by Stephanie's to see how she was doing. She was doing well and I wanted to see if we could rekindle any of our old magic. We become reacquainted, but saw one another less often than in our previous relationship.

AN AMERICAN MESSIAH

I finally break down and file for unemployment. My father had been telling me it was a good thing for me to do for sometime. I had the checks mailed to my P.O. Box in East Greenwich. I had the P.O. Box before I left for Venezuela and I still had time left on it. I took this measure because I didn't want anyone to intercept my checks. I wasn't taking my meds I was slipping back into psychosis. One meeting with my Case Manager Jackie, I told her, "I'm changing my name because my father doesn't deserve to share a last name with me." This wasn't the real truth, but had manifested itself in my mentally ill mind.

Having begun collecting unemployment I watched lots of TV. I can recall watching the Presidential Election between Bush and Gore. I voted for Bush in that election, only because I thought Gore was wrong for the position. I can still see the ballet counters, cross eyed, looking at hanging, dangling, and dimpled Chad's in the state of Florida, which ultimately decided the election.

As I watched day after day, my mind asked itself a question. That question was, "How could the Human Life form be improved?" After some consideration and ruling out my distain for failing inner organs, I came up with an answer. I felt that we humans have a problem. The digestive system is very trouble some. We each have a long snaking track, running from our mouths to our anis. This leaves us, and all animals for that matter, with things –soils and liquids- leaking out and falling out of us at in opportune times. We take special breaks to relieve ourselves of what comes to be one of the more disgusting and vial substances around. Just its offensive odor can be too much to bear.

I thought it would be better to get rid of the digestive track and fuel ourselves with oxygen, as we already do, partially, but modified to an entirety. Exploring this diagnosis I came up with a theory of how the digestive track came about. I chose to believe, something out there in the far reaches of space skewered a whole through us. Perhaps a snake was then run through the damaged life form creating the messy intestine and stomach. Teeth are like shattered bones, protruding from the wound. From this I figured all the animal species are possibly on this planet to heel there wounds. As far as how we would communicate with no mouth. I would have to guess the nose and nasal passage would evolve into a single breathing and communicating passage. As for the urinary track, I would consider this to be an infection to the reproduction organs, which would go away with the healing of the digestive track. Giving one function to the reproductive organs, I believe, could make for more pleasurable sex.

As the Chad's lasted day after day I came up with a human experiment. The experiment was set up into two groups. In one camp they would communicate only with numbers, I viewed them as very scientific. While the other bunch would accomplish their tasks with only words, I saw them as a more natural people.

The humans with numbers, in my mind, would experiment on one another until they reached the point of death, calculating the numbers from beginning to end. Once ones experiment was over they went right to the next guinea pig. The wordsmiths would do things slowly and peacefully. When they needed something they wouldn't count or calculate, they would simple grab a bunch of what they needed and go back for more if it wasn't enough. If someone in camp did try to introduce numbers they would send them out to the thousands (there word for islands) until they felt the numbness instead of numbers. At this point in the late fall of 2000, I had grown a beard for a more natural look. The facial hear was minus the mustache.

Back in West Warwick I found myself rehashing the Wizard of Oz episodes I had put together in the past. I had played the game on several levels, but had not put together a cast of characters for a local West Warwick show, at least not until now. I started with myself, cased as the obvious character of the Lion, as I was a Nittiny Lion. My next move was to make my old football teammate, from my sophomore year, Matt the Tin man. He was an alumni of U Mass whose mascot was the Minute Man. In my mind this was a natural fit. For people who have followed West Warwick football over the last two decades, you know my coach at West Warwick was coach Alves. A Wizards follower would also know coach Alves had a severe stroke after leaving the sidelines. I don't mean this to be insensitive to his family or friends or people who know him, but in my thoughts, at that time, I selected him to the part of Scarecrow, due to the fault of his brain. Again I apologize if this characterization of Coach Alves is hurtful to anyone, but this is how I put things together. Continuing to fill the cast, I had the easy selection of Coach Maznicki, the coach prior to Coach Alves, to the Wizard of Oz. For his name is synonymous with West Warwick football and the football field is named after him. I have to add, for all the games I played football, including Championship games, I've never saw Coach Maznicki at a game or anywhere else for that matter. For my final selection, of Dorothy, I looked out side of West Warwick to a town I thought sounded a little like Kansas. The goal tender from the United States Olympic Gold Medal winning Women's Hockey team, I looked to Cranston and Sara DeCosta. I hope one can see the Gold Metal and Yellow Brick road as not to far a stretch. This is just one of the many things traveling through psychosis with me. Though I was still seeing my case manager and doctor for treatment.

On my next visit to my case manager, Jackie, scheduled an appointment for me to have blood work done to see if I was taking my medication, which I wasn't. She had scheduled it at the IMH. Without numbers I wouldn't have this to worry about, but in this world we do have weights and measures. I knew if I went to get the test my doctor, Dr. Koyfman, would find out I wasn't taking my med's and may send me back to Butler. That's when I started considering leaving again.

I went out with Stephanie for the last time at the Providence Place Mall for some shopping and dinner. That year the West Warwick High football team made it to the Championship. Of course I wanted to see the game and I wanted Stephanie to attend the game with me. I was surprised when she declined. I guess she really didn't want to go, because I grilled her pretty well, but she maintained she didn't want to go.

The same day as the game I was scheduled for the blood work. I decided to leave the state, because I was most likely court ordered by the whole state to take my med's and I didn't want to go back to Butler. I elected to go to Penn State and to the Chi Phi brotherhood. After having survived in Venezuela, I knew I could due better in the U.S. I was also receiving unemployment check to live off of.

My plan was to go to the football game, which had to have been a Thursday night. I would then leave for Penn State the next day. I left with nothing but the clothes on my back. One thing I had to wait for was my unemployment check, which was to arrive the next day after the game. West Warwick lost the game, which made the night seem a little longer. Once that check came in I cashed it and was off to Penn State via a bus out of Providence. I left my car parked outside the new Providence Place Mall, so there wouldn't be a way to track me down. Again I would flee from an unfavorable position.

CHAPTER 13

I left from Providence, purchasing a one-way ticket to Philadelphia, where I knew I could pick up a bus to State College. After the long ride from Rhode Island to the 'City of Brotherly Love', I had to wait until the next day for a bus going out to Penn State. I spent most of the time sitting in the bus terminal watching people rush in and out of the coaches. Once the night had replaced the day, I grew tired and decided I had enough money to get a hotel room. The bus terminal had several hotels advertised and I chose an inexpensive one, $50 or $60, a few blocks down the road.

The room I was given was old and in need of attention, but I knew I hadn't spent a fortune to stay there, so things where relatively priced. I laid down for the first time in two days and it didn't matter much what shape the room was in, I went right out. I got a good night sleep and headed back to the bus station the next morning.

I picked up a ticket to State College and got on the bus headed to Happy Valley. The bus traveled through many towns and boroughs, stopping here and there to drop off riders. As the bus rolled on I was filled with the idea to try out boxing and to box my way out of this mess. The bus had road all day until dusk when the driver stops at the Penn State bus station. I got off and headed to the Chi Phi Fraternity where I planned to gain refuge.

On the way to the Fraternity I stop by one of the many Penn State apparel stores and pick-up a Blue and White PSU shirt to wear. After throwing the shirt on I head for Chi Phi, entering the Kingdom for the first time in four years. The houses structure had not changed much, but all the brothers I knew where gone even the pledges at the time I had graduated had received their diplomas and left the University behind. One of the first things I did was meet with the current Alpha (president) of the Brotherhood. I told him I was considering going back to school to get a second degree, most likely in the field of Art

DAVID MICHAEL

History. Most of the brothers had left for Winter Break, but a hand full remained. He directed me to find a room to stay in. After some time and consideration, I chose to stay in the Tube room or TV room. It was a large room with a fireplace. It was a room the brothers used (also the brothers room) during parties. Other than the brothers who passed out in the room, after a party, no one had ever used it for a bedroom, as I proposed.

As I settled in, almost all the brothers had vacated the building for Winter Break. At most four to five Chi Phi's remained, as the Holidays approached. All the brothers I did meet where all very welcoming, friendly and happy to see a brother from the houses past. Not only did I meet with current brothers, one day a brother from a more distant past arrived at the Fraternity. I exchanged greetings with him and he made it known to me he was considering running for a high position in the Chi Phi local governing board, which was made up of graduated brothers from Penn State.

I can't say I had the same encounter with the President of the current Brotherhood Association. He was a man roughly in his 50's. His name slips my mind. He was there to meet with the other brother I had met, to talk over Fraternity politics. What I can remember is he told me to leave the house at once. I took his demand with a bit of animosity and sarcastically stating in a raised voice, "The Brotherhood is strong!" Meaning they were pushing a brother out into the cold of winter instead of asking if he needed any help. I took his order seriously and fled into the cold snowy afternoon to contemplate what to do.

After some time out in the elements, knowing I had little to no money, I made my way back to the Chi Phi Kingdom. I was hoping he had left and I could find refuge with the current brotherhood. I didn't see either of the two men again, from this point I re-entered the Fraternity to stay. In fact I was almost the only brother in the house. I can recall only two brothers occupying time under the roof. This left me with basically free rein over the building.

Having established a place to stray I redirected my unemployment checks to the House. I walked through the snow to the post office a few streets down the road. When I got there I filled out a movers packet to forward my mail in the P.O. Box in Rhode Island to Chi Phi's address. It took a little time, but the post office came through

AN AMERICAN MESSIAH

with a check delivered to the Fraternities door.

The major hang up I now faced was how to cash the check. When I went to a bank to cash it, they told me I would have to open up an account with the check and then wait four to five days for the check to clear. The problem with the check was it was issued by an out of state unemployment agency, if it was a Pennsylvania unemployment check, I could have been able to cash it then. I didn't have that kind of time, I was just about out of money and was running out of the food the brothers didn't eat and had left behind.

Just when I thought I was licked, I was watching TV when a commercial for a new Federal Bank opening in State College appeared. It was again just a few blocks away as most things in Happy Valley are. I took my check there almost immediately to get cashed. Cash it they did, with no questions or hassle. This cashed check gave me some money to have some fun at the bars downtown, buy some food, some clothes and even take in a basketball game in the new Brice Jordan Center.

One night at one of the bars, while sitting at the bar, my mind wondered as I sat on my stool. I fantasized I was in competition with two other humans in a human experiment, to see who was the best David Garcia subject out there. We where separated by the vast reaches of space in different Universes. We had the same make-ups and story lines to our lives, but where now all at a crossroads. One was accepted and had gone into the military, as I had attempted to do in the past. The other version had gone to Venezuela and found safe heaven in the jungles of South America. He had turned to religion and had become a tribal holy man. The military man, on the other hand, had risen quickly through the armed forces. He was ear marked to become one of the youngest Presidents in history. I gave each one of us a label: one would be 'me', another 'myself' and one became 'I'.

In the military officer mind, he thought it was all about him or me, he would be 'me'. He would think how could something benefit 'me'? The jungle would find the holy man saying "I this, I that," he was 'I'. Myself, I felt like I wasn't always myself or I could do this myself. I was categorized as 'myself' in this group of three. To get rid of one of us I turned to the man in the jungle. I didn't think 'I' would ever come out of the jungles or if he could even survive in the jungles. I would have him bumped off by the local tribes members. I chalked him off as defeated in our game of life. As for the militaries 'me', I set up the Kennedy assassination for him, because in his part of the World they didn't have such a queue, so they would have one now. A young President struck down in his prime. That's how I got rid of the 'me'. This is what my distorted mind had come up with, a game in which I was playing king of the hill with versions of myself and I through them both off track. Getting rid of the other subjects, I was left with "myself" and the beer I had been consuming.

The Holidays where approaching, the House was empty with the exception of one brother. By this time I had the House basically to myself. I'm not sure how or exactly when it happened, but my mind was playing tricks on me. It was telling me Cover Girl model Nicky Taylor was going to attend Penn State University and was going to stop by to see me at the Fraternity during Winter Break. This was the kind of shape my mind had bent itself into. Dilutions and fantasy gripped my thoughts and my mental wellness. Could this happen, Miss Taylor actually attending Penn State? It could, but for her to come out to Chi Phi to see me was more than an unrealistic reach. As the days past and Nicky didn't arrive my thought turned to a different subject.

I had established myself in a room on the second floor, toward the back of the Fraternity, seeking refuge if the Head of the Brothers Association came back. Once I had made myself comfortable in the room and felt safe to appear in the building, I built a fire in the large clubs fireplace, with some wood I found in the back of the House. As Christmas drew to a few days away, I kept the fire going and slept on a coach in front of the flames. I ran out of wood at one point, so I raided the neighboring Fraternities' woodpile. Christmas Eve the final brother left for home. I spent Christmas alone in front of the glow of the fire listening to a radio, the night actually past by quickly.

As Christmas came and went so did my money. I really can't say where I spent it, but it was gone. I can remember rummaging through the rooms of the Fraternity hunting for loose change. Having spent all my unemployment money I was left camping out in the Kingdome instead of going out to the night seen. As I stowaway in the House I started another experiment, this time with lions. As the legend has it or as I know it, the last mountain lion in the region evaporated on Mt. Nittiny. My experiment called for the introduction of young cubs to the mountain, to see if the animals could re-inhabit the mountain. I imagined a bunch of young lions injected onto the mountain. Almost all the lions came crawling, whimpering down the mountain when winter took hold. Though there was one little lion who wondered off on his own to the back of the mountain to hunt and forage. He would chew the bark off the trees, eat the snow and hunt down the small animals, such as rabbit, to stay alive. As years past the young cub grew and grew, working his way up the food chain, hunting down deer. As he survived through the different seasons he grew more and more matured, he even grew a main, something the Nittiny Lion had been void of for decades, more than likely because the Nittiny Lion was a mountain lion. I named this animal Goliath. My imagination produced a vivid image of the lion.

After several years of living on the mountain, all alone, the Penn State scientists plucked him from his home for evaluation. He was fed every day but didn't really know what to do with the butchered meat, he was used to hunting for his food, not brought out on a platter. He was also introduced to lionesses, which was foreign but welcomed attention to Goliath.

To finish the story of Goliath, I have to look toward Penn State. The University would announce him as the Nittiny Lion and could be seen in a large captive setting by Beaver Stadium. I now realize this was just a tale my over productive mind conjured up, but at the time it took up a great deal of my time, fueled by mania.

As this story ended my imagination was unweaving another game. I sat in the back room of the Fraternity attempting to combine my spirit and soul with a warrior from the age of Kubla Kan. I envisioned sending my left hand (the one with the two wounded fingers from the lawn mar) to get this man from another time to replace this hand or arm with his. In fact he took the entire left side, my bad side when considering I could feel the Bi-Polar condition run up and down my left side. I would remain the right. I sat in meditation as I felt our souls and spirits fuse.

After this spiritual experience I had to turn my attention to food and money. I was out of both, but a check was due in the next few days. I think I used my last few quarters to wash my clothes in the washer and dryer in the Fraternity basement. I had to eat, so two days before New Years Eve I went to the Chili's in town and ate a cheeseburger and fries. After the meal I walked out of the establishment and never looked back. I didn't pay.

My next unemployment check was to come after the New Years Holiday. I had no money, but wanted to go out for a few drinks on New Years Eve and that's what I did. First I started by shaving off my beard. I then went out to the *Allen St. Grille*, my favorite bar, where I had something to eat and began a tab for drinks. That evening I drank pints of beer at the bar and started a new game. This endeavor grew from my lack of money. I was trying to put a word or title to the largest amount of money or plain number I could think of. We all know millions, billions, and trillions all of which follow a pattern of 'illion' in their make-up. Something else I did know, because I had stumbled across it in an encyclopedia, was a number quintillion existed. After that I had no clue, so I made up word combinations using what ever came to mind. The first number I came up with was Chitillion Phitillion, which started with the Fraternities letters. After some time of using the labels on the bottles in front of me, I turned to the double ll's in the 'illions' and came up with two ll's in Hell. As one knows the devil is associated with 666 and has a strong hold on that number like no one else could replace. I came up with Hell Fire as a number. I thought of these letters as visual shapes and turned the H to an I, changing the E to a W and then flipped the LL up side down to lowercase rr's, making IWrr. As for the Fire the F stood alone while the I turned to an H, as the r was flipped to an L and the E spun to a W, which formed FHrW. Together that combined to make IWrr FHrW and that is where I got stuck. The night came to a close, as I made no more sense of my game.

The bar was now beginning to close and it was time to buck up. I didn't have money to pay the bill, so I told the bar tender I was short on cash and would pay them sometime this week. They called the police who where on the spot quickly. One of the cops chewed me out, but in the end we, the bar and I, plus the police, agreed I would pay them this week. They took my name and address and I was set free into the New Years night and the extreme cold gripping central Pennsylvania.

On the way back to Chi Phi I came back to my money game and focused on the E Pluribus Unum on money. I took these words and used artistic license with the look and shape of the letters as I did with Hell Fire. I came up with unumuwus buqupudus. I hope one can see the unumuwus, if written is a squiggly line with the US at the end, for United States. As for the buqupudus I hope one can see the b, which is followed by a q that should look like a turned b. The q is followed by the p, which mirror one another, leaving the d looking like a turned p, with u's in between and ending with the US for the United States. That night, after drinking, I lay down and my lights where out.

    The New Year started uneventfully. I spent the first couple of days in the New Year waiting for my unemployment check. The check was taking longer than usual due to the holiday. Though I didn't have money, it didn't keep me from going out to watch the College Football National Championship. I went to *Zino's*, a bar below the *Corner Room* and the *Allen Street Grille*. Again I had something to eat before I started drinking. The bar tender serving me had no problem with me running a tab and spending time throwing darts and drinking. It was the next bartender who did me in. For some reason, in the middle of the big game he asked me to pay my tab. He had me in a spot. He had called for the doorman to keep an eye on me so I wouldn't leave as he called the police. This time the cops took me away.

    I spent the night in a holding tank in the State College Police Department. After a few hours I was placed in front of a Judge. We presided in what appeared to be an office in the Judges residence. He gave me a fine of $300, which I found ironic. If I couldn't pay my tab how could I pay this fine? Since I couldn't pay the piper I was taken to the Bellefonte Holding Facility just down the road. They finger printed me and gave me an orange jumper to wear. I was then escorted to a cell.

    From what I could see through the bars, I was in the second cell on the left if I faced the on duty guard. I also counted 6 to eight cells on each side of the jail. The only time we were let out of our cells where for meals, showers and an hour in the afternoon. During the times I was let out, it was visibly noticeable there was an open holding area above us. There where no cells just bunks and tables for meals. There was a large cage holding them all in. The way they gathered they where to numerous to count. Each level had a Television and at no time did I ever feel more like an Oakland Raider fan than I did when I watched my favorite team play a playoff game on the jail's TV. At one end of the facility there was a weight room, which was open on the weekend. I went in once but it wasn't a true gym, it had pieces of equipment from here or there, but nothing to really train with. As one might take from my description I was there for more than one or two days.

At the beginning of my stay I had to meet with the jails parishioner. We touched on a few subjects before I gave him something I had come up with recently, perfect for the ear of a holy man. I plainly told him if one takes the an 'o' from good one gets GOD and if one adds a 'd' to evil they would get DEVIL. I believe this simple exercise had him think I had a simple belief system and I was all right. I'm pretty sure I was called to meet with him, because I was giving the guard on duty my theory on how Marcus Allen killing O.J.' wife. Being held in the second cell I was in ear sot of the guard.

The days were long and the time out of the cell was valuable recreational time with the other captives. I met two young men there. One was more of a pretty boy, conscious of if he was liked or not. The other kid seemed to talk well and made things simple. My mind labeled both with positions from hell. I'll follow this up by stating, I believe there are positions in Hell to create order and the Devil is much different from say Lucifer, Beelzebub, or Satan. I believe each of these positions have a specific job to do to hold down Hell from breaking loose. I'm not exactly certain of when I started formulating this order, but I recall classifying the simple man as a Lucifer type personality. While I found the other jailbird to be more in tune with Satan's position, one that depends on people liking him only to test the bond with twisted games of loyalty.

To detail what I believe is the high arc key of Hell, I have to start with the top. I'll begin with the one and only Devil, the 666 and the headman in charge. He rules all and knows all about the Kingdome of Hell, and will give you the truth you don't want to hear. Making a lateral move I put Satan, because in his twisted mind the higher he goes the more power he assumes. The Devil allows him to fly higher only to tame him on confrontations. Satan plays twisted games, with lies, and deception, the best at what he does. All one has to do is admit he is twisted and his lies and deception can only get him so far. Making a move down I have positioned Lucifer. Looks like the devil acts like the Devil and keeps things simple like the Devil, but he just is playing the part. He knows nothing and is given the answers from the

Devil. I color him yellow and most of the time I have him hold up Q-cards. He holds down most with a simple approach and his similar appearance to the headman. Making another move down I have placed Damien and Beelzebub. They don't get along and fight back and forth. They don't make much sense and will argue over the smallest thing while making a huge ordeal seem like patty cake, which one might find them playing. They are petty and rude and have very little respect for anything, but the Devil. This raps up my order of Hell. Such things occupied my mind for lengths of time.

On my eighth day in the holding facility I was told, if I pled guilty they would let me go. I quickly pled guilty and they set me free. When I got out I had to walk from the Bellefonte Jail all the way back to the Penn State Campus. This was roughly 10 miles in the dead of winter. I walked and walked until I came to what was about a halfway point, the Nittiny Mall. As luck had it I came across a commuter bus and jumped on board while the driver was away from the vehicle. The driver never questioned me being on the bus and after a few stops along the way; I was dropped of in University Park. A few days before I had been released from jail I had a dream about the University of Missouri football team. This to me was an omen for me to head to Missouri. That's what I did. Due to the fact I was in jail for a little over a week I now had two checks waiting for me. I cashed them both and paid the New Years Eve tab at the *Allen Street Grille*, but not *Zino's* for the ordeal they put me through. I then headed to the bus station to get a ticket to Pittsburgh, where I would board a train to St. Louis, Missouri.

CHAPTER 14

After boarding the train in Pittsburgh, I had one more stop before arriving in St. Louis. I had to change trains in Chicago. This switch left me with a layover in the windy city's train station. During my wait I encountered a man sitting on some steps in the station, in rag tag clothes. I took some time to talk with him. All he did was complain about the cities local politics and how things where run. He was obviously a street person, but he was so emphatic about the city I could see him as the Mayor in some lifetime. Who knows what put this man in this position, but I could see potential in him. If only he could find a way out of the streets and back on his feet. If only he could find help.

I wasn't that helpful hand. I was currently in a pinch of my own. After my conversation I went for a bight to eat. Once the time had elapsed on my wait in Chicago, the next train on the final leg of my journey pulled up, and I climbed aboard bound for Missouri. The locomotive raddled and sway its way down the tracks through the dark of night. There wasn't a lot of rail left between St. Louis and me. The train didn't make a single stop between the cities.

This would be my first trip across the Mississippi River and I felt I was doing it in a more officially way by traveling through the Gate Way to the West. I kept an eye out for the Gateway Arch as the train clanged its way into St. Louis, but the Arch hid in the evening's dark blanket. Perhaps the trains approach was away from the cities land mark, leaving my eyes searching through thin air. The express finally ended my blind steers out the window when it rolled to a slow stop.

The station was small and I made my way through the building quickly. There was a little walk before I actually hit the St. Louis streets. I had no idea which direction I was traveling, but walked into downtown St. Louis just the same. I walked through the night, only to end my exploring by find a hotel room to rest my weary body. It coast around $60, which didn't leave me much to spend in the future, but that was a worry for the next day. The hotel, the Ramada or Radisson, had laundry accommodations and I took advantage of the hospitality.

The problem I ran into was I had no other clothes to change into as I washed the clothes I had on. I solved the dilemma by tacking the sheets of my bed and raping them around me in toga fashion while I did a load of laundry. Luckily none of the other guests were doing laundry that night. Once the dryer warmed my things to completion, I took them back to my room, where I turned on the tube for a half hour before laying down to sleep.

The time I rose the next day is a forgotten detail when compared to the rejuvenating rest I received from a nice warm bed. That first day in the Gate Way city, I enjoyed myself as much as I could, considering my financial constraints. The first memory of the day came in the cities downtown Mall. After finding lunch in the food court I roamed the Mall and stepped into a music store. I per oozed the musical selections, until a band I had always wondered about and listened to sparingly came to mind. Up until then the similarity in the Garcia name of one of the band members and my own kept me from fully enjoying the group. I'm of course speaking of the Grateful Dead and Jerry Garcia. I still had enough dough to purchase a Walkman with a cassette and a Grateful Dead Greatest Hits tape.

I sat down as soon as I left the store to get the items out of their rappers. I played the tape as I made my way out of the Mall and headed out into the sun filled city. From there I headed to the Gate Way Arch for the first time. I recall playing a game where I walked directly under the center of the Arch from the Mississippi River to the city of St. Louis to officially pass from the East to the West. My headphones stayed on, playing the Dead wherever I made my way.

If you're like me and have never been to the Gate Way Arch, here is a guide. When entering the structure one actually heads down under into the earth. Entering the Arches base, a large open area greets its' visitors. Married to this rotunda is a museum. The museum is free, the right price for me. I found the museum to be educational and entertaining. There are talking manikins telling stories and images tracing history. Again I went through with the headphones on. The blue grass style of the Grateful Dead began molding the day with their lyrics and rhythms.

AN AMERICAN MESSIAH

Following my trip through history, I got in line to go up the Arch. It cost $7 for the ride to the top, that's the price I remember anyway. Once I made my way through the rope maze, it was my turn to board the – for lack of a better word – drum. I was one of four squashed into this cylinder. Claustrophobics may want to skip this experience. When all four passengers are ready the drum is then lifted, picked up, or carried upward. Not only is the capsule moved upward, but also it rocks, tilts, or shifts as it makes its way up the long leg of the Arch.

The Dead occupied me as the climb to the summit was achieved. Now at the top of the Arch, I looked out at the city of St. Louis for miles and miles through the crystal blue sky. I took at least 20 minutes taking in the sights; I could see the cities scrapers melt into the neighborhoods on its perimeter. All the while I surrounded the experience with Jerry Garcia and his band. Once I had enough I climbed into one of the drums making its decent.

The rest of the day was spent wandering around with empty pockets. I was tapped out. When the dark of night wrestled away the day, I found myself seated in a *T.G.I. Fridays* ready to order a meal with no way of paying. This is something I had done in the passed and had slowly become an act I starred in before.

I ordered a cheeseburger, which I devoured quickly. I asked for the manager when the bill came. I told him the plain truth, "I had no money, but would pay the tab when I came across some money." He then asked for my ID to make a copy and sent me on my way, with a full stomach.

I put my headphones back on, making my way around the urban sidewalks. As the hours went by I encountered people on the streets asking, "Could you spear some money or change?" I told them, "I have no money myself." This occurred a couple of times and I found it ironic a person with no money was asking another person with no money for some money. It was at that point I told myself I would never beg fore change, no matter what shape or position I was in.

Time made its way to a slow grind as the night hours stood still and I searched for a way out of the January cold. I was able to concoct a plan to go to the Police Station to report I had lost my wallet in my travels. I was hoping they could help me with lodging. It took some time before I was able to find the station. I had to ask people I came across for directions. What happened at the Police Station that night is somewhat a blur, but I did report my wallet was missing and they did help me with a place to stay. A police car dropped me off at a *Salvation Army* in the city. By this time it was dead of night and a floor covered with men sleeping on mats welcomed me. I was quickly taken to an office where I gave my bio to one of the *Armies* helpers. I was given a mat and told to find a spot on the floor, but I found a chair instead. I was just happy to be out from the cold. I stayed awake in my chair the entire night. In the morning the *Salvation Army* provided a breakfast for what had to amount to 50-60 men, 90% of whom had to be homeless. I received a plate of food with gratitude and then walked my way back onto the concrete sidewalks of St. Louis.

That morning I shuffled my way down Washington St. where I came across a *Gold's Gym*. A gym was a familiar environment for me; I started lifting weights at around 13 years old and had spent many years in gyms crafting my workouts. I went there with an honest to goodness curiosity on how much a membership would be. I talked to someone who informed me it would take one hundred sum odd dollars for the membership and $45 or $50 each month. I didn't tell him right out, but I found those conditions to be ridiculous. It's a good thing I kept my mouth shut. He followed up with a free weeks membership.

I exited the gym with the seven-day pass in hand. I played the Grateful Dead tape through my headset with a day of exploration in mind. I stopped by the Mall for a quick stroll, while leaving I noticed a Convention Center. I found my way to the Convention Center Door. I walked along the main corridor, passing door after door. On my way out I noticed a sign advertising a casino, the *Presidents Casino* to be exact. The gate I was exiting hosted the casino sign, which included arrows indicating the direction to the gambling establishment. I didn't see a casino when I passed through the doors, but I kept walking in the direction the arrows pointed out.

The first thing I noticed after I vacated the building was the Convention Center was attached to the dome the St. Louis Rams played in. Following the sight of this huge complex, I spotted another *Presidents Casino* sign, which I followed. Shortly after this sign I bumped into the President's Casino, snuggled up against the Mississippi River Bank. It was a River Boat Casino and the thought of a casino on my map excited me. As much as my own curiosity drew me to the boat, I resisted for that moment to become more familiar with St. Louis. The casino and the sports dome were now added to the Gateway Arch as landmarks.

I didn't resist for long, but as I angled toward the *Presidents Casino* I thought I wouldn't get in with my Walkman. That's when I took the headset and the Grateful Dead tape and put them in the trash. After my first real listen to the Dead ended I have to acknowledge the emotional level the music added to my escape and navigation, lifting my enjoyment, excitement and entertainment through the National Monument and my uncovering of a city will never be forgotten.

Back to the *Presidents Casino.* Once the Walkman was left behind, I passed through the doors of the casino only to be stopped at the final gate. I was halted, because I had no casino card. The usher pointed out where I could get one. My biggest worry was the card might have a cost or price to it. When I applied they gave me a free card with no problem at all.

The ringing, pinging and dinging of the slot machines played to my ears and was the first indication I had entered into a gambling facility. My sight was fancied next with the slots spinning colors. I casually made my way by the gaming tables...craps, blackjack and roulette. I had played all the games back home at the *Foxwoods Casino.* I spent time moving around the establishment before wandering up a set of stairs to the second floor. The second floor was ring overlooking the gaming tables and some sets of slots. Something I found on this level I considered worth its wait in gold, was a free soda fountain. Having no money left, the cups of *Coke* gave me at least one way to put some calories and taste into what was now becoming my second battle with survival.

The casino was warm and a safe haven from January. I past the time by filling my cup with *Coca-Cola* and mapping out the casino. What I found was a buffet one level up from the second level and a lower level beneath the entrance level. I was in for a rude awakening when I was informed the casino closed its doors at 4 a.m. I was under the assumption the casino was open 24 hours like *Foxwoods.* I was directed into the cold night. I took myself by the *Salvation Army* in hope to find refuge from the early morning frost. I got there to late. I was made aware the doors to the shelter closed at 10 p.m. and didn't re-open until 6 a.m. I spent about an hour and a half passing through the winter a.m. air, before I made my way back to the *Salvation Army* for the breakfast. After the breakfast the person who signed me in my the first night told me I should meet with one of the councilors to see if they could help me. I took heed to his direction and signed up for an appointment with a councilor.

I hung around the *Army* waiting for my turn to come and at the same time stay warm. This was also the first time I got a look at some of the men taking up residence. It was a motley crew at best. Some men appeared to have no function and/or purpose. They just hung around. They where in far more need than the *Salvation Army* could supply.

My time came around taking me from those men taking residence at the establishment. I was seated in front of a blond haired woman in her thirties or forties. Her name slips my mind, though she was of great help to me. On this first visit with her, I believe I told her the story I had lost my wallet. I also told her I was collecting unemployment checks; that if mailed to the *Salvation Army* I could possibly get out of this mess. She gave me the O.K. to route the checks to the *Army*.

The one thing I had to do to even get my checks set out, was call the automated service in Rhode Island which would register me for a check that week. I had missed the last one due to the absence of a phone to call on, but the councilor allowed me to call the Rhode Island unemployment center. I called and registered for the next unemployment check. Next I had to get to the post office to fill out a change of address from my P.O. Box in East Greenwich to the *Salvation Army* in St. Louis. I asked her directions to the post office and she gave me her version of direction.

From her office I moved myself in a southerly direction, using the Mississippi as my point of reference. I had to ask some people on the way, "How do you get to the post office?" With some direction I hit pay dirt. I went to the counter and got a change of address card to fill out and returned to the post office.

A bigger discovery of a Mall close to the post office was added to my landmarks. I could be wrong, but my memory recalls the *Union Station* as the Malls title. Again it was a warm place and I walked around poking my head in and out of some of the stores, but kept to the main drag. Adding this landmark I became more and more familiar with the town. This was a nice little shopping venue, but the casino pulled me back in. I hit the streets making it back to the *Presidents Casino*.

Once on the boat I drank several free cups of *Coca-Cola*. I really couldn't get enough of the stuff. This day I made curtain to leave the casino before the *Salvation Army* closed for the night. That night I slept on the floor on a mat just like the dozens of other men. As the scores of men signed in for the night, paying the quarter charged to gain refuge, I got my change from a slot machine a gambler hadn't thoroughly cleaned out. My mind went to work making characters out of some men in the shelter. I envisioned some of the rag tag city soldiers as figures from the Civil War. I saw them as parts of great hero's. I saw Abraham Lincoln, William 'Tecumseh' Sherman, and Ulysses S. Grant, as well as, Rebel Robert E. Lee. I didn't think of them as the actual men, but rather pieces of those historic men, left behind as a remembrance to me of how hard things could be. I could see characteristics of each man in a *Salvation Army* soldier. There was a tall thin man with dark hair, like Lincoln. There were several bearded men, though only two captured my mind as Grant and Sherman. As Lee had a gray white beard so did one of the gentlemen sharing the *Salvation* 'Armies' roof with me.

That night lying on the floor, packed head to toe with down and out men took some adjusting to do, but I did end up falling asleep. The following morning, after having breakfast, I went to the gym were I had the seven day pass and took a hot shower! I didn't have a towel, so I drip dried the best I could before slipping back into my clothes. I took some time in the gym before I slipped back into the cold.

It was then back to the casino boat. Some how and I don't know when, I started the habit of looking into the slot machine trays to see if there were any tokens left behind. This practice was good for a few bucks a day. When I wasn't peaking into the slot trays I would stand around a craps table. During the weekdays the casino wasn't that full and I could watch the games with no problem. Some *Coke* as the day passed then back to the *Army*.

Somehow in my mind I re-named the *Salvation Army* to 'Uncle Sam's'. I guess I took the S in Salvation and the A and M from the Army to come up with the nickname. I spent another night there and in the morning received a free warm meal. I also stayed to talk with the councilor. I wanted to call the Chi Phi house to see if they had possibly received one of my checks or better yet I was still waiting for the document with my name change on it to come through the mail around this time. I was hoping my change of address would have taken effect before this could happen, but I had to check. When I called, one of the brothers looked for me, but saw nothing.

That day I spent the morning hours in the 'Uncle Sam'. The councilor must have told one of the people working there I had artistic ability, because someone asked me to draw something for them. It was a church. I got about half way through the drawing before I was told to leave the facilities, along with the rest of men, as was customary on each day. They mopped the floors once the shelter was empty.

That day I visited the downtown Mall. I had no money to purchase anything, but it was heated and it took me from the elements. I grew board with the shopping center quickly and found myself out on the freezing streets. When the sun was out winter didn't feel as harmful. That afternoon I traced my steps back to the 'Uncle Sam's'. I found, after hanging around the outside of the building, they re-opened around 3p.m. When the doors opened I went in and took a seat. There was a jacket I had noticed, handing from one of the bunks. The *Army* housed an additional 20 bunks or more in a room abutting the outer floor area. I hadn't yet cracked the code on how to get a bunk, but I noticed a black leather jacket had remained untouched for at least three days. I could use another layer to ward of the cold, so I walked over to the coat and put it on. I even waited in the common area to see if anyone would claim this garment, but I had no one approach me.

I then walked out strolling down Washington St. to the *Presidents Casino*. I walked around with my new leather coat, like I owned the place. It gave me a look. My hair had grown long, pulled back and unwashed for days. I was unshaven from one day to the next and sported some stubble. I sat down at one of the bars and caught a glimpse of the news. George W. Bush was to be sworn in at his inauguration the next day. This sparked my sense of humor. I could watch the Presidents inauguration from the *Presidents Casino*. How could I pass up the irony, it was almost like being a guest. I made it a point to myself to make it to the casino early. This coincidence pushed my thoughts to another instance where I was placed in a spot. I flashed back to my interview in Maine, where I was brought to

AN AMERICAN MESSIAH

Waldo Hospital. I had thought of it in the passed, but on this day I gained a special laugh. I had thought as a joke to myself, I found Waldo, like the books *Where's Waldo*. Well I found Waldo in Belfast, Maine. Put that together with the opportunity to see the President on National TV from his casino.

The next morning I quickly made off to see the Presidential inauguration of George W. Bush. I waited several hours in the lower level of the vessel. I took a seat at the bar and watch in delight as the President was inaugurated. It made me feel I was in the right place at the right time. Once the event had passed, I took a stroll around the establishment taking a glimpse at the gaming tables before I wondered into the city.

I carved a new path directly up the gut of the St. Louis urban district. I came across a help wanted sign at a pizza shop and attempted to fill the vacancy. When I was 16 I worked for a pizza shop, *Checkers Pizza*. I delivered pizza mostly, but they did teach me how to make a pizza. I was asked to fill out an application, which I did. I put my *Checkers Pizza* experience, while using the Chi Phi address as my home. After finishing the application, I was brought into the kitchen to make a pie, so I did. I don't know if the manager was impressed, but after the pizza came out he gave me the whole pie and told me to come back tomorrow to see if I got the job.

I left with an entire large pizza all to myself. This was a treasure for someone eating one meal a day. I couldn't just chow down on the sidewalk, so I took it to the eating pavilion in the Mall. I was able to get down half the pizza before I was full. I was then faced with the dilemma of carrying this box around with me until I got hungry again or to just trash it. I took a few moments to decide before I deposited what was left into the trash.

The next day I stopped into the pizzeria, as asked, and was notified I wasn't the right person for the job. The next few days followed the same patterns, until I got to the weekend. The casino was open 24 hours on weekends. I spent a lot of time around the craps tables or looking down from the second level at them. At the time I had formulated a system I felt could increase my odds, but I had no dough to test it out.

That Friday while looking down at the gaming tables a man stepped to the side of me. We exchanged some light conversation, mostly covering strategy on how to play the games. His name was Curtis. We formed a quick friendship and he quickly became my guide to the city. I followed him like a lost puppy. That night we spent the entire night on the boat, both killing time.

The next day he got me on a shuttle bus, of which I had no idea existed. The shuttles where run by the casino, picking people up and dropping them off at hotels and other venues. We got off our shuttle at a hotel, where Curtis was able to obtain passes for free food and gambling on the ship. We then got back on the shuttle system to go back to the President's Casino. That afternoon he treated me to the Presidents Buffet. My condition spiked into a new mental game as I ate. I was attempting to categorize foods in their food groups from soup to nuts. The items that challenged my thoughts and added humor to the game where: an egg is nothing like an eggplant, they even have opposite colors, and ones a vegetable and one is produced by a foul. There not even shaped the same. I was also attracted to a comparison between the pea and the peanut. Though they both grow in a pod their textures, colors, tastes and categorizations are quite different. I followed that thought up with the potato. To me the potato is more like the peanut than a pea. They are both brown and grown in a similar fashion, in the dirt, from what I know anyway. This led me to believe the potato has been denied long enough and I categorized the potato as a nut and not just any nut but the king of nuts, because he is miss interpreted. This is one of many games my mind toyed with in this span of time, but none stand out as I chronicle my steps.

Once Curtis and I finished the buffet we split up for the day. I spent the day harassing the bartenders, asking them to read the unumus buqupudus I had concocted. At this point I thought I had this unumus buqupudus owed to me and where else to let the cat out of the bag than a casino.

I caught up with Curtis later in the day. He had more q-ponds for the boat. This time he had free burgers and fries. We redeemed these tickets in the lower level. I didn't even know this part of the ship existed. The lower level had a fast food area tucked into one of the ends of the boat. It didn't take long before I noticed Curtis hustled to get these tickets.

That night we left the casino, though it was open all night, to a motel quite a distance from the gambling establishment. Somehow

Curtis had come up with enough money to sleep at the motel that night. We split the bed, with no funny business and both slept soundly. The next morning we where awakened by the cleaning lady. Curtis gave me a hand full off money to give to the motel owner for another two hours. The owner told me we where three hours late and kicked us out after taking the money I received from Curtis. Curtis was somewhat upset I had given the owner the money he gave me when we where getting kicked out any way. He got over it quickly and we made our way back to a casino shuttle pick-up.

That afternoon I watched my beloved Oakland Raiders lose to the Baltimore Ravens for a ticket to the Super Bowl. As I watched the game a good-looking female accompanied me at the bar. She was also a Raider fan. A roommate she had had was a Raiderette. To my chagrin she left before the game was over.

This night Curtis introduced me to another shelter in the city. That night, I remember vividly, a man approaching me as I lay on a cart. It was a scary situation; he had come from one end of the building to harass me. I had no idea what this person's problem was or what he wanted. I was in an unfamiliar place, with only Curtis to back me. I don't even think this man was speaking a language; I couldn't make out anything coming from him. All I know is he retreated after a few anxious moments. I was tired and did fall asleep after this strange encounter. When morning broke, Curtis and I headed for the exit, where we where given donuts on the way out. Curtis showed he had been around this block a few times.

I managed to find my way back to the 'Uncle Sam's' on Washington St. to see if an unemployment check had found its way into the mail. When I asked the councilor informed me nothing had come just yet. I did sit with the councilor, who wasn't too many years older than me. In a way I found her attractive, but respected her position as a person with some compassion to be helping these street dwellers and I needed her help to get my checks. I made a call to the Fraternity too erg a brother who picked up the phone to send any of my mail to the *Salvation Armies* address. I followed the visit with a trip to the *Post Office* to see if the change in address had occurred and to see if a check was waiting to be sent out. They assured me the change in address had occurred, but no mail or check had been delivered yet. The check must have been sent to the Fraternity before it could be routed to St. Louis. Most probably buried in the mailbox.

The *Post Office* sits around the corner from the *Union Station Mall*, so I stopped in. I canvassed the Mall, which appeared to be an old railroad station. While there I applied to a *GNC* supplement store. On the application, when questioned on references I put down Arnold Schwarzenegger, and Jack LaLane. I didn't put their names down as a joke, rather I was recognizing the history of body building and the two figures making the most impact on the sport of weight training. My illness allowed me to make wild connections without questioning them. I never returned to the *GNC* for an answer.

That evening I came across the bar seen just up from the Mississippi River banks. They didn't ride along the banks, but it was a short walk to the River. I sat down in a bar, early before any crowds formed. This gave me the opportunity to talk with the bar tenders to ask them if they knew anyone in need of a roommate. She offered no one, but I spent most of the night at this bar hanging out taking in the crowd. As long as I stayed at the bar I still ended up back on the gambling boat.

While in the casino I walked around the joint playing the part of a casino informant checking out the establishment. I know I had nothing to do with regulating the casino, but it's what my mind came up with at the time. Once the gaming facility closed for the night I was forced to walk the city grid. That night I had to add another landmark to my mental map. *Bush Stadium,* home of the St. Louis Cardinals. I traveled further into the night coming across yet another marker. The *Savior Center*, Ice of the St. Louis Blues. As I passed the hockey building I found a five-dollar bill on the cold pavement. This was a bit of a found treasure for me at this point. I made a path to the *Seven Eleven*, buying a bag of chips and a drink with money to spear.

I would have liked to share my good fortune with Curtis, but I didn't bump into him that night. I had also missed the curfew for the 'Uncle Sam's' that night. I was out in the cold. As cold as it may have been I was thankful of the weather, because it hadn't snowed one single time in this part of Missouri. I kept myself moving through the winter air fighting back the elements by walking, keeping my blood flowing.

AN AMERICAN MESSIAH

In the morning when the *Salvation Army* opened it's doors I was there waiting. I needed some warmth and wanted to inquire on my checks. Once again the checks or check was a no show, but I did stay until they mopped the floors. After the brief stay outside I re-entered the shelter and waited to see the councilor when a young man asked if I could do his portrait. Word I was an artist must have spread and I accepted his request. It took all of 15-25 minutes before I captured his likeness. Once I had finished the portrait I waited for my turn to meet with the councilor. It was late enough in the day that the mail would have been delivered for that day, but no sign of my checks. By this time I had to call in for my next check anyhow. I used the councilors phone to make the long distance connection to Rhode Island's automated service.

Again, down Washington St. I walked to the *Presidents* gaming facility. I made my usual rounds to see what I could find in the slot trays. I found a few tokens and combined it with the money I had left over from the fin. I used the findings to get food on the lower levels fast food area.

I had been connecting people to one another the way I had in Venezuela. I would see someone looking like they should be meeting with some other person I had spotted in my travels. Sometimes as far back as my visit to South America. These could be friends and family from other lives not quite making the connection this time around. I thought by connecting them in my mind it made for a connection that would help them in this and other lives. At this same time I was trying to use the ping, dings and clanging from the slot machines to break everything down until things worked harmoniously or as one. I thought the machines could make the connections as they crunched out the combinations of numbers. I felt this would lead to a more natural flow to everything and it would be me to line everything up for this harmonious flow. In my mind I was making myself well with this logic.

The casino must have noticed me on the riverboat day after day, because they put an abrupt halt to my visiting. They approached me by the slots and told me I was being banned from the casino for "Buffalo Scalping". They explained fully, I had been hunting for tokens left in the slot trays. When they had me in the holding area, I was a wise ass and told them to ban David Michael as well, because I was having my name changed. To be honest, the papers had more than likely been drafted and sent to me for the name change, so I didn't know my own name. Honestly my name was more than likely registered in Rhode Island as David Michael, but my ID read David M. Garcia. Anyhow they escorted me out, never to return. I had missed the locking of the 'Uncle Sam's' for the night, so I was thrown out into the cold yet another night.

CHAPTER 15

There is something I've failed to mention up until this point. On the other side of the Mississippi River, anchored along the Illinois side of the river, another riverboat casino can be found. The *Casino Queen* is in clear sight from the *Presidents Casino*. I neglected to mention it, because I never planned on visiting the riverboat. Having been tossed from the *Presidents Casino*, the Casino Queen's lights never shined as bright, as I began looking for a way to get over the Mississippi.

All I could see is there was a highway bridge to the left of the *Presidents Casino* and a highway bridge to its right. I elected to travel over the bridge to the right. The traffic flew by as I began walking across, on what the bridge had as a break down lane. The cars came one after another, racing past me as I hoped not to get hit. It was as dark as night gets while I navigated the dangerous highway. While clinging to the barrier marking the edge of the bridge, a taxi stopped and pulled in front of me. I let him know I had no money for a ride. He asked me were I was going and I answered the *Casino Queen*. He then told me to get in and not to worry about the tab as long as I didn't mind making a stop on the way. I accepted his generous offer. If he was getting me off the tar and into the taxi, I had more than enough time to make a stop.

I forget my friend's name, but as we drove along he asked me a surprising question. "You don't mind if I smoke a little crack, do you?" It was his taxi and I was getting a free ride, so I told him it was fine with me. He then proceeded to put a glass tube to his lips, lighting the end and then puffing away at it. He never asked if I wanted a hit and I was relieved. I do have a poor opinion of the narcotic, but if that's his poison of choice, I'm not going to stop him.

After putting some road and rock to the journey, we stopped at a house. It was a descent property judging from its distance to the city.

A woman came from the house and got into the taxi. She was introduced as the cab drivers girlfriend. At this point I didn't care who she was, I just wanted to get to the casino. The yellow cab then made its way out of the neighborhood and back onto main drags. Just as I started to make out the lights from the Queen, he stopped and dropped me off on the riverbank, but a little ways away from the casino. Beggars can't be choosers. I was somewhat happy to be out of the taxi, but more relieved to be on the correct side of the river.

I walked along the riverbank, if I remember correctly, along some old railroad tracks. It didn't take long before I approached the boat. This was a much larger facility. Along with the boat on the water, the *Casino Queen* also sported a hotel, so when I got there I had to walk all the way around the hotel before I could get into the entrance.

There wasn't any one thing that caught my attention when I walked in. There is kind of a tunnel taking a guest from the hotel area to the casino boat. I passed through the casino stopping here and there. I did sit at a slot, where I gambled the little change I had in my pocket. The change went quickly, so I did some more exploring. I left the boat and approached the woman working the front desk for the hotel. I asked her how much it was for a room and if I could be billed for it later. She let me know the rooms ranged from $65 and up and there was no billing, only cash and credit. I asked about the billing trying to score a room for the night.

I did check the time and it wasn't yet late enough where the *Salvation Army* would shut their doors for the night. I exited the complex and hailed a cab. I told him I wanted to go to the *Salvation Army* on Washington. The cab made it there in good time, but I had no money to pay him. I told him I had a check coming and would pay him in a few days if he could give me a way to locate him. He frowned upon this idea and called the police to intervene. This all began to unfold in the 'Uncle Sam's' parking lot. I felt ridiculous as the men from the shelter watched me being handcuffed and put into the cop car.

I was taken to the police station, where I was finger printed and escorted to a holding cell. I spent the night alone in the cell. I didn't sleep and never really tried. Attempting to measure time was a futile act. There was no clock or windows to look out. It was a consistent crawl through the night. The most exciting event was when I came across some grease, ash, or soot. I put my two surgically repaired fingertips in the black substance and left some fingerprints on the wall, to prove I had been there. I used those fingerprints because they are unique and easy to read due to the scaring. An officer did make his way through the cells maybe twice. There was a hallway running in front of what I would have to estimate was six cells, for them to check on the captives. After the mountain of time had eroded away and the morning replaced the night I was set free.

My steps from the police station led me around the city, until I ended up at the 'Uncle Sam's' in the afternoon. I received some of the best news in some time when I met with the councilor. An unemployment check had come in. I know I ran into problems at Penn State trying to cash these same checks, but I noticed a pizzeria with a sign in the window stating they would cash all checks. I couldn't recall exactly where the restaurant was, but began hunting down the location. I had a general idea of its where about and was able to track it down. They cashed it with no problem. I now had a couple hundred bucks to help me climb out of this whole.

I was going to take this money to the *Queens Casino*, but checked to see if shuttles were there to get over the bridge, in a safer fashion. I asked at one of the hotels if there was a shuttle to the casino and they confirmed when I was handed the times the shuttle picked up. I waited with anticipation for the shuttle. When it came I got on and road my way to the Queens door. I began my stay at the casino, by renting a room in the hotel. With the room I was given $5 to gamble, free breakfast buffet and a free shrimp cocktail on the boat, but that could wait. I found my room and immediately lay down on the bed. It had been some time since I had a nice clean bed to rest on. I didn't lay long. A shower, a nice warm shower with soap and shampoo was in my grasp. After showering I put myself on the center of the bed and took a long nap.

When I awoke it was night and I got ready to enter the casino with my loot. First I would indulge in the Queens Buffet. I sat and ate for a good amount of time, filling my belly until I could eat no longer. It was now time to enter the casino with some money to gamble with. I had concocted a system for the game of craps, so off to the craps table I went. For those who know the game: I placed $10 on the 5,6 and 8 with $5 on the field, to cover all the numbers, but 7. This would ensure me $5 every roll as long as the 7 didn't come up and I would place $20 on the Don't Pass as insurance incase the 7 did come up. It really only works when there are several roles with out ending the shoe. I was at the table a little while before luck turned the screws on me. Once that was over I had my free shrimp cocktail and went to my room empty handed. I crawled under the covers and fell asleep in a nice clean environment.

The following morning it was difficult for me to leave the hotel, but I ate at the breakfast buffet for free before leaving. After filling up I boarded a shuttle to take me back to Missouri. I was right back where I started before I got the check, but it was time for me to call for the next one. Back to the Uncle Sam's I went. I met with the councilor who allowed me to call and I could expect to have another check sometime next week.

The weekend came quickly and it was Super Bowl weekend. The Baltimore Ravens would battle the New York Giants. This would be the first Super Bowl in my memory I didn't watch. I was up in one of the bunks of the Army, where I could hear the game as at a whisper. The Bi-Polar illness entertained the rest of me. There was a corner of men in the large room with the bunks. My mind was reminiscing. It put together a story line, where the men gathered in the corner and myself were forgers in another life. Not any forgers, but money counter fitters. I was tangled up in the story, convincing myself that in a former life we would print the money, then hop on trains to random destinations to launder the fakes. We would buy small items to break the twenties into smaller legal bills. We would then return to go to the casinos and gamble. My mind was telling me they where placed here, knowing they had succeeded in St. Louis in a past life attempting to prove they where in the right place at the right time, but failing without my involvement. In a strange way it made me feel valued or needed. This is an example of how my thoughts built confidence in what I was doing out in the middle of the country. I was fighting for my *life,* the one I had to live for many years. I was unhappy with the position I was forced into back in Rhode Island and was attempting to make a new try.

The Super Bowl, which was won by the Ravens, marked the end of January. February came in with the same cold air as the previous month, but I was grateful there had been no snow to this point.

AN AMERICAN MESSIAH

Having replaced one casino with another, I was starting a new pattern. Now having knowledge of the shuttle system I could travel safely from the hotels to the Queen. The problem was once I was on the boat I would stay on until the casino closed at 4 a.m. The shuttles where long gone at that time and I found myself walking over another dangerous bridge. It wasn't the first bridge I traversed. Rather it was the bridge on the other side of the two casino boats. There was little area to walk and I made curtain I looked each car past me. Sometimes cars did look like they would swerve just to get a rise out of me, but I made it by foot over the expansion several times without incident. Once I was over the bridge in the wee hours of the morning I would move around St. Louis to stay awake until the 'Uncle Sam's' opened.

During the day I sometimes visited the Mall, where I found some really good prices on clearance clothes. Of course I spent most of my time on the Queen. Spending so much time on the boat I felt Queen Elizabeth was taking care of me, providing me with a shelter and on occasion her buffet. I have to confess; I once snuck into the back entrance of the buffet and ate for free. On two other instances I order a meal, finished it and made my way to a stair well to the next level, never paying for the meals from the Queen's sandwich and beer restaurant in the back of the second floor.

In my mind the Queen (Elizabeth) was looking over me. There was one day in particular; I was looking out one of the windows on the boat, gazing at the beautiful view of the arch and the Mississippi River, which flowed at its base. The sky was a crystal blue. A question came to me, asking if I could imagine a better me somewhere off in the heavens and I did. I could envision a story carrying me through Penn State, 4 to 5 inches taller, as a Nittiny Lion on the football squad. Not only on it, but a fullback who was honored with the Heisman Trophy. I could fantasize this better version could be drafted by the Oakland Raiders, contributing to NFL Championships. I then through the hat of this me into the political ring finding votes to put Dave in a Senators or Congressman's seat. Perhaps even a Presidency could be a much better me, but I was working on the role off Messiah. Perhaps my negative experiences could be turned in my favor. What doesn't kill me will only make me stronger.

I thought to myself I was part of this other story as kind of a test run to improve on. This would be the dream way I would have wanted my life to travel, but I believed my current path was taken to prevent me from a possible injury as a Penn State football player. An injury as severe as a broken neck could be a possibility. Where I don't find I could have won a Heisman, I do believe I was talented enough to contribute to the team. Again I believe Penn State finished #2 to Nebraska in 1994-95, because I was there in Happy Valley, but not recognized as a winner. Something came to mind during this daydream. If I were to ask a father whether he would want his son to win a Heisman or a Pulitzer Prize, which would be picked? I'd bet they would go for the Heisman.

I have to admit being more familiar with the city the time picked up. A week passed and another check was delivered to the Army. This time I played things differently. I cashed the check at the pizzeria, the only place accepting the note in the city. The first thing I wanted to take care of was my housing, which I had none. I searched in Real Estate books, but found only houses, no rentals. I then looked in the newspaper classifieds, where I noticed a room to rent in the *Mark Twain Hotel*, in the city, for around $100 a week. That caught my attention and I was off asking people on the street for directions to the hotel. I found it eventually, working the details out with the gentleman at the front desk and was given a room. It had no kitchen, only a room with a bed and a bathroom.

The very first thing I did was lay down on the bed. I then took off to the drug store across the street to pick up some toiletries. I also picked up a box of coffee cakes for about a dollar, to snack on. I paid and took everything back to the Twain. When I got back I took a shower. This was a COLD shower. I thought maybe they where out of hot water and completed the bone chilling cleaning. It did feel good to be clean, but I would have to ask about the water. Following that, I put myself in bed and I stayed there for about a day and a half.

As I lay there, relaxing, I slowly began to build on a passed subject. My memory reacquainted itself with my Michael Irvin. I believed him to be very important to the future. When he came to me, in Butler Hospital, I put him in many different rolls from the first man teleported to a general in a Civil war between North and South America. This time I envisioned him as the first man to enter the Alternate –next- Universe. To leave Michael for an instance, my mind theorized on the make-up of an Alternate Universe. As I had done in

AN AMERICAN MESSIAH

the past I used the properties of our Universe and logically formulated the opposite. As our Universe is shrouded in a dark black setting, I deduced white would fill a different theatre. I also projected, perhaps, a galaxy with nine or ten purple spheres orbiting a single planet. The purple spheres would be the opposite of our sun in color, and this single planet would sit in the same place like our sun with purple sun holding it in place. Taking a big picture view of this there is our black tank and their white tank and Michael Irvin would be the first to travel from one to the other. My biggest fear is the next Universe is a bright white that would blind eyes not evolved to it glow. I tell him in my thoughts to close his eyes and do the best he can, knowing the glow most probably comes with heat to destroy the mission.

I lay there reconnecting with past thoughts. I landed on an old subject, but made it bigger and at the same time more manageable. I looked at the black and white opposites and thought about the chessboard. I imagined several Universes, black and white cells of experiment. Each monitored by some higher power. Perhaps God or Gods. I looked at this infinitesimally once again, as if it was all in one machine or computer to be altered or experimented with. The test blocks of black and white cell or tank strictly placed side by side may theoretically create the checkerboard pattern, but I would have to wager on a looser system with unequally sized experiments. I also looked at this practically. I viewed this as a symbolic order, a way to travel from one Universe to another. Moving officials, Popes, Messiah and Rooks, if not Kings and Queens, to solve matters with out conflict through the black and white Universes chessboard, as if knight where sent to Queen.

These paragraphs don't reflect the true time and process involved in these theories. Rather they represent the full body as uninterrupted thought. This continued as I rested. My thoughts where focused and able to continue work in this vain. I had always believed that one shouldn't mix religion and government. I then thought to myself that the Pope and his counter part, as I would recommend him to be: the Jew, are men of religion. That sparked me to make the Messiah an agent of government. The two Messiah's would be the heads of all government. This was exciting, but it left out my Visroi. What was the subject for his mastery? This didn't come to me as quick as a bolt of lightning, but after fishing around I had the Visroi's toy. I looked at him as a man of business. When looked at religion, government, and business are the three big categories running earth. To this day, I challenge a subject not ruled or covered by the three. I use the King and Queen of England, preserving the Monarch. This Kingdom was now prepared, if only in mind, to take on the future in a safe playful manner. This proves "I'm only Playing!" A large chessboard would be used in formal playful negotiations, to be viewed by crowds or watched on TV. This would allow visitors from any part of the heavens or Earth to engage in a peaceful exchange of information.

Two days had passed before I pulled myself from my bed. I had some money left and made a decision to purchase some close at the Mall, from the clearance I had noticed. As I looked through the rack of clothes I couldn't help but notice the blue jeans with the American flag for the pants' label. I got a closer look at the $60 Ralph Lauren jeans and could only covet them as I returned to the clearance clothes. I was foolish in purchasing an item. I bought a pear of jean shorts thinking and hoping spring came a little earlier in this part of the country. The shirt I bought is unmemorable to me. A sweet shirt rounded out my spending. On the way out I treated myself to lunch in the Mall. On my way back up stair to my room I stopped at the front desk and asked about the hot water. We solved the problem. I wasn't using the handle in a way that would choose hot water.

The first thing I did when I returned was take off my old dirty clothes and hop into the shower for a warm treat. After a good half hour in the shower I jumped back into bed. I took on a totally new topic, the Animal Kingdom. I know we do our best to communicate and teach tricks to them, but what if we could get them to help us build. This may sound humorous and on a level it is to me also, but the animals have a representative that can speak, even if they are mimicking. Parrots have the gift of speech. I would like to see some studies with say the parrot and the ape. It appears the ape has been chosen as the next in the evolutionary chain. Someday I would just like to see the animals communicate without help. After mulling over several simple symbols to give direction to the animals, including top, middle, bottom, left and right, to help them understand how to build, I came up with up or down, yes or no, deny or confirm, higher or lower, and more or less. These answers or signs would all be given with the same very *complex*, thumbs up and thumbs down. I do believe animals are in the same boat humans are. They got here some how, just like we did. They have the same make ups: blood bone, skin, muscle and hair.

I rolled out of bed put my new shorts on, while it's still February, and headed out for the casino. It was only mid afternoon at this time. First I wanted to stop by an apartment building to see one of their apartments. I couldn't believe I was shown a one-bedroom apartment with a beautiful view of the Arch for only $500 and change. I didn't have the money as of yet, but when I did this is where I was headed. I then took off to the *Ramada Inn* I had stayed at my first night in St. Louis. A shuttle bus ran from there to the Queen.

As I waited in the lobby I struck up a conversation with the women at the front desk. Her name was Carla. I mentioned I had just finished looking at a place to live and I was out in the cold. She graciously offered to help me fined a place to live. She gave me the time she was getting out of work, so I could meet with her. She then gave me a discount sheet from the hotel. The same card with free offers the *Queens Casino* gave their visitors. The shuttle then arrived and I boarded. While in the boat I killed time waiting to meet up with Carla.

I was back on a shuttle headed for the *Ramada Inn* to meet Carla. She was just getting off when I arrived. She took me back to her house on the out skirts of St. Louis. She changed and took me to lunch at a bar she had to be familiar with judging from the conversations she had with some of the people. After filling our stomachs, she took me to a friend of hers house. He and his friend, both I'd estimate to be in their 50's, smoked some grass with us and drank some beers. Our conversations bounced all around the map, with the two older gentlemen telling a story most of the time. It was the first time in some time I was in a social setting. One thing I can remember is sitting in Carla's car with one of the two men. I can recall having to hold myself back from spouting of that I was the Messiah, but I didn't and I'm grateful for that. The thing that troubled me was I couldn't say with any guess where we may have been going, but the night ended when Carla and I made our way back to her place. She shared her bed and more that night. She left early in the morning for work, leaving me behind to rest.

I watched a lot of QVC in the morning, feeling as if I had made mental connections with some of the girls or models on the show. I gave them directions to the *Casino Queen* if they wanted to meet with me. This lasted for a few hours until I made my way down to the living room. I turned on the TV there and watched some more QVC. While the show paraded item after item across the screen, I put together what I thought would make a good 24-hour channel. I envisioned a cable channel allowing people to appear on TV to exhibit a talent or show themselves off: tell a story, sing a song, dance around, perform a stripped tea, read poetry, etc., etc… It would be a live show with no prizes, just a way to get on TV with whatever one wanted to do, a 24-hour entertainment channel.

I changed gears rather quickly to a Messiah topic. I was asking myself what could I do to begin to prove myself as this governmental leader. It came to me I should get to an undeveloped territory and provide a first class government, which would put them on the map. I thought Greenland would make a nice country. It isn't a fully developed country, but in the same token the country has established a root or base society to overlooks affairs. It is also a pretty substantial piece of land in size. I'm not exactly sure how I would go about this transfer of power, but I planned on using as much of the United States government as possible. I would call the new government the United States of Greenland, and would put U.S. Presidents on the money. No-where on earth does it say I can't copy another countries government and it should be obvious at this point the United States of America provides the highest standard of living for its people. My reason for this would be to unify the two countries at a later date. At the time this was my best plan.

I was lying on the couch when Carla got home and she greeted me with a shrieking, "Get your feet of the couch!" This disturbed me in such a way I wanted to get up and leave, but I didn't. That evening she took me shopping to get a more appropriate change of clothes. I was fitted with a pear of Levis and a shirt.

I stayed there with her for about four days, until Valentines Day began to make its approach through the calendar. Carla was generous, and caring enough to try and help me, but at the same time I couldn't see myself getting any further involved with her. One day I got up and walked out the door, walking all the way back to the city and my one room apartment.

The following day I received some bad news, just when I thought I was going to be getting some financial help from unemployment, they pulled the plug. I had returned to the 'Uncle Sam's' to make the call for the next check when I was notified my benefits had been cut off. I was told when I was put on unemployment I would be getting benefits until April. I called around and got connected with someone who told me I would need to apply with the State of Missouri, since it was where I was living. LIVING, is hardly what I was doing, but I had to accept the decision. I was directed to the local unemployment office, and to make a long story short they couldn't help me.

My apartment in the *Mark Twain* expired after the week and I was back on the *Casino Queen*. I can recall some of the nights on the boat I would eat crackers from a chili and hot dog cart, because they where free. I would put different condiments on them for some flavor. I would have either mustered or mayo. I knew the mayo had more calories to it and the mustard tasted better. I avoided the *Ramada Inn* to pick up the shuttle. I found another hotel to wait at down a few blocks. On the boat I considered different approaches to prove myself as a worthy Messiah. I looked at the current state of politics and saw a divisive line drawn between Republicans and Democrats. I had felt this way for some time and hoped one of the newer parties would catch on to break the two party system now in place. I put stock in creating or fathering a party. I thought about what each party's purpose was, I did know they each called the country a great Democracy or great Republic. This got the gears turning, I thought of a great society, but that would lead to the Socialist party. I came up with the Civilists party representing a great Civilized country, made up of civilians. I dug up the old Federalist Party; we have all heard of the Federal level or perhaps a great Federation was to catch on. There where more like the Nationalists of this great Nation but nothing really grabbed me until I came up with the Populists.

I'll recall sitting at the bar in the lounge watching the TV, when the Populists Party took stage. The represented the population, a great Population. It's head a second side to its coin. This could also be seen as popular people, making the elections a popularity contest. I went to work on the Political animal to represent my group. As I thought more and more I had a few animals in mind. That is when I thought to create my own animal. I gave this good thought. I combined what I thought where the very best the animals had to offer. Not only did I use wild animals, I added myself and/or humans to this interpretation. I fused the head and back of a lion with the bottom jaw and underbelly of a cobra and the arms (hands) and legs to the beast where human. The best part of a lion in my opinion is their mane and golden skin as well as its instincts. A cobra can slither on its belly to attack its enemy. The hands of a human are in my mind what separate us from wild animal friends. They can't create tools, write or operate machinery. I used different combinations of the Populist and came up with something like the Sphinx when combining the lions paws, arms and legs with a human face. I believe the Sphinx wears a snake, cobra, on his head. I also used the cobra head and back with the human torso and lion paws and legs. My first interpretation was my favorite and the connection with the Sphinx was like being honored by a past society. I did leave the boat in hoping to give birth to my party in St. Louis, but was told I would have to do so at the state capital of Missouri in Jefferson City.

Sometime at this point my world was about to expand ten fold. For sometime I had noticed a commuter rail that stopped at the Queens. I had always assumed it cost something, but one day I was led to believe differently. To curb my curiosity I climbed the stairs to the boarding area. The railcars came by and I got in and sat down. No one questioned me for a second.

I was transported out of St. Louis all the way to the Airport, about 15 miles away. There were stops on the way, but I can only remember the *Union Station* Mall, the University of St. Louis and a hospital. My first visit in the airport I got something to eat at one of its restaurant, left without paying and made my way back to the commuter rail which took me right back to the Queen.

While on the Casino Queen I began putting something together and it wasn't a small thing. I began to put together what I called a Mega-Plex. It would be the ultimate entertainment venue. I put a casino together with an amusement park and all its' rides. I thought the carnival kind of games went well with a casino. As a side thought: while spending time at the casinos, I looked at the slots as brainless. I would like to see something that requires skill to the gaming industry. Video games. I would like to see a kid win some money if he was talented enough to solve the games. A video game casino may be possible. Added to that would be sports stadiums, like football and baseball. One could place bets on the games at the casino. Accompanying the stadiums would be a concert hall and movie theatres. Maybe a horse track could be included. A Mega-Plex could include it's own teams, perhaps even their our boxers or other athletes. A total entertainment spectacle! While I'm at it, a petting zoo or a whole zoo may be nice. Bring the whole family. I envisioned these Mega-Plexs all across the globe, competing with one another. Smaller cities without sports teams of their own would be chosen to host such an endeavor.

As I was mentioning earlier my territory was expanding rapidly. On one occasion, I can't recall if the girl at the front desk at the casino hotel had told me or it was announced a shuttle was bound for some town. I boarded the shuttle headed to somewhere I hadn't heard of. It dropped some gamblers and myself off at a strip of malls, restaurants and hotels. The shuttle traveled further to the same kind of setting. I didn't get off that first trip; I stayed on the shuttle and was dropped off at the casino. The next morning I took this shuttle to one of the stops, a hotel near the shopping and entertainment venues. I spent my day at the mall, just taking in the new see nary. As night fell I went to one of the restaurants, maybe another Friday's, had dinner, took off without paying, got back to the hotel and took the shuttle back to the Queen.

As I expanded beyond the St. Louis area, my mind began to tell me I should take advantage of my new methods of travel and move on to a new venue. That's when, after a week or so of just shipping myself off to a new land, I hopped on the commuter rail headed for the airport. The rail snaked its' way down the track, stopping at points in between. Its' final stop, the airport, was my destination. I wandered around the terminal, taking a seat here or there until there was little traffic. I then fell asleep in one of the seats, undisturbed until I awoke the next day.

I did more exploring the next morning, in which I came across shuttles. I had no idea of their destination; I did my usual thing and jumped on like any good vagabond would. This shuttle took me to a hotel. While in the hotel I asked the front desk for a map of the area and she produced. I spotted the *Ameristar Casino* in St. Charles roughly eight miles away. This got better every stop I made. First I had the *Presidents Casino*, followed by the *Casino Queen* and now I bumped into St. Charles, as in Prince Charles. I began to feel these where test area for me to navigate, with obstacles from each figurehead at each stop. Forget where's Waldo, that was like a warm up. How could I deny this connection? I looked at the map, noted what routes I needed to follow and was on my way. I started walking along the highway on what was a nice warm day for the start of March, I hoped for an early spring.

I traveled in the breakdown lane of the highway. I found my way over hills and valleys, neither of which extreme. I walked and walked, putting my design background to good use as I stepped one after another. I envisioned what kind of coat I would really like to have right then. Some day I promise I'll have this coat. It is simple to put together, but needs to be worn out a head of time. All I wanted to do was get a jean jacket cut it's sleeves off and wear it over a black leather jacket, though brown may look nice. Maybe some day I will sell such a coat. It's very biker or rebel with out a cause look.

Carrying myself down the free way I made out a Motel just off the long strip of tar. It was at kind of crossing between highways. I wandered in and found my way into the dinning area of the building. There was no one else there, but me. This was a bunny; I had eaten without paying several times now. I did feel bad, a young girl was my waitress and she was nice, but after eating I made curtain I had a direct shot at the door and I took off.

Once I bolted, I headed up some more miles before running into a *K Mart*. My clothes where in a retched shape at this time and I felt I could possibly get some clothes at the *K Mart*. I picked out a pear of Route 66 jeans and a yellow button up shirt with short sleeves. I took them to the changing room and put them on. I got up opened the door to the dressing room then headed to the door without a hitch. No one seemed to care or notice what I had done, so I made my way down the highway.

It took me longer than I expected to reach the *Ameristar Casino*, but I did finally navigate my way there. There were the usual sounds coming from the gambling sphere. To me, the establishment had a kind of western feel. My eyes gravitated to the large screen displaying the NCAA basketball tournament. The thing I recall the most, is my Penn State Nittiny Lions were matched up with my High School Sweethearts Providence College Friars. In the distant past, before I was diagnosed with mental illness I brashly attempted to mentally control the brackets creating a scenario were Penn State and PC would make the Finals. Both teams would be considered Cinderella stories and I hoped would re-ignite our relationship. This time they met by chance in the opening round. This did remind me of her, but she had taken up with one of my former friends. Not Matt the football player, rather Matt playing cards in the basement. There will always be times when I think of her. I can only hope she has not erased all we experienced together.

I stayed on this riverboat as long as I could, until 4 a.m., after which I was asked to leave like everyone else. The environment was still flooding the air with cold as days began to move through March. As I did in St. Louis I walked around to keep my blood circulating to keep some warmth. Walking around I came across a *McDonalds* and a *Waffle House*, side by side both looking for help. I sat for some time before I went to the *Waffle House* in an attempt to get a job. After filling out an application and talking to the person in charge I was hired and would start that very day. The one thing I would need to do is buy a black per of pants, which they lent the cash. They would take the money from my first check. I took the dough and walked up the street to a store, where I bought the pans.

I returned with the pants, put them on and started my day. They started me with small things at first, but then they unloaded boxes of onions they wanted me to peel. I went at it for a while until I got hungry and I'm pretty sure I was told I got my food for free. Therefore I went to the grill and cooked myself a cheeseburger. When I sat down to eat it one of the employees, a man pushing his 60's took a seat next to me and invited me to his place after work and I gladly accepted. I returned to the onion again, fighting back the watery eyes. I chopped a lot of onions that day. I also went to the grill again for an omelet. After chopping more onions, I was told to leave and I wasn't needed. The only silver lining was, I may have a place to crash for the night. The man who had invited me to his place was waiting for me and we made our way back to his place.

When we got to his one rented room in some women's house, I took a seat on the floor, after he asked if I wanted to lay-down on the bed. I was exhausted and tumbled into a deep sleep quickly. This is somewhat embarrassing, but this man startled me. He was trying his best to get my pants off. He had already undone the button and pulled down my zipper. He was trying to get gay with me. I immediately grabbed him by the throat, more like the neck. I wasn't trying to hurt this man, because I could have. What I was doing was holding him at an arms length, waiting for him to stop, but he did persist. I think he may even had tried to sneak a kiss, but I denied him forcefully, but in no means in a way to do him harm. It took some time before he quit and he did apologize for his over cheers and we did become friends. We didn't spend the night there; rather we went to the casino boat.

We where dismissed from the vessel at 4 a.m. as usual. The days in March had begun to erode into the months' center. I can't recall how I was keeping track or noticed, but the ides of March had arrived. March 15, 44 AD, Julius Cesar was slain by Brutus. As this day moved along my condition fancied the time paradox, it wildly conjured up imagery of a twisted Brutus coiled to strike the unbeknown Caser. I was still traveling with the gay gentleman from the night before. My thoughts grew wilder when my friend took me to lunch. I couldn't help myself. I had to order the Cesar salad. When it came I help Brutus from his seat to plunge his weapon into the Roman leader.

I'd like to note what I consider to be a strange time in history. According to what I know and have gathered; Caser and Christ lived basically in the same time period. If what I know serves me correctly, my friend Christ was crucified by the Romans in the early 30's of AD and Caser stabbed 44 AD. This leaves 10 to 15 years in both their demise. I can't think of any time the two had been linked together, I don't believe it was Caser who ordered the crucifixion of Jesus, then again I don't really know when his rein began. With that said, if the two were left to live their natural lives, it is with most certainty they would have to co-exist and perhaps the two together could establish the positions with a man of religion-Jesus, a man of government-Caser, and maybe they could recognize the use of a man of business. When these two figures fell, so did the Roman Empire.

In mentioning the Roman Empire, as an artist, I would like to point out the Renaissance took place at the end of the Roman Empire. A peaceful movement that has out lasted the blood shed of the Romans. Rome has collapsed to a tiny area of Italy, while the enlightenment of the Renaissance astounds to this very day. This is a shining example of how fighting, bickering and war continue to fall short over and over again, while creativity can make such an impression on a person, it may change the way they think. In my opinion the religious masterpieces of the Renaissance moved viewers so much they yearned to read, so they could read the stories they witnessed in paint, as told in the Bible.

After lunch I was taken to a local bar. My guy who was now taking me around always introduced me as his heterosexual friend. I didn't mind it; I just thought it was uncalled for. We attended two bars if my memory serves me correctly. One night had rapped itself around day and we once again visited his one room apartment. When we arrived the women who owned the house was up in arms. She didn't want me there she was calling the cops. As soon as I heard her say she was calling the police I took off and that was the end of that.

The next few days I spent on the St. Charles Casino and when I was sent to the streets I stayed close by. Though spring had begun to attack winter the early morning was still frosty. There was a *Denny's* restaurant just up a hill. I was up to my usual trick when I stopped in on a late night. I ate and left again without paying. The good thing about *Denny's* is it more than likely takes sometime before the waitress checks at the register at the front door to see if you paid there. At *Denny's* the check can be left, paid on the table or on the way out. I chose neither and walked through the door.

The following morning I attempted to put in a days work at a resource center offering a day off work. I was turned back because I didn't have a social security card. They gave me direction on how to get a temporary card. From what I remember it was in St. Peters. I walked the few miles to the Social Security office, where I obtained a temporary social security document. On the way back I ate at another restaurant without paying. I made my way down the ramp to the highway when an officer pulled up behind me. I thought I was pinched, but the officer asked if he could give me a ride. I accepted quickly and he took me right to the door of the temporary employment service.

By the time I got back they had no more jobs for the day. That evening I hit the *Denny's* again without any repercussion. I was the first one at the employment agency the next day, but I fell asleep in a chair and missed the jobs being passed out. Later I slept in a gazebo not far from the casino. Actually it was somewhat still on its grounds toward the exit. I again wondered what my legal name was. I still carried my license naming me David Michael Garcia, but I know the papers to severe the Garcia had to be completed. This wasn't a true change of name. I was really shortening it. I began to try and truly come up with a new name, one that would fit my role as Messiah. This isn't the first time I had come up with this task. I learned in art history classes about a man who strength came from the earth as long as he was in contact with it. Therefore he was as strong as the earth. His name was Antaeus. One day Hercules came to him to see who was stronger. Hercules pulled Antaeus from the earth taping him of his strength. This would prove Hercules was stronger than earth. I like the story and was sympathetic at this point to the fallen strongman Antaeus. As Antaeus was once on the top and fallen from his perch, so was I taken from my high, disappointing the people who knew me? I would take this for a first name and would turn once again to the Art World for a last. There is a word in art, vanitas. This means vanity the way I learned it, it is a symbol one would place in a portrait indicating a vain subject. The object placed in the painting would be a human skull. In most books one is most likely to find images of fruit somewhat torn hastily. Vanitas can also refer to flesh. I can't imagine a better last name than Vanitas. Antaeus Vanitas would be my name, if I had to choose.

I walked around the slots mostly, to hide out. I did roam the gaming floors, taking peeks at the craps tables. I was out on the floor one morning when one of the security guards took me by the shoulder and told me I couldn't stay there any more. He said he had noticed me a few days ago and I hadn't been playing any of the games. He said he was going to help me. He took me to a security car and told me he was going to bring me to the *Salvation Army* in the next town.

CHAPTER 16

I was lucky to arrive at the 'Uncle Sam's' when I did. They had an open bed. From the start I could see this Army was a leap from the one on Washington St. A woman checked me in, and made me aware of the shelters rules. Most of the rules involved keeping everything clean and neat. The big rule was; in order to stay at the *Salvation Army* one had to look for work. After meeting with this *Salvation Army* representative I was shown to my bunk. I shared a room with another person down on his luck. He wasn't there when I climbed up to the top bunk to get some rest, but I did meet him later in the evening. I met the rest of the men the following morning at breakfast. I would guess there where eight to ten of us in all.

This Army not only provided a bed, but three meals a day. They also had two bathrooms each with a shower. They where also equipped with a washer and dryer, which had me rap a sheet around me, once again, to clean my cloths. As I stated this was a whole other world from the St. Louis shelter. A small lounge, with a TV provided some entertainment. The fact was they had maybe ten guys to look after, as the one in the city had 50 or 60 men seeking refuge.

Once I had settled in I began to consider what I thought was the current state of government in the United States. It didn't take me much time to separate the President, Senators and Congressman from the people I believe that actually make the difficult decisions. In my mind the Pentagon has a pulse on everything from foreign policy to protecting the President. I can't imagine the country functioning in this day and age with out the inelegance provided by this entity. I keep these stewards separate from the politics of our elected officials. I imagine this is the group who has final say in a nuclear situation. The President can't just go fire a nuclear weapon when he feels like it. The Pentagon monitors such situations. Our elected officials are there to push agendas and provide the people with a better standard of life, not keep an eye on all the moves made nationally or around the globe. The Pentagon must have the first and final say on crucial matters affecting us all. They must carefully advise our politicians on how to run the country.

Having spelled my point of view out I began to wonder what kind of positions make up the Pentagon. I could see some Generals, military people, CIA Agents and FBI men. My mind curiously wondered if perhaps they had a position of God, just to cover the title. I would have to think the roll of God would be difficult to get an opinion out of. One wouldn't want God to have too much power.

I ran with this over my first couple off days in the 'Uncle Sam's'. Not only did I wonder about a position called God, I hoped a Devil could be established. Then I thought we should supply our planet with an official God and Devil of the United States Government. I would establish the positions when they're young. I would try to find a God by power of persuasion. I would have orphaned infants raised into the position of God, while one was needed, until the Pentagon selected a suitable God. In essence he would be recognized as God right away. The United States Government would then raise the child, isolated from the rest of society. People all over the world would be able to visit God to pray or give gifts, just for a moment. He would most likely hear confections making him wonder what people did to themselves out there. He would be spoiled and showered with all the gifts and prayers, only to know the small world around him. He would see the rest of us through TV and he would be televised 24 hours a day on the God channel. After growing into an older man he would be rolled out into society to, hopefully, do good and great things with his high profile position. There would be a God or two in line just incase God passed on.

As for the Devil, he would also be anointed at a young age, taken in the same manner as God. The big difference would be in the rearing of the two. The Devil would ride in an infinity loop from his youngest years in a crib and beyond into his adult years. I suggest this round and round motion to symbolize the Eternal Kingdom of Hell. The motion of traveling in this loop his entire life should pacify him to such a great extent; he would throw fits when the loop motion stopped. I even envisioned a loop traveling into space, as a vessel, which would open up and deliver the Devil into a future space colony to strike fear into them. This took a few days of imaginary work, but I think it may be interesting if these titles where brought down to a more realistic level. As a final thought I could look after them as if they where my own children, if only I could raise myself to the level of Messiah first.

As I mentioned I would put the so-called Devil in an infinite loop representing the Eternal Kingdom of Hell. In contrast I have a line from a prier that has stuck with me. It goes, "thy Kingdom come thy will be done on earth as it is in heaven..." To me this sounds like the end of the kingdom, where in my mind I would rather an Eternal Kingdom that spreads. I admit to have more of an affinity to Hell then Heaven. If one looks into society they may notice the existence of the Duke Blue Devils, or the Arizona State Sun Devils or even the presents of a hockey franchise named simply the Devil's from New Jersey. Earlier I made mention of a gray devil, which came to mind at this point. I can't think of any instances where God is the example of strength in athletics. Though I will bring to mind the Angeles of Anaheim, who play baseball, I guess that's the closest mention to heaven in sports. I use these examples because I am sports minded individual and I haven't seen any examples of these teams produce un-sportsman like behavior, cheating or sinister soles. In fact the Blue Devil's run one of the more clean and successful teams in NCAA Basketball history.

I'm attempting to make the point God is somewhat soft in my mind, on the other hand it has to be admitted the Devil woops so much ass people desperately avoid any kind of encounter with him, because they know the Devil runs the show. I do admit that Satin is a twisted, manipulative, and a show off. I believe, as the church teaches, Satin should be rejected, but the Devil is unfairly slandered and dumped on. The Devil is strong and mindful of all going on in his Kingdom. When I think of God I think of an old man floating in the clouds. How old is he anyway? Another question is, when one dies do they show up in heaven at the age they died or is an age assigned. I can't imagine the problem Heaven must have with incoherent, crotchety old people. God also works with no logical explanation, called miracles, which don't happen to often. I pose the question, "If God and the Devil where to switch there positions, swap Heaven and Hell, which would rule and change the Kingdom from Heaven to Hell or Hell to Heaven. I don't believe God could keep the residents of Hell captive, where the people in Heaven should be easily tamed do to their cushy life style. One also should consider the Devil inherits the soles God castes away from Heaven, the Devil doesn't have much say in who enters his Kingdom he does his best with God's rejects. God would have no chance changing Hell into Heaven. He could have already done so, but he has cast all those people into Hell when he could have worked a miracle to get them into Heaven. Put everyone in Hell, because one is more apt to see a wild party in Hell.

I'll admit, with the overwhelmingly lopsided slant to God in our current state of worship, I think it is probably easier to land a better position in Hell. I don't prey or worship the Devil. I just like him better. God's the one hung up on worship and prier.

I figure if I commit my lives work believing I'm going to Hell I hope to get a favorable position with some power to it. With my point of few, I believe I'm already just destined to Hell and can't due much about it, but if some chance I end up in Heaven what glory there will be. In my mind Heaven and Hell may just be part of the black and white test cells or tanks (chessboard) I had laid out.

I would add, the course for this planet was pointed out long ago. Good would be what was taught, but this doesn't mean there is no evil. In fact I do believe true evil has the same bad rap as the Devil. He is evil and does a good job of it. I suggest good and evil actually go hand in hand, one the answer to the other. The problem in my eyes is evil has been so stereo typed as a misbehaver that an evil person can't live a peaceful life. Not all evil acts poorly, for I see the wrong doers as bad not evil. I find bad to be very out of control. I think even the good must understand evil to counter and control bad.

Getting back to the story line, to stay where I was I had to at least look for work, so I headed out to the part of town providing a shopping district. It was in walking distance. I applied at a bagel shop. This place was wall to wall with attractive young woman. I hoped to land this job as a bagel maker. I also applied at a *Red Roof Inn* hotel. Neither of which called me back.

My shoes at this point had begun to come apart. I knew there was a *Payless* in the strip of stores, so I decided to take a risk and thieve me a new pear of shoes. I barrowed my roommates coat with out asking and tied it around a tree in a small wooded area. I walked into the *Payless* shoe store, looked over the selection of footwear, found a pear I liked looking to be my size and put them on. I stood up; leaving my old kicks behind and headed for the door. I made it about 40 yards out the door before I heard a women yelling out at me. I stayed calm, continued walking away from her, ducking behind cars as I traveled to my roommates coat. I hid in the wooded area until I felt safe. I put on the coat to alter my appearance and headed back to the 'Uncle Sam's'. The Messiah 'paid less'. I paid nothing to be exact.

The weather was now producing some cold days and some warmer days as March rolled on. A day or two later I applied at an employment service in town. They had a test, I found easy and they gave me my choice of jobs. I could either make baskets or load coffee machines into boxes. I chose to load the coffee machines. The company was located in St. Charles. The Army also had bikes to lend out. On my first day I packed a lunch in the 'Uncle Sam's' kitchen then took off on a bike to the coffee maker company. The mornings still had a chill, with the cool air freezing my hands making it difficult to carry the lunch. I managed to find the address given to me and was ready for my first day. I met with the manager to kick things off. I had to supply my driver's license and Social Security information. Luckily I had obtained the SS info. back at the one-day employment opportunity center.

After sitting in his office for a good hour or so, I was taken to the floor and introduced to the people I would be working with. I introduced myself as A.V., which stood for Antaeus Vanitas. Once that matter was cleared up and I convinced everyone I was A.V. we began the task of rapping the coffee machines in plastic and then lifting and dropping them into boxes. It was somewhat tedious, but the day past quickly. At the end of the day I found my way back to the shelter for some dinner.

It occurred to me there where a whole lot of cities and towns in this area with Saints. There were St. Louis, St. Charles, and St. Peter that I knew of. This got me thinking, if I where a Saint I would be recognized as a serious candidate for Messiah. I also altered the names of the cities to Satins Louis, Satins Charles and Satins Peter. It made sense to me, as well, that Satin would have a problem with multiple personality disorder. The real twisted soul in Hell is Satin not the Devil.

I made the journey with a bike and lunch in hand, for the rest of the week. On the weekend I thought about what I was doing and how much I had earned. I calculated I had a little over $200 dollars coming to me. It was at this time my thoughts where interrupted by, what I considered to be Queen Elizabeth. In my mind she demanded I not show up another single day for that job. I was to make like I was going to work Monday and Tuesday, then grab the check on Wednesday at the employment service. Then cash the check and go to the *Harrah's* casino with the money and your knowledge of craps. I could see her roll the dice and rack in the chips.

    I did as the Queen ordered, for in my thinking I was her royal subject, loyal to the crown. I made it through the weekend and made like I was going to work on Monday and Tuesday. There was a taxi driver staying at the 'Uncle Sam's' who gave me a ride to the *Harrah's*. He and another gentleman from the Army accompanied me to the casino. I looked around awhile before I implemented my system to craps. I was hit early with loses, while the other two men watched. I left the table with some of my pay still remaining. I did this in an attempt to loose them, but it didn't work. After a while they wanted to go, but I had none of that. They left and I went back to the craps table. I lost a long hard battle, but I left the table with enough money to eat at the buffet, which was a small victory.

    I made curtain to take my time while eating, I didn't want to fill up to quickly. Though my mind was full with entertainment. I begun to list or make note of the history of what I considered my most unique and valuable asset. My hands, the part I used in the construction of the Populist animal. I'll start with the operations to my left hand, due to a lawn mar accident. I would have to believe the success of this delicate grafting, alone, would set me apart from the vast majority of people. My fingerprints on my left middle and ring fingers have been altered from this undertaking, and should be identified as my fingerprint rather quickly. The skill of my fingertips on my right hand to create artwork separates me from the average human. Playing baseball I was a catcher. That means I caught almost every pitch from the pitchers, foul balls and hits not included. I also held a bat hitting a few home runs. I know for a fact the vast majority of baseball players never hit a single one. In football I was a running back and rapped my hands around the pigskin, at times one carry after the other through an entire game, which led to touchdowns. I have a good idea of how many

AN AMERICAN MESSIAH

players score touchdowns and I am curtain most players never do. In track and field I through the javelin, the shot put, the discus, and the hammer. Be it only a couple of times competitively, throwing the hammer alone puts me in rarefied air. When I throw it in High School I remember only five to six states even allowed the through it. All the weights I've lifted, clutching the bar adds up to a whole hell of a lot of reps, weight, and calluses. What's ironic, I was considered to have bad hands on my football team and was thrown to sparingly.

My hands continued to fill my mouth with buffet until I could eat no more. I climbed out of my seat and made my way back to the casino. I watched the roulette wheel spin and I did formulate a system, but had no money to play. What came to mind was a game most people have heard of, Russian roulette. After analyzing the 'game', if the trigger is pulled for a fifth time and the gun is in hand, turn the barrel at the opponent and fire, he knows he has the one shot left, he may just turn the gun the other way. I would also suggest firing one into his head if the trigger is pulled for a forth time and gun is in hand. The best way I could think of to play the stupid game, would be to hand the bullet over to one of the participants and the gun to the other, both leaving to go their separate ways.

My mind continued the 'play' with guns and took suicides into account. I've seen guns pointed at the temple or in the mouth, but after consideration I would like to enter my official United States government way to shoot ones self in the head. Take the gun put it about an inch behind the ear. Aim for the front temple on the opposite side of the head, to have the bullet travel through both hemispheres of the brain, as well as, damaging both up and down.

Harrah's casino would be my home for a good number of days. When looking at the *Harrah's* name I couldn't help but turn the last 'h' upside down and getting rid of the last 'a' to spell out Harry's. Harry is the name of the third prince in line for the British thrown. This would make four consecutive casinos I could connect with either the President or a member of the Royal family. I have always felt Harry would make the best King of the lot. I have no mind for his brother William, next in line after Charles. William makes good for the paparazzi, but I see him as a spoiled prince. Harry plays a second fiddle, which I believe grounds him and from time to time a wild side surfaces out of this prince.

DAVID MICHAEL

Even better, the *Harrah's* (Harry's) was located in a part of Missouri titled Earth City. It appeared to me I was navigating from one Royal pit stop to the next gathering clues to unite the United Kingdom. These thoughts played through my imagination as the time spent in the casino evaporated, hour-to-hour and minute-to-minute. Somewhere in these blocks of time I made my first stab at a plan to unifying the globe. I took the Star of David, of which I always had an affinity for, as someone named David should, and put it to use. The star if broken down is made up of a triangle pointed down and a triangle pointed up. I took those two triangles and projected them on to a map I envisioned. I took one point and anchored it in Washington D.C. for the North American representative. From the U.S. capital I anchored another point into South Africa as the dark continents representative. Attempting to form the first triangle of power, the third point would be found in Russia, I had no certainty of the where about of the Kremlin in Moscow, but knew enough that a triangle was established and Asia would have it's mouth piece. The second triangle of power started in England to serve Europe. The country and continent of Australia would be represented my Sydney of Melbourne. The final point would lie in South America, hopefully in Brazil. All I had was my mental map of the continents, but felt good if needed I could put together two interlocking triangles of power to possibly dominate and unify the planet using a signature star.

I was in the casino for a few days and had to pull off another eat and run situation. The gambling establishment hosted a few restaurants outside the gambling areas, so I popped in on one did my usual thing and got out of there unscathed. On a separate instance I would like to share, I was denied access to the gambling portion of *Harrah's*, because the man at the turnstile said I had been drinking and could smell the booze. That wasn't possible, but I may have smelt from not bathing for a few days. Anyhow I was upset because I hadn't been drinking. Just the same Harry's had two sides to the casino and I gained entrance at the other side. As I mentioned I wasn't in Earth city for long, but Harry's supplied a lot of play.

There are two items that filled my troubled thoughts before my stay at *Harrah's* comes to an end. First off I considered the Pope and Jew to be the Kings of religion, the positions of Messiah the Kings of government and the Visroi the King of business. With this said I was faced with the dilemma of what kind of crown I would where in a formal gathering. At first I designed a headdress running low in the front, about an inch in height. From the front it would rap around the head slowly climbing to a five to six inch point in the back. Some kind of gem would sit in the center of the back point. It didn't take long before I through it on the scrap heap and went with something more disturbing and simple. In a tribute to the thorny crown of Jesus, I would wear a simple chain around my head. I would also attach another long chain to the right and left temples to drape around my back. I do this in tribute to the Indian Chiefs, as their headdresses ran along their head to their back. Not much to it just a simple chain.

The second question developing in my thoughts: is my condition a form of evolution? This was a very radical idea I took very seriously. Was it possible? I had to think yes. Even the doctors agree there are cells being produced at a much faster rate than normal. If everyone was producing cells at a faster rate, it's possible in my thinking things would run faster and maybe smoother as everyone shares the same mind set and one another's thoughts. I have also heard here and there humans are currently evolving, but how is a mystery. At this point I had to also acknowledge the classified illness may have given me a channel to receive information intended just for me. Information lost on the layman or healthy minded individual.

I never confirmed the condition as evolution, but if it where there is a great injustice handed to the people who suffer from the stigma of being mentally ill and its treatments. I refrained from an answer, because I would hate to pop into my next life out there and be blamed for giving the human raise on earth mental illness screwing up their whole existence. I'll make a final pitch for the illness being evolution with the common knowledge evaluation of humans: we only use 10% of our brains. The mentally ill may just use more.

As I once again tried to travel through the turnstiles I was stopped by security. Once again I had been noticed by the security over seeing the establishment. They took me to a cab and told the diver to take me wherever I wanted. This I remember, how I ended up the next day at the Employment Services door in St. Charles I can't for the life of me remember. Maybe that's what I asked for, but it doesn't make enough cense for me to have asked to do this at night, but I'm sure I was there the following day.

DAVID MICHAEL

This time I had my ID and proof of my Social Security number and was ready to put in a days work. I was by passed by the person handing out the days work and queried why? He was giving me the assignment of cleaning and straightening up the office. I then went to task. I began by mopping the floor, which was followed by getting the table and chairs in order. I then moved behind the counter to neaten things up. The more difficult choirs would now eat at the time. I painted the bathroom walls and door, which took some time. The bulk of the day I found myself cleaning out a closet with a metal shelf in it. Once I had cleared the closet of debris I was directed to take the metal shelving out of the closet and paint it by hand. It was your run of the mill gray metal shelf about six feet tall. I painted it white, out in the back of the building and left it to dry. My day of work had ended and I was cut a check for around $35 from what I can remember.

It was early evening when I left the Employment Service. As soon as I left I made a B line straight for the airport to catch the rail back into St. Louis. It took a few hours of walking before I hopped on the rail. I got off at the stop in front of the downtown Mall. At this point I was hungry and wanted something to eat. I had an un-cashed check and figured if I had something to eat I could co-sign the check to pay for the bill. That was my plan. I chose to eat what may have been named *The Spaghetti Warehouse;* the name had Spaghetti something in it. What I had to eat is unimportant, but when it came time to pay the bill I told the waiter what I wanted to do and he went back to his manager for approval. When he came back he had the change from the difference in the meal and the check. I left him a good tip for his trouble; he couldn't have been more than twenty years old.

I left with a good ten to fifteen bucks. Traveling through the city, I made a stop at another restaurant in an attempt to contact the only person I knew in the city. I riffled through the phone book until I thought I had found Carla's number. Using the house phone I realized it wasn't her number when someone else answered. Following the call I showed up at the *Ramada Hotel* she worked at, but she wasn't there and they wouldn't supply her phone number. Stepping to the curb a shuttle bus pulled up and I jumped on. I resisted the temptation of the *Casino Queen* and chose to take the shuttle down the free way to a shopping district.

When I got off the shuttle it was pretty late. None of the Malls or shops where open. Early April brought some slightly warmer weather, but the nights where still raw. That evening I bought a loaf of bread, picked up some free newspapers and grabbed some matches from a convenience store. I then made my way down a street, through the parking lot of a factory, over some railroad tracks and into a wooded area. I gathered wood and kindling and began to light a fire to keep me warm through the night. The wood was somewhat damp so it took some time before I got my fire going. I had learned how to build and was trusted with a fire at the young age of 11 or 12. There was a wood stove in the house I would light up after school. The fire grew in intensity and I sat close to it to keep warm. The night filled me with sleep as I rested, seated on a log with my head slumbered on my crossed arms which sat on my knees. I was out when out of nowhere, as if it where a reaction, I plunged my left hand directly into the flames into the hot coals. As I gained my faculties I coiled by arm back. Luckily I responded quickly enough that only my finger tips hand slightly burned. I had never felt anything like this in my life. The only thing that could rationalize this action, after experiencing it, was possession. I have no other explanation for this bizarre occurrence. I do believe words like possession exist to explain such freak phenomenon and at this point I could have been possessed by anything out there.

    I didn't abandon my fire, rather tended to it and made curtain to stay awake. I ate some bread to try and keep something in my stomach, as well as, give me some energy. When the sun lifted its way into the sky I put out my fire with some dirt and headed to the Mall. The Mall was open early, but the stores remained closed until 10 a.m. I tried to catch a quick wink on one of the Mall benches, but was continually awaken by the old people doing their laps around the Mall. In fact I could swear they would shout something in my direction denying me any sleep.

    The gates went up on the storefronts at ten. By that time I had joined the elderly on their walk way. I spent a good part of the day at the Mall before deciding to head back to the city. I went to the shuttle stop in front of a hotel and boarded the next shuttle to St. Louis. I hopped off the shuttle and made my way to the downtown Mall. I knew there was a buffet in the lower level of the Mall and I had a few dollars left to fill myself up pretty well. I had a few plates of food before I paid and left. It felt strange paying for my meal and not having to sneak out looking over my shoulder.

With a full stomach, I jumped another shuttle headed to a shopping district. I arrived at a Mall with just enough sunlight to look around. Once the sun had been forced out by the dark my exploring of the strips had come to a slow stop as I found myself in front of a church. I always considered the church as a means of last resort, a refuge to help the needy. I considered myself to be struggling long enough were the church could intervene. It was growing later and later as I entered the church of St. Albert. The lights had all been extinguished with exception to the candles of prier. Though my opinion of God and worship are not the healthiest, I believe I do have strong faith in my friend Jesus.

Time past as I sat in this religious oasis. There was never a time I felt I should kneel down and prey, I don't think that way, but my years of CCD, respect for the good in church and relationship with Christ open wells of tears running down my cheeks. An uncontrollable sobbing filled my body. I was spent. I cried for the position I was in. I asked for no miracle, rather some guidance or help from Christ.

The tears continued to stream, as I lit several candles at the feet of Mary's idle. I then crossed the center of the church to its statue of Jesus. I lit no candles, but took my license and added it to the pictures of the diseased left adorning the candles. I gave no prier, but left my ID as a symbol of the end of my past life. By now my change of name had to have been recorded, though not received. I would search for a new life for myself in my travels. I wouldn't say I had been resurrected, rather reinvigorated.

The tears had stopped and it was very late as far as I could tell. I would never forget this night, one can only prey for a moment as spiritual as I had experienced at St. Albert's. If no one had bothered with me by this point I thought I could likely spend the night without a problem, so I went to one of the back sitting rooms and fell asleep.

I was awoken the next morning by a gathering in the church. It was early morning Mass, of which I attended. Following Mass, some students of what had to be a St. Albert's Catholic school occupied a small portion of the pews and I sat in on it. Once the class was through I exited the church after the children. I then built up my courage and went to the rectory to talk to the priest. I knocked on the door and he invited me in.

I sat with him and told a story where the people who knew me did not appreciate me. I told him I was traveling looking for a school to attend, which was one of my original thoughts when I left Rhode Island. I finished our conversation by asking him for a few dollars to feed myself. He was gracious enough to donate to my cause, and I thanked him for hearing me and for his generosity. I took the money went straight to the Mall in sight and had lunch. I then hopped a shuttle bus back to St. Louis.

Once in St. Louis I waited for the rail to come and pick me up at the *Casino Queen*. This trip would be different. I was going to take the rail further into Illinois, to its final stop. I traveled on the commuter rail to its end. It dropped me of in a small town for which I can't remember. I did a good deal of walking before a bus stop was in short distance. I checked out where the buses where headed. Somehow in this gathering of direction, I was able to find a bus headed in the same direction as a *Salvation Army*. After climbing aboard the bus, which made several stops on route to Belleville, I was dropped off virtually in front of the shelter.

I was checked in, as all the *Salvation Armies* will do before lending a hand. I was shown to a bunk in a room of two bunks, with only one other stow away. He was a man possibly in his 60's. He gravitated to me starting at our initial introduction. I was then welcomed to the cast of characters staying at the 'Uncle Sam's' in the common area in the lowest level. There was some old TV show on one of the men was watching. He was lying on the couch- this is an important fact. Other men sat around in chairs watching. We were lucky to be served three meals a day.

As I had mentioned I made quick friends with my roommate. I can't recall his name, but I do recall sitting in a *Burger King* close by, paying for a drink and refilling it at the soda fountain. From the very beginning he was trying to talk me into driving down to Columbia and smuggling drugs into the country. I wasn't into it, but I heard him anyhow. That was his focus and my focus was to start a political party. At that very moment I was a Cool Moose, a small party in Rhode Island. I always thought the party had a future as a political mascot or animal. I asked him what he thought if a few small parties united to form say a Civilest Party and used the Cool Moose as its animal? I wasn't ready to drop a ton of heavy Populist Party concepts on him, just something he could look at. I wanted to get a barometer of his political interests. He was as receptive to it as I was into smuggling drugs.

In my passage of time in this 'Uncle Sam', I began to consider a life as a priest, which I would use as a springboard into politics. There was a day I was assigned work from the Army to help a man clean floors. In our conversation I mentioned I was considering the priest hood as my calling. I was quite serious at that time. That day the man never got around to doing the floors, but he did do a lot of running around for errands. I was paid nothing. In fact there wasn't a whole hell of a lot of places to find work in the area.

My final day at the Army was short. I woke up got dressed and headed down to the common area. I lay down on the couch and was told to sit up and I ignored the messenger. Again I was told to sit up and I was defiant. When I showed up there was a man lying on the couch, why couldn't I? That is when the person on duty came down stairs, as he commanded the first to times over the intercom. He told me, "If I have to tell you to sit up one more time you're out of here!" The smart ass I am responded, "How about a third?" That was the end of his rope and I was escorted off the primacies. That's when I turned my back on St. Louis and the surrounding area and began to wonder on foot.

I just started to walk, plain and simple I started to walk. I had no destination, but didn't care. I had no money, but didn't care. I decided to walk as far as the road would stretch.

CHAPTER 17

I walked and I walked… I kept a constant pace. I was in no hurry and didn't want to tire early. Traveling up a slight grade, my first memory was of a playground with swings, a slide and ample room for young people to play. I took a breather and noticed for the first time in my 'pursuit of happiness'; clouds blotted out the sun. Precipitation in the form of a mist would accompany me as I began to walk again.

The road featured a bend or two, but offered no real change in direction. The mist continued as night found me pulling into a shopping district. I had expended some energy without eating anything that day and I began to shut down. I scrambled for shelter, but it was late enough for stores and shops to have closed. If I where more familiar with the area perhaps I could have escaped the elements. I stopped in a convenient store tired and cold, peaking through the isles of goods. I had found refuge from the weather if only for a brief spell. I sat at a table to rest. As soon as I sat I struggled to stay awake. The girl at the counter took a long while before questioning me. She was sympathetic when I told her I had begun to travel by foot. She was gracious enough to permit me to stay in the store for the night. I landed in a 24-hour convenient store and was lucky to have a caring sole running it. I was in and out of sleep as I sat at the table, the in and out of costumers made sleeping difficult, but I did get out of the wet and cold as well as rested my legs.

I was back on the street early in the morning. I was hoping this girl would further lend a hand, but when her shift ended so did my recuperation. The next day was filled with sunshine. The morning evaporated with the puddles from the previous days moister. When stores opened, the *Barnes and Nobles* in the vicinity captured me. I looked around and toyed with some of the headsets, which played samples of CD's before finding something of use. A map to indicate where I was and to direct where I should travel unfolded in my hands. Today I can't tell exactly where in southern Illinois I was, but I do recall pointing myself in the direction of Kentucky, south of Illinois. That's the best I could do with the map, seeing I had no money to buy it.

It was then, just before I left the *Barnes and Nobles* as I looked for an avenue to lead me into Kentucky, that Prince Charles re-entered the picture. Though it wasn't as a member of the Royals. Another, previous, life had planted images of a friend. Not just any friend, but the other Messiah. I was given memories of a duo, walking the country, as I had begun to. The visions told stories of the Prince and I in and out of trouble. One would rescue the other. We were two wise guys with not much too loose and the world to gain. This brought questions. Why was he not at my side this trip? How did he luck out to get in the Kingdom as part of the bloodline?

I took these questions with me to the street. The answers entered my mind in the same channel of thought. I saw Charles in my position. Traveling alone carrying the Messiah's burden with nothing but the cloths on his back, with a continuous struggle at every point. I envisioned him breaking down as I had done, clamoring, "Why, oh why?" and crying, "This is unfair". With that, in my mind, the heavens answered his tears of unfairness, by guiding a large comet from the far reaches of space. The planet was found to be so wrong to him the existence of the planet would be destroyed by this hurling seed. For the comet would plunge into the center of the sphere, fertilizing the orb ending the cries of Charles. Existence of the heavenly body would be wiped away, with the exception of Charles himself. He would take on the life of the newly fertilized life, gestating with his mother, Queen Elizabeth II. He would be reincarnated as a King as compensation for his unfair situation as Messiah.

I could see my current situation was better than Charles', because I thought of him as an ally, even if he doesn't recognize this offering. In my opinion the Monarch is more governmental, than religious or business oriented. I do consider the Royal bloodline to be a critical cog in my pursuit to organize the planet.

I left *Barnes and Nobles*, which I call 'Barney Rubbles', moving through the business area I stumbled across, before heading south. I found it funny, if I was asked where I was I could tell them, "I am in a northern state, headed south, on the west side, east of the Mississippi. I took the positioning and distanced it from the build up. I strolled along until I came to a small town several miles from where I had started that morning.

I couldn't tell where I was if they pointed it out on a map for me. I hadn't eaten in some time and noticed a church as I stepped through town. Again I went in, but there was no one there to greet me, so I looked around making to a small kitchen in the building. I had some soda from the fridge, there wasn't much else to consume. I then went looking for someone who might help me and I found a priest to talk to. I told him the same thing I told the first priest, 'I was not appreciated and was searching for a college to attend.' After which I mentioned I hadn't eaten in some time and asked for a few dollars to get something in my stomach.' As the first priest had, this religious gentleman gave me what I remember as $10. Again I was very thankful for the Fathers generosity and headed off to get something in my stomach. I didn't have to walk long before I got to a *Sub Way* sandwich shop. I ordered a large sub and when I was done with the first half I contemplated whether I should eat the other half or save it for later in day or evening. I decide to have it then, I didn't want to carry it. I wanted to tank up for the big hall ahead of me.

On the way into town I had passed a sign saying I had 20 some odd miles to the next town. Exactly where I was I'm not sure, but the towns of Marissa and Sparta where stops on my expedition. I was tanked up and ready to go. A high sun was above me. Again I paced myself. I thought I could make it into the next town without a problem as long as I kept a good pace.

It was dusk when I got to the small town, in between the two I was attempting to cross. There was just a small diner in front of a small community and I stopped in to see if anyone could help me. The two girls working there did their best to put me in touch with the priest they knew, but he was of no help. I have to thank both of the girls, who pulled crumpled dollars from their pockets to give to me. They also gave me a free burger. This generosity came at a time of need and I can only hope they receive this thank you.

Once I recharged my battery I marched on down the strip off tar. The night filled the sky with an open slate. The moon and the stars were my company in this stretch of open land. It's strange walking a line of road as long as this one in the darkness. Nothing seems to move. It's like treading water. Even the cars seem to be the same, speeding by with no thought of giving anyone a lift that late. Hell I couldn't even tell how late, late was, but it felt like an endless number of cars passed me by. As my hips began to feel the slow grind from pounding of the pavement, each car felt like its pistons wore on my hipbones.

Alas the end of the road was in sight I could see lights in the distance. The problem was it must have taken another hour or two to get to the lights. Once in the town I looked immediately for a church and found one rather quickly. I found one, but this one had its doors locked. I was back on my feet headed down the strip of the small town. Everything was closed for the night and again I found my way to a convenience store, which was open for business. It was small, made up of maybe two isles. I stopped dead in those isles staring at the snacks. I was asking myself if I should just drop to the floor in a desperate sign for help, but I didn't. I just kept to myself gazing at the snacks.

After about ten minutes a police officer came and picked me up. I told him my situation and he rushed me some miles away to a 24-hour *Wal-Mart*. I found a space in the back where the food court was, which was no longer serving for the day, sat down and rested my head on the table. I kept my head down close to the front of the court, so I wouldn't be visible. I rested for a few hours, after which I got up and walked around. Comparing this *Wal-Mart* to the ones in Rhode Island was no contest. This one was two to three times bigger, maybe more.

The size of the warehouse like structure started the wheels turning, as I went up and down the store isles. I always thought the rate of space exploration was slow considering man plunged into space in the 60's. It is now roughly 40 years since this achievement had been met and I have to look the history of manned flight to make my point. The Wright brother's first flight in the opening decade of the 20th Century was crude and the advancements in aviation from that point to the 60's saw man travel from the Wright brothers' bicycle shop to landing on the moon. The evolutions from the rockets of the 60's to today's modern Space Shuttles are a dramatic leap in design. Though the only memory of space travel in my youth was the Challenger explosion in the 80's and I haven't seen much, if any, change in the modernization of spacecrafts in my existence.

My opinion sparked a suggestion on how to get moving into the final frontier. I was amazed at how large the *Wal-Mart* store was. I thought the government should build huge hangers, even bigger than the shopping center providing me shelter. I would implement the draft, giving young adults the opportunity to serve their country in NASA and spark an attack on space. They would be drafted into the space program, made part of a noble endeavor. I envisioned young people building space vehicles in an enormous and modern model T type assembly line. They would have to account for a very small portion of the crafts, but they would have to work closely with their pears to connect A to B and B to C and so on. After one had taken part in a number of successful constructions of space ships, that NASA representative would be eligible for space flight.

The deserts of New Mexico, Nevada, and Arizona came to mind as large open areas for such an undertaking. The nice dry climate, not a producer of many storms, should play host to the launch of said vessels. Mega-Plex's could be provided, making down time a fun experience. I'd pay them well, so they could have money to waist at the Mega-Plex. I would recommend prices surrounding these facilities stay cheap. These people would be there to get into space not build a fortune.

I could see portions of a ship designs handed over to some young person to manage, understand, repair, and connect to the portion designated to some one else. I considered these thoughts for some time, walking through the endless sections of this 24-hour *Wal-Mart*.

Staying on space travel and exploration the artist in me produced an offering. The question of, 'what should be the first thing built on the moon?" After some deliberation with my creative parts, I came up with a monument to symbolize the moon landing. The size could be changed from one plan to another, but the modern sculpture would be constructed with a material with four sides, with all the same dimensions for each side of a long segment, like a 4x4. A circular or octagon base would anchor the project. I would attach 8 legs or more to the base, which would extend upward from the base into a point. One of the pieces would sit in the center of the joining legs. This piece would be held in place by the legs, suspended, partially extending up and partially extending down. The piece pointing downs head would make a point, representing the landing or touchdown of the moon mission. When assembled properly this work should resemble or mimic the capsule used in the moon landing. To finish things, I would color each side of each piece a different color as an exiting offering to the heavens as man prepares to travel through the Universe and beyond.

Not stopping there I followed up with a plan to build a base on the moon. I kept it very crude and simple to accomplish. First I would build a landing strip. How? I would use the old school rockets. I would simply blast segments of runway into space, to be gathered and placed on the moon surface. I would most likely be taking a risk with the next part, but it is so easy to accomplish in my eyes. I would shoot a nuclear sub into space or a modified version of a sub to sit beside my landing strip. It's airtight but I'm uncertain if the water surrounding a sub is needed to produce the oxygen in a sub. Oxygen tanks could be sent up if that's a problem. That's as far as I went, maybe someday we will do something exiting with the moon. I can't recall any one saying we couldn't.

Back at the tables in the food court, resting my self for the next days walk, I noticed more people than I would have expected shopping at night. The store was still far from crowded by any means though people where there. I sat with my head down just waiting for the next day to arrive.

Arrive it did. The day was so much easier on traveling by foot. The early sun puts a little step into your pace and the body all together feels more alert. As I had before I began walking, hoping to be headed south, though I needed to go southeast to reach Kentucky. That morning walking on some back roads a dog started after me before his owner gave him a shout. I passed through a patch of growth tangled and twisted with thorns and trees. That was followed by a piece of land I could only wish to have a camera for. They open country area looked like it had swallowed up VW bugs. It was like a large mogul field, for those who ski.

I walked a distance down this endless bumping of land, when someone pulled up beside me and asked if I wanted a ride. I may have hesitated for a fraction of a second, but I jumped in his car with thanks. He asked me where I was headed and I told him south. As we passed these lumps on the sides of the road I asked the driver what they where? He answered, 'They are from coal digging.' There where spots of silence as he took chunks out of the walking I would have done. I was very mindful to watch his every move no matter how slight, one never knows what to expect when picked up by a stranger. He then asked me if I wanted to smoke some grass with him? I accepted his offer and we took hits from his bowl as we made it further to my next destination. It was a mid-day high ride and it was a good, unexpected buzz. He traveled quite a ways with me or even went out of his way for me. When he dropped me off he pointed out a direction I should take. Again I had no idea where I was, but I was high, it was a nice day and I didn't car where I was. I took the advised route into a town called Carbondale. I walked straight through down route 51, but as 51 kept going and civilization ended, I stopped in my tracks and turned around to get more familiar with this well developed area.

I found out quickly this was a college town, home of the University of Southern Illinois Salukis. I wondered around the surrounding build up of restaurants, businesses, and stores before taking a seat on a bench someplace in town. The thought I may have stumbled across a college for me to attend crossed my mind. I ended the day on the out skirts of town in a Mall, dodging the rain.

I found myself looking through the men's summer cloths selection when an employee asked if I needed some help with anything. I told her, an older woman approximately in her late 50's, I was looking for some summer things, but wouldn't be buying at that time. She continued to show me some things here and there and I went back to her for help. I was hoping she could see I could use a helping hand and did bother her a number of times before leaving to take a look at the rest of the Mall. I didn't make it far before I sat down at a bench. After a short time I elected to return to the men's section to speak with the employee.

The next thing I know the police where at the door, but hesitated before entering. They entered the building, but again waited to move. I casually looked at some clothes, trying to blend in. Another employee must have fingered me, because she never left her station. The police then moved in on me and escorted me out of the Mall. I was asked where I lived due to the fact I couldn't supply an ID and I gave him the Chi Phi address. I answered his question to what I was doing in Illinois, with the truth. I was traveling.

It was to my surprise when he took me to a Hospice near campus. I had looked to see if there was a *Salvation Army* when I came to town, but there wasn't one and I had not in my most creative vain considered a Hospice as a place to find help. I was dropped off by the officer and interviewed before gaining entry. They also asked my address and I gave them the Penn State address. What surprised me was they wanted to help me more than I expected. Their solution involved getting me a bus or train ticket back to Happy Valley. I was all for it.

I was then shown to my room, which I would share with two other individuals. I laid down following the tour of the Hospice. Once my head hit the pillow I was engulfed by a horrible dream. I was trapped in theatre, being castrated by a few women. I cried for help and wondered if my cries where heard by the others. I returned, with relief, to consciousness. My first thought was this may have happened to me in a past life and it was jarred from my memory. Another rational explanation I had come up with was a theory I had developed in the passed, but could explain this episode. I have some belief when one sleeps they transmit their daily events to other characters around their test cells.

In other words one individual, while sleeping, releases their daily information to other individuals in the same test pattern, while also receiving valuable or sometimes frightening information from other subjects in a test parameter. I suggest our dreams are events being carried out somewhere out there and some poor sole relayed his horrifying experience to me. I also felt it took place in Medieval time and may have been a failed past life.

I got up and watched some television with the others after my rued awakening. The TV was shut off not long after I sat down to watch. This sent everyone to bed including me. I went to sleep with some hesitation, but sleep through the night without another nightmare.

The next day, after breakfast, I was more surprised with the Hospices than the night before. They told me they where not going to try and get me a ticket to back to Pennsylvania and asked that I leave. I didn't fight them I did exactly what they wanted me to do and I wondered off into town.

I took my first good look at campus. I recall a statue of what may have been the schools founder on campus. I made a trip to the registrar to pick up an application; I found the student center on campus and the athletic offices. I took to the football field, which was being used for a track and field event that day. I stayed to watch. I couldn't help but notice the train passing by from time to time.

As dusk broke, I found my way into a bar, a college bar with lots of room. I had left my ID behind long ago, so I had slipped into the party before it started. I ordered a drink with the money the girls had given me somewhere close to the town of Marissa. I drank it slowly in an attempt to have a drink with me, so they wouldn't get on me for just hanging around. Students began to trickle in a little at a time until the establishment was in full party mode. There was a big crowd, but nothing I hadn't experienced before at Penn State. Though I wasn't expecting such a gathering of people. This was a positive experience, a definite plus for the school in my mind.

Toward the end of the night, actually closing time, I was trying to talk to a girl when I was being told to leave. The bar had emptied out onto the streets by this time and this guy was just doing his job, but I didn't like what he was saying, so I spit a small red drink straw I had been chewing on in his face. That may have been stupid, but stupid I'm not. I took off before he could gather a bigger bouncer. I didn't run I just walked quickly to the door and mixed in with the party on the street.

The streets emptied after some time and I found myself seated at a table in a small pizza shop. I couldn't order anything, but it was busy enough with the late crowd that I had nice warm place to pass part of the night away. I left once I thought I was being noticed. There was still some foot traffic, but the streets had been mostly abandoned that night. The train station was just blocks from where I was and I decided to see if I could possibly crash there. I had heard the trains passing through all day and walked by the station earlier. It was a very small station, but I got in and dozed off until early morning.

In the morning I walked my way away from campus across from the Mall to a shopping plaza. In the plaza was a *Kmart*, which I began walking around. I was able to get a shave at the *Salvation Armies*, but my beard had begun to look raggedy. I thought a clean shave went a long way in giving the illusion I was grooming, even if I had begun to give off a body odder. With this running through my mind I took a razor with refills and went to the *Kmart* bathroom, where I shaved and put the razor in my back pocket. Again I was undetected when I walked through the doors. I would go on to keep the razor in my pocket.

I found out a Saluki was a kind of dog, a kind of gray hound if my memory serves right. I was kind of disappointed in the pooch and began looking for better mascots. I had been thinking about all the nomadic walking I had accomplished in the previous days and thought the Nomads may be a formidable foe. I continued to formulate, trying to produce the concept of winning. The best I could due was, the Victorians as a victorious bunch. I would make note and mention it once I talked with someone from the athletic department.

Shortly after, I was in the athletic departments building. I found the football office on the second floor and was asked to wait for someone to help you. I told the woman at the front desk to call me A.V. It took sometime, but a coach, I believe the defensive coordinator, came to my attention. I gave him my football resume, verbally, and told him I would like to play for the University. He brazenly told me they where not looking for recruits and sent me on my way. On the way out I intruded on a coach and one of his players weight training, a female player. I watch as they worked out so as not to interrupt, but when they finished I bounced a weight training modification on him. I asked, "Do you think the bar could be replaced with a chain?" I told him it could develop better balance and strength. He didn't give an answer from what I can remember, but I also asked what he thought about a Nomad or Victorian as a mascot. Again he had nothing. Before I left I asked a favor from him and he granted it. I asked if I could take a shower. He showed me the way and handed me a towel. It was a good feeling having the warm water cascading down.

After the shower I left the building, but didn't make it to far from the athletic department. I went out into a large open area lay down and took an afternoon nap. The sun was nice and worm now that spring was bottling up winter. I actually felt I got burned when I woke up. When I did it really hit me I needed something to eat.

I knew what I had to do it was just a matter of what restaurant. I found a good place to eat not to far away from campus. It wasn't a national chain, rather a restaurant home to Carbondale. It wasn't burgers and fries or pizza. It was likely the best restaurant I would chew and screw from. Never the less I ate well and skated out onto the street and down the road.

The day had begun to end when I neared the University. I sat on a bench somewhere in between campus and town. I had picked up matches to help me turn my jeans into shorts. I burned small wholes in the jeans then carefully tour the pant legs off until I wore shorts. I picked a white flower as I walked into town. I wore it in my ear and twirled it in my fingers. I sat on the sidewalk beside a fire hydrant and watched the people go by. I watched it get later and later and later, with the sound of trains passing through town. The idea of jumping onto one of the trains as it came by was a serious consideration. As serious as I was I opted not to take such a risky gamble. I could fall from the train as I tried to get on and they may stop the train to kick me off.

Instead I slipped into an open-air bar. I sat and relaxed, while putting my flower into a beer. The bar began to close shortly after I stopped in, but I sat until I was the last one out. In converse from the way I was treated at the other bar the guy cleaning up asked if I would like to smoke some weed with him and I accepted. He told me to wait in the back while he finished up. After not to long he came to the back and we smoked a Jay.

I thanked him as he left me there. It was already late in the night at that time, but I carried my buzz for a long while. In fact I stayed up all night walking straight out of town, only to turn around as I had planned. I walked with bear feet for quite away. In my mind I did this for my friend Christ. I may not have walked with a cross, but I thought of Jesus that night.

The next morning arrived with a stunning sunrise that snuck out of sky line and the telephone and cable wires. The flaming ball was unmistakable. Again I wished to have a camera. The next day took me to the student center or student union building. I was there early and nabbed a muffin from one of the carts. It had a chained gate around it, but I was able to grab a muffin close to the side. Once that went down I laid down. I found a green couch in the TV room and fell asleep. When I woke up I found myself steering at one of the small red dots making up the pattern on the couch. I rationalized this behavior. I told myself I had to go all this way and endure all of this to look at this red dot. If I never found this red dot I maybe left incomplete with the un-blossomed thought of this red dot in my mind, preventing me from following the script. I made this an indicator I was in the correct place at the correct time. I then left this couch, knowing I would never lay eyes on that red dot again.

Again the night produced itself in a timely manner and I had made it easily into the library, where I was in a chair in and out of sleep. The next night I was unable to repeat my stay in the library and I found myself on the tennis courts pushed up against the fence which was fixed with plastic sheet to block the wind. The weather as I mentioned had begun to represent itself and I hoped I could make it through the night. I didn't sleep soundly, but I did get some rest.

The next day I got back into the library and found my way to the inter net. I looked up Chi Phi and was able to get a list of all the fraternities in the country. I then looked for the Chi Phi closest to me, in southern Illinois. There where two. There was a Chi Phi in Bloomington, at The University of Indiana and another brotherhood at the University of Western Kentucky Military Academy. With this in hand I left Carbondale.

Night fell quickly and I found myself walking in the dark in the middle of nowhere. I remember coming to an intersection and seeing a sign pointed to Giant City. With a title like Giant City I had to see it. No travelers past as I walked my way through the night. I thought I would see some lights or buildings of some sort before I came to a sign welcoming me to Giant City. It was as if someone had pulled a joke on me. Giant City was a park or campground. I took this in stride and entered the park. I ended up in the area designated for RV's, there where big slabs of concrete laid out in an orderly fashion. There may have been one camper on the grounds.

It was late no matter what time it was and I originally tried to fall asleep on one of the slabs of concrete. I chose a spot far from the RV, making it more difficult to be spotted. It was a colder night from the night I slept on the Saluki's tennis court or the wind that was blocked by the barrier on the fence that night was giving me shivers this evening. I got up and looked for another place to make camp. I noticed the restrooms the part supplied and noticed they where a pretty big structure, so I went in to take a better look.

AN AMERICAN MESSIAH

I couldn't help but noticed the amount of insects dead on the floor, but I noticed some shower stalls deeper into the facilities. I checked the water to see if it could produce hot water before thinking about a shower. Hot water came streaming from the showerhead and I took a nice long shower. I may not have been able to clean up with any soap, but the heat cascading down was exhilarating. I can't begin to estimate the length of the shower, but it did continue to produce a source of heat I enjoyed for a long duration.

Once I turned the water off I put my clothes back on after allowing some time to drip dry. That night I took up residency in one of the shower stalls. Though it wasn't the most comfortable way to get rest, it was void of flies and kept me out of the elements. I decided to leave the structure early in the morning and headed out early.

I marched around the park until I bumped into some kind of information center for the park. On the way in a few deer crossed my path. Once I poked into the station the park supplied, I found brochures and maps. I perused a map before leaving with it. Finally I could get a sense of direction. I took my map and headed out of the park.

Devil's Kitchen was one of the more tempting sights I passed that day. I walked up a pretty steep grade later in the day. I climbed to its summit before continuing a down ward trend. I ended up in a small, not even, town with just a couple of old storefronts on the way. I stopped into a deli just to sit and get my bearings straight with the map. As I did the guy behind the counter offered me a sandwich and I told him I had no way to pay for it. The kind individual gave me a ham sandwich for free. I thanked him several times before hitting the road.

Not long after I came to a stretch of road heavy with traffic. I took my shirt off to get some sun on my body as spring began to warm things up. Not long after following this road I came across a side country road headed in the same direction. A few cars past me by, but I kept walking. On the way I came up on two bulls grazing. As I passed I didn't know who was watching whom, but as I crossed directly in front of the two, one of them sprung a leek that went on and on and on. I thought he would never finish. I was truly astounded by the amount of urine that bull produced. Any how I'm a Taurus and I felt those two bulls where good luck.

DAVID MICHAEL

I traveled further and further down the lonesome stretch until I stopped to rest my feet at the side of the road. I rested on a small bridge stretching maybe 10 yards over a brook. As I sat there a car stopped and a women asked if I wanted a lift. She was kind enough to give me a lift and I jumped in. She road for some time before letting me off in a town named Anna. Before I got out I asked her if she could spear a dollar. She gave me four quarters before putting me back on the curb. I took that dollar to the first convenient store I came across and bought a bag of cheep chips. I devoured the snack food.

After those chips I was like a junky looking for a fix, they got the digestive juices flowing and I took a seat in a *Pizza Hut*. I ordered a sandwich off the menu, which I know is an odd choice in a traditionally pizza restaurant. It didn't take long for me to down the sandwich and I was faced with my waitress, who I did find appealing. I told her straight faced I had no money to pay. She called her manager out and he took me to the counter, telling me he was going to call the police. When he went to the back room I could have left, but I was so exhausted I thought the police may actually try and help.

The officer arrived quickly. After the manager explained the situation the policeman asked for my ID, which I couldn't produce. He put the cuffs on me and escorted me into the car. He asked me the question of what I was doing and I answered traveling. He drove around for sometime before taking me into the station. Next I found myself in a holding tank. I started off as the only one in the tank. A poster of tough looking men lined up behind bars with type reading something to the affect off, 'Meet your new friends,' steered at me. I actually wondered if I was going to meet anyone that could, honestly, become a good friend. After several hours, the tank housed three young guys. If we had conversation it was kept to a minimum. I felt like I was in the holding tank for an awfully long time. My wait ended when I was put back in a cop car and taken to the Jonesboro County Jail, charged with theft of service.

CHAPTER 18

The anticipation and fears of what loomed ahead filled me with curiosity and withdrawal. The first formality was the exchange of my clothes for an orange jump suit. I was then supplied with a thin mat, light and heavy sheets, a towel, a role of toilet paper and flip flops. A guard then opened the door to the main holding cells. He escorted me down a hall, to a door. My mind was racing with both illusions and expectations, as I was about to face the realities of jail.

From the second the door opened and I got my first look at my new home, to the walk up the stairs to my cell on the second floor, I could sense tension. Once in my cell I put my mat on the empty top bunk. My cellmate came in and showed me how to tie the sheet around the mat. He left as I hopped up onto my bunk to get some rest. In about five minutes time my cellmate returned. He reappeared demanding I take a shower. Over and over again he shouted get in the shower and I ignored him. With that, he was a guy right around my age and a little bigger than I. As his cries fell on def ears he grabbed hold of the mat I was laying on and proceeding to pull me from my bunk. Once I got my feet on the floor he took a swing at me landing on the side of my head. From there I didn't get a chance to swing back or retaliate, the cell was flooded with inmates. The crowd forced me from the cell to the isle in front of the cells. I can remember being forced to the rail, holding on for dear life hoping I wouldn't be thrown from the second level.

Some how the bomb was defused and I rushed down the stairs to one of the tables in the common area. My cellmate tossed my mate and sheets from the second floor cell to the floor of the common area. As I sat there the juices where flowing while I attempted to calm down. This was my welcome into this jail. The most frightening thing about the ordeal was I had no friends to back me up. It really could have been much worse. Responding to the demand of my cellmate to get into the shower, my first thought was there is no way this guy is going to get me bent over in the shower as an introduction or some kind of initiation. When I looked at it for a second time he may have had a point that I wasn't seeing. I may have been on the streets, without washing, for so long I was producing a stench he couldn't tolerate. I guess my thought was I'd rather be a fighter than a lover while being imprisoned. For what its worth, I noticed a razor blade, not a shaving razor, on the windowsill of that cell. It may have been a good thing I got out of there.

 I spent a good hour to hour and a half sitting at that table while I vented. One of the much older inmates broke my stare. He helped me get my things into his cell. He had no roommate, but he told me I would have to sleep on the floor. After sleeping on a similar mat on the St. Louis *Salvation Army* floor I had no problem with his request. Almost immediately after settling my mat on the floor I lay down for some rest. The old man, who wore a hearing aid, left me to rest. He was a little guy who had to be in his 60's. His hearing aid reminded me of my sister and as I had played in the past I considered this to be a possible relative of hers in a past life. I took this to such an extent; I began cleaning out the intercom system, which had been clogged with toilet paper. I was under the impression this may help my sister and my new cellmate hear more clearly if I opened up this clogged passage. I used great care in this cleaning. It made sense to me at the time.

 I rested all day and all night, only meals took me from the cell. When I came out for my meals I had a reoccurring imaginary story play out. It was the story of David and Goliath. For the longest time I saw a ball hit off Goliaths head. It happened so often I made David and Goliath friends, just playing a game where David would through the ball off Goliaths head. Playacting, Goliath would fall to the ground. This played in my thoughts over and over again. I began try to make some kind of explanation for this repetitive theme. One guess was; if David through the ball off his head and Goliath went down it meant he was in some kind of trouble or to confused to continue and David should cut his head off. It is part of the story were David does take the head of the beast. Another suggestions is David may just daze the beast, Goliath, enough were he can decapitate him. This was really the first time in my life I gave thought to the story, with exception to the works of art I came across in college which where dedicated to the tale.

There was another rear occasion I left my cell, and that was to take a shower. I showered early in the morning when there wasn't much steering. Other than that I stayed in my cell relaxing. This went on for maybe a week tops, when I was summons from the cellblock. To me I thought I was going to be released. I was very wrong. What was happening was the powers that be where relocating me.

I was taken a few doors down to a different cellblock. This was a much different holding tank for the structure. I would now experience an open cellblock. To give a description of the holding facility, there was an upper level housing bunks. A cage or screen extended up to the ceiling, which had to be around 25 feet or higher. The cage also ran from one staircase to the other (there was a staircase on either side of the upper level) I would have to estimate it held about 50 criminals. There was a smaller lower level housing maybe ten men on the wrong side off the law. There was nothing fencing them at the ground level bunks. A much larger common area, than my first stop, occupied the majority of the cellblock. The shower and bathrooms where separated, but beside each other. Both were open, everyone was in plain sight at all times. The shower may have had a curtain.

I made my way up the stairs choosing an unoccupied bunk to take up residence. It was up against the back wall almost in the center of the row of beds. My introduction into this part of the facilities was like night and day. I couldn't help but notice or even ignore three young captives wrestling around the bunks below me. Once they grew tired and needed a rest from there horsing around they took up conversation with me. Some how from there I found myself engaged in a hand slapping game. It's a game I had learned in my junior high years. A person would hold their hands out, palms down, while the other player holds his hands palms up beneath the other combatant's hands. The person with their hands under the other person's hands would then, at any time, try and slap the tops of the others hands before they could be pulled away. This game changed into a game with a similar premise, but a much greater level of pain if ones hands or fists in this matter failed to pull away to safety. Standing face to face the players would extend their fists to the opponent's fists. Once their knuckles butted one another one was chosen to try and hit the others knuckles. If one missed the other would have his turn.

I played these games with a guy who couldn't have been more than 21 years old. I have to admit this criminal got the best of me. He was a big individual, not enormous but big. He was heavy, but not really fat and had to be close to six feet tall, a naturally big and strong individual, kind of like a farm boy. He and another young, but big, inmate had forged a friendship which was evident. His friend was taller, but thinner. He wasn't skinny he had wide shoulders and a body one might find on a monster. These two troublemakers had become my allies. For the third guy I mentioned, these two just enjoyed picking on him, though he was another young and big person.

I noticed at this point my feet where a mess. They bleed in some spots, while other spots had skin coming off from blisters. This stay in jail gave me an opportunity to rest my feet and body. I also was provided with three squares a day.

At night they passed out medications to some of the prisoners. They didn't give any to me and I felt this was a good thing, an indicator I was doing well. Later in the evening once the television and lights were turned off, the slapping of dominos on the tables and the general sound of conversation made it difficult to fall asleep. After some time I was able to fall asleep, until one of the inmates had an announcement to make. He felt he was obligated to let everyone in the cellblock aware of what he had just done. To quote this man, he blurted out "I just had sex with another man in the shower!" That was the last thing I wanted to hear. I'm glad he was so proud. After the announcement I quickly went back to sleep.

The days that followed where much the same. What I found to be one of the more difficult tasks as a new guy was finding a table at mealtime. I had to guess most of the seats where pre-arranged by the prisoners. One day I found myself eating with my tray on the bottom of the rail of the staircase. The rest of the time I was able to find a seat.

I saw a few guys get battered around by a swarm of inmates. Early on when I did get a seat one of the criminals inquired: Where I was from? What I was in for?, etc… When he asked about my family I answered to him, "They are like a bad accident." I kept the same answer for anyone asking, because my family had forced me into a corner I didn't want to be in.

AN AMERICAN MESSIAH

In those first few days I began to unravel a plan or concept to redefine the world. I'll began by giving a pet peeve and maybe this approach while make people more conscience of their world. The concept of the world, in my mind, has either been confused or needs to be up dated. In my mind the world is not earth. Earth is just in the world. I lend this example. A child has a small world that grows larger and larger as their boundaries grow. I ask the Question: Did everyone just stop at earth? Aren't all the planets in our world or even the galaxy for that matter part of the world? Our boundaries have expanded past earth. It also seems to be a struggle for people to say earth instead of the world, as if the earth is a more difficult subject.

During my stay at the Jonesboro County Jail I tackled the mastering of the Universe. I stayed with my consistent theme, where the British Monarch rules. Therefore I used England, Great Britain, and the United Kingdom. I began with Great Britain. I gave all the darkness and black in the Universe the distinction of Great Britain Great Britain will stretch as far as the darkness travels, so as one travels through space they travel through Great Britain. The title of England would encompass the same island it does currently on earth, the same island housing the Throne. To cap things off I used the United Kingdome as a tool to unify any Universes or test cell we may encounter as we travel through space and the unknown with another Universe or test tank.

I played some cards with the young bucks I sleep near. They played a game called Spades. I picked up the game easily. It is a simplified version of High Low Jack I know. I made an attempt to teach High Low Jack, but it was shot down quickly. After playing cards while laying in my bunk I wondered the last time playing cards where changed or how whom ever came up with the spade, diamonds, clovers, and hearts. It got me looking for an alternative deck of playing cards. Sticking with my game, I checked to see if it would be possible to put the Pope or Jew, the Messiah, and the Visroi, in a deck while keeping the king and queen. A small alteration to a deck of 52 would make this possible. The 10 would need to be occupied by one of the positions. The 10 is the only double-digit card and would go nicely with a Visroi. I lent the Ace to the Pope or Jew and suggested the Messiah replace the Jack. The funny coincidence is there are eight number cards left over to act as pawns. Theoretically one could play chess with this form of cards, but I didn't stop there. I wanted to change the symbols on the cards. I didn't even have to think when I came up with the cross as one of the symbols. Replacing the lucky clovers I found the horseshoe to be a good exchange. The next two symbols where not as easy. I had guns and bullets run through my mind before settling on a hatchet or tomahawk. My final mark for my cards would be difficult, but after some consideration I decided on a simple circle, dot or spot.

Some days passed and I had no word of how long I would be held. The constant grab ass between my young friends and my desire to get a better view of the television from my bed caused me to change my bunk. I went from the center of the back row to the left, all the way to the staircase, in the front row (against the cage). Again I had a top bunk, though I really wanted a bottom bunk. This move would alter my stay in more ways than one. Yes I had an unimpeded view of the TV and I had distanced myself from the antics of the younger inmates, but I found out quickly the leader of the three, the individual I had played the hand games with, became disturbing and irritating. He may have begun as a gesture of fun. I normally wedged my flip-flops under the mat at the end of the bunk, when for the first time he grabbed one of my flip-flops and slapped the bottom of one of my feet as I lay face down watching the tube. I let it pass, but began putting my flip-flops at the other end of my bunk, where my head rested.

As my stay carved further into the calendar I lost track of days. To that point two things I saw on the television surprised me. For one, an occasion where a soft-core porno graced the screen late one night and on a separate evening the prison treated us to a World Heavyweight Championship match between Lennox Lewis and Hasim Rahman. I remember being stunned when Rahman upset the champion Lewis by knocking him out.

I spent the majority of my time in my bunk resting, healing my feet and regaining strength. In addition I spent time on my mat attempting to give an honest and accurate version or scenario of how global dominance or unification could be accomplished.

My first real revelation came to me when I thought North and South America could be unified under the government of the United States of America. My logic was simple. I looked at the two continents as less powerful than a United States that governed them both. I would attempt to sell the fact the word America would be used as a preordained higher order representing both landmasses. It was destined to be by the mapmakers who established a North and South **America** and our fore fathers who elected to go with America, rather than North America or some other title when configuring the government. I view the United State as a higher order of either of the two continents.

I also could see battle lines. If unification with our friends to the North turned to blood shed, I could see the natural battle line sitting in the center of North America. The Great Lakes interrupt the countries enough that another battle between north and south could hamper progress. I would expect some type of conflict any time one government swallows up another. I expected another conflict between north and south to break out further in a time line. The obvious forces from North America may run into a South American resistance. Again I turn to Michael Irvin to be my possible hero to end the disturbance.

I also sell the fact the United States government would provide a better standard of life for the people of both continents, with free education, a strong military, better jobs and wages, protection, and higher standard for achievement, not to mention the development of athletes for sports.

Once I thought it possible to unify North and South America with little blood shed I pointed my thoughts to Africa. Africa has been laid out in such a way it I almost want to tame the Dark Continent first. The countries aren't laid out as the state in the U.S. Where the U.S. started out with smaller states in the northeast and had states grow as they traveled west, the African continent has a blend of large and small countries throughout the map. As much as I wanted to say I think dominating Africa was possible in my lifetime, I could only see state hood for maybe a third of the continent.

By this time at least two weeks had passed and I heard nothing, but at night they continued passing out medication without any mention of me. Somewhere around then I elected to make Abraham Lincoln my mental health doctor. I was after all in Illinois, the land of Lincoln. I'll follow up with something that may be shocking to some. Abraham Lincoln suffered from mental illness. Further I consider Lincoln to be one of the more tragic figures in history, even more so than Cesar or Kennedy. He lost the vast majority of elections he ran in, endured mental illness, he couldn't prevent the Civil War, once the war ended and he kept the Union together he was shot in the head. As my blemished mind considered the story of this man, I anointed him the real King of the United States Government, who arrived to over see and preserve the Union. I could see him in the distance wearing a little crown.

Whack! This time I was smacked on the ass. He took the flip-flop right off of my foot as I lay on my stomach with feet in the air. He laughed and again I let it slide.

Goliath re-entered my thoughts. This time around I made him God. I took the G in Goliath and gave him the middle name of Oliver. His last name came to me as Davidson. Use those initials and one gets G.O.D. Pushing the limits a little bit further I saw him as a leader in another world who went by G.O.D. just like earth had the trend of F.D.R., J.F.K, and L.B.J. I did notice only democrats or dummy-rats as I like to call them, found it cool to go by their initials. Going a touch further in my mind, I looked at what Apple computer was naming their computers. Last time I noticed they where up to the G.4. This led me to this theory. If Apple computers continues to name it's computers with a G followed by a dot, followed by a number they would eventually reach the G.500, which is to long a number. It would look sexier if they turned to roman numerals. That would make this computer G.D. My mind gave it a go for the little dot to be construed as an O. This would lead to a superbly designed computer, if one evolves it 496 times into the future. Creating a master computer not only with a memory, but possibly language, judgment, and logic. Our biggest fears come true. A giant computer that thinks it is God, ready to go out of control.

This intrigued me so much I went back to Goliath making a connection between God, the computer, and the presidential lettermen. I hypothesized each of those leaders was a reincarnation of a computer from a distant land with initials that mean God in a different test tank or cell. The strange thing is these guys showed up as the computer was in its' infancy. From what I know, in World War II the Germans invented the first computer to keep track of weapons, F.D.R. right on Q. Getting back to Goliath. It doesn't bode well for the character that is infamous for taking a shot to the head. I had to put the two together and say Goliath Oliver Davidson is possibly about to take on the role of J.F.K., who took a bullet to the head by an assassin, for a developed society in some other test cell out there, similar scenario of a blow to the head from David.

The toughest part of jail was loosing track of how long I was there. At the very beginning of my stay we where given the option to go to exercise and I did on occasion. We where taken to an indoor basketball court. Most of the time it was just myself and a few other dudes, sometimes just me. Once a few weeks had gone by they took us outside to a fenced in area. Once that started I was up every time. The weather had broken and spring filled the air.

I recall being outside thinking about the animal kingdom as a part of the chessboard. After all the lion is King of the Jungle and I thought it wise to include the beasts. If at any point man encountered a being that wouldn't make any concessions in language, I would recommend bringing the King to talk to. The lion also says something I can't understand, but I know I'd loose the argument.

Continuing I did put together a Kingdom for the lion on the board. I gave the tiger the position of rook; the cheetah appears to make a nice bishop in my mind, while the panther could iron things down as a knight. I continued this process with the entire animal kingdom. The lion is King and I selected the long and elegant giraffe as queen. I believe the turtle was my selection as bishop, the gorilla makes for a knight, and the elephant would round out the field as rook.

There where chess pieces and a board in the cell block, but the game was lost on the criminal mind. Which leads me to another concept dealing with jail and education. Military schools are an option in educating ones child, but there is a price tag to such a decision. Having been in jail for what had to be close to a month, my opinion of jail had changed. Even with the fight from my first cellblock and the bullying I began to encounter in this cellblock, I considered jail to be an all right place. This led me to a concept where a child could be left at a jail school from the ages of 5 to 18. The government would provide the education. The government has to build schools anyhow. Just lock up the little trouble makers while there young. As far as being afraid to leave a child over night, again a military school shares the similar burden of looking after the students at night. My philosophy begins to differ with an academy from there. The kids would be separate by age and the same loose, hanging out all day, answer to no body atmosphere a prison cellblock has would remain. There would be no forcing of anyone to pay attention if they chose not to. Following that, a teach, in fact the thought of a different teacher each day entered my process, would teach the same thing every day, so as to drill it into the young minds. I do mean the same thing day after day. A teacher would have more time to cover the whole lesson and I believe there are important things one should be exposed to and there are other things that are forgotten before a kid even reaches his house to study. I honestly can't remember and just plain haven't come across at leased 80 to 90 percent of all the stuff I've been exposed to. I really do think the same thing taught day after day by an enthusiastic fresh new professor each day would seep into the minds of these students. Each age group would face different information. As far as the teachers, I would hope some of the parents would like to teach for a day and as the students graduated they may choose to come back and teach for a day. This would cut the cost of teachers. Books would be supplied. I also have to introduce athletic teams to the developing young people. I thought these kids could have an upper hand in athletics just because they came from a 'tough' Jail School. I'll end by stating a jail student could be pulled out of the program whenever their parents deemed necessary.

    Standing in the common area, it came again. A slap on the ass, this time he used one of his own flip-flops. I was steamed and wanted to have it out, but as I rushed down the stairs behind him one of my flip-flops came off. After retrieving my footwear I had calmed, but planned retaliation for this behavior. When he went to rest in his lower bunk, I went up to him and slapped him in the face. To my surprise he stayed in bed with no response. Another morning I woke up with shaving cream on my face. I knew who did it, but couldn't be sure, so I just washed it off. I luckily wasn't being roughed up just annoyed by the childish antics.

    A more pleasant moment in my stay saw me draw a portrait for one of the prisoners. I don't recall how he came to me for the portrait. The only other thing I had drawn was an anchor, which was early in my stay. I would guess he was asking every one if they could draw, trying to get a hit. Well he found me and I accepted his request.

    It didn't take long. I had lots of time anyway. It came out rather well and he was happy. He had found me playing cards, something I was doing more and more of at night to kill the time.

I may be guilty of attempting to seize the position of Messiah and I've witnessed the title in any thing from rock songs, religious speech, to the bible, with an almost desperate cry for someone to fill the void. On this pilgrimage I always had an answer to combat any thoughts of doubt, but there was something crucial to the position I had to address. I didn't know how to spell Messiah, so I tried to sound it out and make a game of it. I knew it started with an M, but the next few letters kind of played there way to my final version. I can recall I wanted the silent 'j' like the Ba*j*a California enunciation. At the time the Baja also looked like a descent state to add to the Union. Back to the topic, the aja portion of Baja would anchor the center of this title. I gave an indication of where I came from using Mass as in Massachusetts the State bordering Rhode Island to the north and east, giving me Massajah. I would add an 'h' to the end, because I did know the original spelling did end with an 'h'. That gave me Massajah. I particularly enjoy the two ss's and three a's. I realize I'll get grief from some, but when they're the Massajah they can spell it the way they want. I thought this might be a good way for one Massajah to differentiate one from another. With this finished spelling off Massajah I remembered the pawns or knights as I renamed them to demonstrate and indicate the position that put the Kingdom in order. With that I named the original eight pawn positions Messiah's. Same title different spelling for the people who would say I spelled Massajah wrong.

I was now doing time. I don't know what the hold up was, but I had to have been incarcerated for three weeks or more and I had heard nothing. Time was my issue and I began to look at the time barrier earth had just past through. The new Millennium had arrived now without debate. I recall some individuals pointing at the New Years of 2000, while others held out for 2001. At that time both had passed and we where all now in the future. Some of my thoughts coming up as we passed through the deadline without any mishaps like Y2K. I had put a lot of mental energy as we approached a big checkpoint looking for a possible black president and a possible woman president. I felt I answer the call if anyone cares to know J.T. Watts as the possible first black president. He even sounds right in my mind as a Republican Representative from Okalahoma. As far as a woman president the best

I could do was Christie Todd Whitman the Republican Governor of New Jersey.

I also included in this year 2000 check up on earth was well under the deadline when it came to leaving earth for the very first time in recorded history. Looking at it differently we may have just snuck under before the number. We would have been well under the mark if manned space flight took place in the 1600's, clearing the bar by 400 years. While earth had the clock run well into the 1900's. 40 years isn't long when considering the time man has occupied earth.

Another topic I know others where curious about was what to call the first decade of the new Millennium, for instance the 30's, 40's, and 50's. After toying with this question I was able to come up with a solution for this new decade. I believe the new decade should run into the next by two years enabling us to call the decade plus two either 'the first dozen' or 'the early dozen'. This would allow the teens to naturally follow the 'down dozen'.

Our president over the 2000 thresh hold was Bill Clinton. I'll state I'm no fan of Bill. His presidency was rocked by a scandal with an intern 25 to 30 years his junior. To be honest I only hope I'm still getting girls in that age when I'm in my 50's or hopefully older. There where also other examples of his infidelity, which leads me to this. Bill likes his women and I hope not too much. All I'm going to do is put together a true sentence concerning Clinton. "Bill Clinton is caught between the Bush's." There was George Herbert Walker Bush before Clinton and George W. Bush following Bill. In my mind this tells me Bill is going to have to face some one in his next life to answer to. It wouldn't be that bad if he hadn't boldly faced the country and lied about his relationship. Why would he lie, does he have some past and future lives to worry about.

Only because the topic of Mr. Clinton has come up, I am going to sling some mud his way. "It's the economy stupid." This was the president's mantra for his presidency and maybe legacy? Well stupid is as stupid does. I hate to fill people in, but any president could have sat in Washington in the 90's and looked over a robust economy. Bill was the beneficiary of several inventions and advancements in technology.

Maybe I wasn't listening or paying close enough attention, because I have no memory of the Clinton administration directing a huge number of people to buy a computer. Computers are the wave of the future and Bill didn't invent the computer, at least not that I know of. I give props to another Bill, Bill Gates for fueling the computer boom. All those people buying all those computers may have had a small impact on the economy, because "it's the economy stupid." Continuing: all those dot com stocks pushing the bull market. At least his V.P. Al Gore *admits* to inventing the inter net. "It's the economy stupid." Without Clinton the dot com boom surely would have never got off the ground, fore he lead the dot comers showing them there way onto Wall St. A cell phone is kind of fun. You talk into it like a telephone, but it has no cord so it can be carried anywhere. I know of a whole lot of people who invested money into the cell phone, which isn't a one-sale deal. One also has to purchase a plan and pay minutes each month. I like the cell phone because it reminds me of Star Trek and captain Kirk pulling out his cell phone to state, "Beam me up Scottie". Another invention provided by Bill Clinton. Again the DVD player took off. It's kind of like the VCR, but more futuristic. The Disks are like my CD's, but plays movies instead of songs. I can't remember anyone buying into that until Bill gave the go. My final, "it's the economy stupid" advancement was the SUV. People love their SUV's. Maybe Mr. Clinton bought an SUV that turned the economy on. I guess William Jefferson Clinton was lucky to sit in the Oval Office during an exiting time of discovery and invention. Just don't tell me "it's the economy stupid" when people where investing in the future, not skirt chasing.

My birthday passed and I was no longer the 27-year-old genius who changed the world, but I continued to imagine the globe and different thoughts on how to peacefully unite earth, fully knowing I couldn't make everyone happy. It wasn't until I began looking through history for Massajahs who never realized or matured into the position. George Washington was the first leader I considered and posed the question why a President and not a Massajah for the leader of this new government. I did wonder if the thought ever entered the legends mind. I do believe Abraham Lincoln would make a fine Massajah, if only he where given the opportunity to contemplate a next step for the government. I looked at the Russian leader Nikolai Lenin, whose strokes may have kept him from a larger system of government. The great Michelangelo or DiVinci where so talented if they where championed by the government as Massajah's I'm pretty sure people would have accepted it. Napoleon is a pretty good example of a man looking for a unified government. Kublai Kan conquered the majority of Asia and may have ruled over the largest area of land in recorded history, a definite Massajah candidate. It wasn't until I considered a president, a democrat even, who I respect a great deal. In fact Woodrow Wilson was the very first leader to lay out a plan or system to govern for the entire planet. His League of Nations was the first global unification plan. This struck me so deeply I resurrected the League of Nations. When analyzing the environment of the planet to be dealt with, a combination of a land and water, I found the United States governments' best plan to tame earth would be the League of Nations. This combination of land and water lead me to slightly modify the plan to Leagues and Nations. Leagues would represent the oceans and water while Nations would deal with land.

I had no maps or even anything to write on, but I proceeded to fill my imagination with the images of the planet I was exposed to in my years of education. My ability to create art and its visualization process, allowed me to produce artistically accurate fantasy to work from. The North American continent, specifically the United States, would grace my mental easel the majority of the time, as the familiarity with my country of origin was greater than with other parts of earth. Though I do believe the images of the rest of the globe where well represented in my mental gallery.

It baffled when I actually began to think it over, there have been so few, if any, attempt to bring earth together, when everything has already been laid out and agreed upon. The current maps of the planet represents the boards shared by the vast majority of governments. Few boundary disputes have yet to be settled. The imaginary lines are on display for all to see. The biggest problem I see, with the exclusion of language barriers, would be all the different titles given to the head of each country or nation.

I chose to work with the Nations label, in the Leagues and Nations, first. Asking myself what separates a government from being a Country or a Nation? I've heard them used as interchangeable terms and it is here I'll make my first modification or judgment. In my quest to satisfy the entire population of earth I considered an entire continent to be considered a Country when the body of land is recognized and a leader is established for such a Country. Remember a Country would be an established continental government. As for a Nation, they would represent major cogs in a level currently established through out the Globe, but only the most productive and powerful Nations appeared in my thoughts. To give an even dispersion of control through each Country I followed up something I had noticed the continents had in common. Using first a North American Country, generally speaking three governments occupy the land. Mexico, Canada, and the United States. I quickly turned the thought to Asia where three Nations grabbed my attention quickly. China, India, and Russia make up the majority of Asia and I would note the potential Nations. Moving to South America I was able to see, again three Nations to govern the Country. They are Chile, Argentina, and Brazil. Once I had made it this far I turned to Africa fully aware the Country had a sprinkling of sizes and power to the landscape. I made the decision to put an almost perpendicular shape in the heart of Africa to establish three make shift Nations. Australia was given the same treatment, but in two vertical borders providing the magic number of three Nations. I fully anticipate the previous two Countries want to establish their own three Nations, but at the time I had nothing better than my imagination to hypothesis. Finally Europe. It was difficult to select three Nations, because they are so many Nations rich with culture. I eliminated Italy only because the Pope already takes up residency. Nation one would be England, with the German Nation, and Nation of Greece to follow. Spain and France where on the map, but find leadership under the English Nation. What I will call States – Peru, Japan, Italy and others– which fell short of becoming a Nation will reside under the protective umbrella of one of the three Nations found in each Country (continent).

On the other hand I established Leagues over the water covering the planet. As a Nation was made up of three parts, I stuck with the theme and 'equal' sharing of control with the plan of three Leagues for each ocean. Being aware of longitudinal and latitudinal line, I through symbolic lines on my minds oceans to give ideas of how to regulate the water. The water really didn't have much to consider, but I found States for the oceans. Each block in the latitudinal and longitudinal grid would form a State. With the larger landmasses running the big show, I take the bold move of adding the rest of the contestants for

Nationhood to Statehood. This should by no means cheapen the history or society created by one of these newly found States and I make a move those hundreds of leaders may enjoy. While working I couldn't help but attach positions and titles to the pecking order.

I began moving the titles of Prime Minister and President from the level of Nation and Country. Something jammed in my head offering a new title for the ruler of a nation. It was hard to take the President off the level of Nation the current Union had amounted to, but Indian Nation grabbed my attention as well as the Commander and Chief title. With a tribute to the Indians I would call upon a Chief to run each Nation. The Prime Minister shot up to the level of Country, while I reluctantly, but in the same token delegated the title of President to find a State to run. It troubled me to give this title a State, but I envisioned this position in the United States government to become more youthful and take on the roles of a kick ass fighting force. When all the Presidents are called to action all levels of the Leagues of Nations should beware, as they are the only common thread on land or sea.

Again block of the grid covering the oceans would also be a State with a President. As far as each League I found most of our current sports leagues to be run by a Commissioner, so I went with it and gave each League a Commissioner. Each ocean was now hungry for a leader and a Mariner sounded like he could emerge from the high seas.

This was the easy part, providing the local levels consumed much thought. Keeping an equal amount of levels of government for both land and water was difficult, considering the Leagues had no rulers or established boundaries.

Again, I was smacked with my flip-flop, but this time I went after him. I got in his face giving him a shove or two and he may have shoved back, but I let him know he wasn't funny. After that he stopped harassing me.

The presents dented filled my thought, again and again until I made the connection. My question of why George Washington didn't pronounce himself a Messiah after breaking the British was getting a response. The answer to the question was being received clearly. The present is dented as in the President...present dent... Washington and the founding fathers where unable at the time to establish the United States government through North America because they where not getting or receiving the whole plan. I don't have the last clue of when the title President was introduce, but my mind told me Washington and the others coined it, as a sign to the future. The present is dented and there is more to come.

I made another connection I was being held in an official United States government facility. I then took the position the directions for the next stage of United States government could be focused directly on the Jonesboro County Jail for me to attempt to decipher.

Reconnecting with the Presidents of the United States who would be a head of an individual State. Three Chief's one for each Nation occupies a Country, which encompasses a continent. A Prime Minister is a Countries or continents best man. With States being the common theme on land and water, a plunge into a League, which also comes in three, has a Commissioner for each of the three Leagues. Once in the ocean the presents of States unify the globe, as the Mariner of an ocean controls the salt water.

I spent a lot of thought on a tear of government I found to be important to the co-existence of all governments. I never liked the uneven distribution of the size from one State to State to another in the U.S. Also carrying a factor would be the presence of an experiment in government. After deliberating back and for I finally gave a new level of government the Territory. Region was a thought, but is to commonplace when divvying up land. Again due to my familiarity with my home country I proceeded to make Territories. I had a group of States tagged the Original 13 States for the east coast, which would introduce a number into a governmental experiment. The west coast had me thinking of the Red Wood States. The 49er States may also look O.K. The Mississippi State could produce a line of states through the center of the Nation. I saw the Blue Grass Sates down South. The Plain States would be considered for the heartland, even better the Heartland States. There are states hugging the lakes in the Great Lake States. I hope it is obvious I attempted to give creative names with some numbers and some colors to the mix. Again all I had where mental maps to conquer, but allow me to embellish on the Territories, I had put a Primer in charge of, as I have looked at a map and made some lines. As much as I liked the Original 13 States, the Appellation States lend themselves much better when making borders. The Appellation States contain: Maine, New Hampshire, Vermont,

Massachusetts, Rhode Island, Connecticut, New York, Pennsylvania, Delaware, New Jersey, West Virginia, Virginia, North Carolina, South Carolina and Georgia. These States have far more states than the other Territories, but all the Territories are relatively comparable in size, which I was going for. The Gulf States, which include Texas, Louisiana, Mississippi, Alabama, and Florida, formed when The Mississippi States conflicted in a few different ways. The Blue Grass States, I had to have, are represented by Kentucky, Tennessee, Missouri, and Arkansas. The Great Lake States Wisconsin, Michigan, Indiana, Illinois, and Ohio all make contact with one of the Lakes. The Heartland States in the center of the Nation is comprised of the Oklahoma, Kansas, Nebraska, South Dakota, North Dakota, Minnesota, and Iowa. The Big Sky States are made up of Idaho, Montana, and Wyoming. The Four Corner States lie in the southwest, getting their name by having the four states come together at one point. They consist of Arizona, New Mexico, Colorado and Utah. I enjoyed the inclusion of a number enough the 49er States would include California, Nevada, Washington and Oregon. Eight Territories make up this Nation with a Primer for each.

While thinking the Territories through, the thought of using the NCAA conferences for some of the Territories lead me to create another level simply put, Conferences. For the leader of each conference I put a Provost in charge. Each conference is already established and in my mind the NCAA is the greatest pool of thought on the planet. The past, present and future in the NCAA most probably deals with just about anything. I want the ability at my fingertips to call upon great minds to solve problems. This was easy because as I stated the Conferences are already established. The Pac Ten, the WAC, the Big 12, the SEC, and the Big Ten cover most of the Nation. Montana, Wyoming, North Dakota, and South Dakota need a Conference and the East kind of tangles up in a couple of Conferences needing some work, but shouldn't be a real problem. A possibility in response to a Conference could be a School, as in school of fish and an academic institute, for the aquatic side of the ledger. A Captain could lead a School.

Having cast Regions aside I took them off the scrap heap and tossed them into the oceans. They would mirror Territories with the exception they are on water and the other on land. Do to the fact there is really nothing established to outline this level I continue planning for the point when living beneath the ocean is more appealing and common. I also believe building beneath the sea would lend it's hand to experiments for space. A government for the ocean may also regulate vessels traveling around the Globe. I do hesitate but I place an Admiral as the head of each Region. Admiral had been in my mind since the *Presidents Casino*, where I wasn't even close to formulating the Leagues and Nations.

Local government gets a little bit more difficult as I have heard of all of the following as forms of local government: Commonwealth, Borrow, County, City, Town, Plantation and I offer comparable levels for the sea.

I experienced the term Commonwealth in Massachusetts and again in Pennsylvania. My understanding, which comes from looking at the word, means there is some kind of sharing of wealth through the area, or state. This came rather quickly on this end. I thought a Commonwealth would make a good tax collector, along with allocating money when needed, a way to keep track of wealth in wealth out. The moneyman. I liked the size of the Pennsylvania Commonwealth more than Massachusetts and recommend a Commonwealth stay in close range of that size to be distributed throughout a Country or continent. It was a no brainer when I looked at a Count as the man behind the money. I went further adding a Roman numeral to each Commonwealth to keep track of them. As an answer to a Commonwealth, a League may find what I label a Trove, as in treasure trove. They would have the same Roman numerals to anchor them down, but I wanted to have some more fun with this and I put a Pirate to look over each Trove.

Working further down to smaller jurisdictions I've come across three local level governments that seem to be close in size. The County, the Borrow, and the Plantation. First off I recognized the full state name of Rhode Island and Providence Plantations. One can also find Counties, but no Borrows in Rhody. I had a Borrow in central PA, along with a Commonwealth, which RI does not. Therefore I chose to use them all. I decided to use the Three Counties to fill each Borrow. As for a Plantation, I had Three Borrows fit into each Plantation. It sounded so good in my mind for there to be a Governor of a Plantation. The Sheriff of the County was my logical choice for a

County. As for a Borrow, my imagination was captivated by a brash young person, an All-American boy, an over achiever, who would look over Borrow. I was in stitches when the Zorro of the Borrow tackled any other contestants for this position.

A city and a town would keep their Mayor accountable, but an ocean may see a Manor and a Major for that Manor as a version of a city or town. Moving up to the level of Colony. A Commander of the Colony would put one half of the Commander and Chief in the ocean at a lower level, where the Chief was on land at a higher position. Presidents would run on the tear of State, located in between the Chief and Commander, giving him range high and low.

An Aquarium could mirror a Borrows' strength. A Scout of each Aquarium would fit the same bill as a Zorro. There would be three Aquariums in a Colony. With the last remaining entity being a Tank. Three Tanks would be arranged in an Aquarium. The leader of such would be a Poseidon.

To recap and lay things out here are the levels and their leaders:

Country – *Prime Minister*	Ocean – *Mariner*
Nation – *Chief*	League – *Commissioner*
Territory – *Primer*	Region – *Admiral*
Conference – *Provost*	School – *Captain*
States – *President*	States – *President*
Commonwealth – *Count*	Trove – *Pirate*
Plantation – *Governor*	Colony – *Commander*
Borrow – *Zorro*	Aquarium – *Scout*
County – *Sheriff*	Tank – *Poseidon*
City or Town – *Mayor*	Manor – *Major*

I neglected to divide the globe into its two hemispheres, East and West. The control of these hemispheres I gave to the Title of Emperor, but I also divided earth again, by its equator giving each half to a Kan as in Kublai Kan.

I spent no time looking for Senator and Congressman, because representation would come from a leader, as one goes up and down the power structure and they could be added later. As one goes from the group of six or seven Prime Minister, the leaders are more numerous and should represent what they are leading. The present U.S.

government almost works that way; with the major difference being a Governor of a State doesn't represent his or her State. Representatives do, but they do come from established portions of their States that they represent.

If the question of were the Massajah fits in this high arc key has come to mind, the Massajah has the power to at any time create boarders called Masses, as in a land mass or masses of people as well as Mass as in Massajah, to prevent a war from spreading past said borders, focus on a sag in a regions economy, or stomp out hunger within a Mass.

Though the Massajah lives on the planet, he is on the Kingdoms board and runs the entire government not any section. To get a better idea, I didn't stop at earth. I looked to the moon and the red planet. To me bringing a Czar back to power was an easy fit. A Czar of the moon felt good.

As far as the planet Mars, the planet which seems to be selected as the next planet to be inhabited by humans, I did some planning. I had a vision of a Mars with white stripes of light with the planets natural red surface remaining exposed as red strip in between the white. Theses strips would look like the red and white stripes on the U.S. flag. I could also see a strip of blue running around the center of Mars with white stars sitting in the blue.

As for a crewed system of government, the planet would be run by a Federate. The vote of Con-Federate or a Sans-Federate would elect a Federate of Mars. Part of my logic for this system was to promote healing in the south, which continues to shows signs of scaring. Getting back to a vote of Con-Federate or Sans-Federate. The word con in Spanish means with, so if one liked a candidate they would vote Con-Federate as a vote with or for the Federate. A voter may find they disliked candidate, therefore they would give a Sans-Federate vote against this candidates run for the Federate. Basically it is a vote down or up, but explaining further. As we just vote yes for one candidate, in this system, a voter would vote yes or no, sans or con, for a number of politicians an a vote for each candidate for that matter. The person elected would get the most Con-Federate votes, but would also carry a number of votes saying no. Maybe two or three Federates could come out of this system, to share the post. This could also be very embarrassing to see how many votes against a candidate came out.

Back to the construction of the planet Mars, I considered the white strips to be colonies I call Millenniums, as there are other words with two or more meanings like: a horn one toots and a horn on an animals head, a Millennium could now mean a passage of time or a space colony. I would number Millenniums and would leave an alley in-between each Millennium. Those alleys would be called zones. Again States would be drawn on the planet, as the consistent theme in the spreading and use of the United States government. I am suggesting States remain the unifying characters on all the planets as we progress further and further into space. That is about all I got to but I did put a Lord at the helm of Mercury. I believe at my young age I could see and perhaps over look such an undertaking over the next say 50 years. Maybe longer as modern medicine expands mans life expectancy.

I have to take a step back to the Leagues of Nations plan and bring the political parties I selected and created to go with the many different levels. The first thing I did was exclude and send the Democrats out to pasture. Their ideas are stale and they are petty when it comes down to something the Republicans want to pass. I also attempt to give enough parties that more people will get involved, as the Leagues of Nations will need more candidates.

I will begin with my party affiliation at this time, the Cool Moose party. I put together an entire level of competition for this level. The parties are as follows: the Rhino's, the Hippo's and the Loosie Goosie's. The Loosie Goosie's resemble the Cool Moose's with the over abundance of 'o's to make up their names. The Rhino's and Hippo's also carry an 'o' in their spelling. An 'o' is consistent through out this level.

I thought a level represented by only animals would get people ready for parties with a political animal. And if the Loosie Goosie party doesn't sound like fun for people with young children and gives an idea of a person that never grew up. This could be a very fun level.

To get the young adult who doesn't pay much attention to politics because they are not part of it, they aren't even on the bottom rung of the political ladder I offer three parties to choose from, the Rebel's, the Radical's, and the Revolutionary's. They are all good parties to get that angst out, make some waves, and be part of the government.

It was difficult to go through the previous parties with out including one of my favorites, but first I have to comment on the Republican. I like the Republican especially the GOP, grand old party, they've attached to themselves, but I had looked up their party in the past and noticed they define themselves as a war party. I would like to do away with such destruction. Though war is a somewhat necessary evil. Further when breaking down Republican I thought it sounded like re public again and re at the beginning of a word usually means again. I had myself doing the public over and over again, but if this is part of how the Elephant work, practice usually makes for a better production.

With the Republicans in mind I deliver the party I really enjoy for the younger crowd, a party putting one in training for the Republicans and this would be the Prepublicans. A party affiliated, but not part of the GOP.

I have thought of great things for a Freedom party, but I look at it as a feel good party at a lower to middle level. Not to say a candidate couldn't represent the Freedom Party on a National or Continental level and win. In fact any of these parties could carry a candidate to any position, but the parties should give an idea of a politicians ideology and level for competition.

Moving up to the more powerful parties. I dig up and re-establish the Federalists, the Socialists, and the Communists. I believe these parties can find a better place in a larger system.

As in my suggested Prepublican Party be a starting point for Republicans I started a chain of parties with ties to another. I begin with the Freedom party that would connect with the Federalists. As in the similarity of 'o' at the animal level, the 'F" which begins both parties spelling are a link. Following the Federalist I evolve the Federalists into the Phederalists. This change in spelling indicates not everything stays the same things evolve. For example old was once spelled 'olde'. I enjoy the fact old is in the past with a different spelling, it implies the party does consider the past before moving forward. The Rhino is picked up as the political animal at this time. Enter my Populist. The P in the Phederalist party matches that of the Populist and I introduce my combination of lion, human, and cobra. This would be the highest level of politics.

Another group whose position deserves consideration as a full-fledged party are the Humanitarians. The people who monitor the human condition through out the globe would represent this party. I could see Humanitarian issues swing votes quickly.

My final Party would be the Ruling Party. I project them at a high level. It wouldn't be a bad idea to put some kind of rules together to form some kind of up dated document to supply proper conduct in today's global community.

To give an idea of the parties and the level they should represent:

Humanitarians   Populist

Republican Communist Socialist Ruling Phederalist Federalist

Cool Moose Loosie Goosie Hippo Rhino

Prepublican   Rebel   Radical Revolutionary Freedom

Once I came up with more parties for the United States government I began to change the names of the continents indicating the mastering of the planet. This came to me as a game. Somehow the rules made mention: only a failed businesses letters could spell out the names to represent the seven continents. I had one. My Meadows Design was a registered business never getting off, so I proceeded to tackle the globe.

My first and most patriotic came from the W in Meadows. I again began with the place I was most familiar. The North American Country would dawn the name Washington for Washington D.C. and the State of Washington where not enough. To South America and the 'a' in Meadows to observe the title of Amazonia from its Amazon River. Asia would find the Orient as in 'o' as a new residence. As far as Australia, I used the islands sprinkled across its northern edge. The Easter Islands would take an 'e' as Australia would become Easter. Europe was difficult, but I settled with 'm' for Mediterranea after the Mediterranean Sea. Africa would take the 's' in Meadows make its desert even grander as the Dark Continent would be considered Sahara. The remaining letter of 'd' would make Antarctica the Devil's Hand.

From there I renamed the earth. I wasn't very creative and we already use this when speaking about the planet. I thought a natural fit would be planet Global as in a globe and global economy. Not stopping there I looked at Mars and did my best to throw a name on that planet. Using the same logic as Global, I deduced there are models of Mars and found the name Model would continue the theme.

While giving these two planets a new identity, my logic handled the issue of what would happen if we encountered beings from space? It made perfect sense to me for our planet to direct such visitors to colonize one of the other uninhabited planets in our galaxy. The fact they had the technology to travel into our world would demonstrate the presents of a higher intelligence and ability to share, from a safe distance, their cultures, advanced technologies and peaceful willingness to participate in the mastering of our Universe.

Staying focused on beings from other worlds, I don't see how, in this day and age, when humans are in space, doubters struggle with the belief of intelligent life out there. I'd like to point out we share our planet with thousands of different animal species and would like to suggest 'space aliens' will more than likely take on the characteristics of another species of animal.

I admit I don't believe we will encounter a sophisticated being while exploring space. Rather I would lend my theory; we will come across small insect forms of life at the beginning gradually work up to more sophisticated alien species.

Jail for the most part is a grind with the same old faces and routines, but I consider it worth mentioning I created an image while in prison. I styled a look making me one of them. When I shaved I carved in a few man chew style mustache, Hulk Hogan type, into my face. I also sported some heavy sideburns, chops. I would run the razor with one stroke down my cheek in between the mustache and the chops. My hair was at a long length, as well. I thought my look to be appropriate for an inmate who had been incarcerated for a month or more at this time.

I, again, spent most of my time on my top bunk, where the thought, games and images flowing and intoxicated my mind like wine at a bacchanal. My Oakland Raiders kept me drunk with movies. It resembled the game where the actor Kevin Bacon is used to connect with any actor buy connecting him with an actor in a movie Bacon was in. That actor is then used in another movie to connect with the next actor to connect with another actor in another movie. I believe this is accomplished with six actors or movies. The game is called the Six degrees of Kevin Bacon. It may be five or seven degrees I never really thought it out.

With this logic I offer Darth Raider, Darth Vader who attends Raiders games. One may find other movie characters in the stands on a football Sunday in Oakland, perhaps the Alien from the *Alien* movies, or the Predator from the *Predator* Films. At this time I embarked on a game to create a greater film fan base for the Raiders. The rules where simple: for a movie to be selected it had to be made up of a collection of at least three movies, they had to have a dark Raider quality, and I would have to use an actor from one movie who appeared in one of the other movies, but an actor wouldn't have to be in all three or more films to be used.

I will start with the Star Wars movies and use Harrison Ford to connect with the *Raiders of the lost Arch* films. I connect with the *James Bond* films using the original Bond Sean Cannery who was in one of the *Raiders of the lost Arch* movie, maybe the third, as Indies father. Returning to the *Bond* productions, Christopher Wilkins appeared in *View to a Kill* and gives a performance in one of the *Batman* film. Selecting Arnold Swartznagger, as Freeze, from the *Batman* films he appeared in the first *Predator*. In the first *Predator* show one can select Carl Weathers who played Apollo Creed in the *Rocky* works. Sylvester Stelone stared in almost all the *Rocky* fights and can connect with the *Rambo* family of films. Stepping back to the *Rocky* movies, Rocky's wife was also the sister of Sunny and Michael Colion in the *Godfather* epics. Revisiting the *Predator* movies, at the time I wasn't able to use them because there where only two movies, but as I write I have the knowledge of a third *Predator* movie, which pits the *Predator* against the Alien in *Predator vs. Alien*. This movie allows me to add both the *Predator* films, but also the *Alien* movies. Using the Predator movies once again, one can find Danny Glover in the second show. Danny was Mel Gibson partner in the *Lethal Weapon* features, allowing the *Lethal Weapons* to be added. My final entry is Mel Gibson in the *Mad Max* creations. As a review I will list all the films from this exercise: *Star Wars, Raiders of the lost Arch, James Bond, Batman, Predator, Rocky, Rambo, Alien, Lethal Weapon and Mad Max.*

When I came across the Bond Movies, I thought it would be great if as the Massajah, I could show up as a character in the Bond films pointing out the correct directions for James. From there this took on a whole other life. I made it part of the job as Massajah to appear in as many movies as possible. I envisioned a cameo type appearance, just a common link in the film world.

I didn't keep track, but a good month or so had passed. I began playing a card game I had learned at Penn State at night. The game involves creating kingdoms with the Ace, King, Queen and Jack making a suited Kingdom. I would read the cards to tell a story, like taro cards. A diamond would indicate money, the spade war, the clover luck and the heart love.

I considered the topic of same sex marriages. I came to the conclusion if the people getting married didn't have sex with one another it may be a good thing. I could see marrying a good friend, one who would know there could be something wrong if they didn't see or hear from the other. That person would know something may be wrong and look for the partner. I could see creating all kinds of mischief a partner could help one out of. In fact graduates of the jail school may need such a kind of relationship, someone to lean on, to get them started and out of troublesome positions. My final thought was same sex or same gender marriage may be better than marriage between man and women.

Then one day between 40 and 50 days, it happened. As sudden as that, I was told to gather my things. The judge would see me. They put me back into my street clothes and got me to the Court. I don't recall what the judge told me, but I was released.

CHAPTER 19

After being released an officer gave me a ride, but he didn't take me back to Anna, where I committed my crime. For some unknown reason he took me to Carbondale. The exact part of the college town I was set free in is a distant memory, but I recall walking around the now familiar streets. I was back in the same position I was in over a month ago. After spending some time doing time I can see how some people keep pushing the limits of the law. In jail your somewhat taken care of, meals and housing are supplied. Some individuals may not have such a guarantee. Though the daily captivity and the same surroundings can get to a person.

I formulated a plan to try and collect some money. I felt I could go door to door asking for contributions to help stop homelessness. It would be the truth, even if the money would help me personally. I went into a grocery store close by to see if I could get an unwanted empty cup or can to use in my newly found philanthropic endeavor. I even came up with a saying, "You don't know how much difference you can make until you get off your *can*."

I walked through the market searching for a free container to collect with. While passing by the coffee bean dispensers I spotted bags to put the coffee in. I grabbed one, looked around with a little less focus before leaving the store with my coffee bag. I turned the bag inside out hiding the graphics on the inside and exposing the white interior. I was now ready for the next day.

Night had put the day to sleep and I was hanging out in the general area of the grocery store I had found the bag in. I sat on a rock wall across from the store enjoying the fresh spring air and watching the cars go by until it was late enough for a passing car to have no company and the street to itself. I had also settled in across from a *Blockbuster Video*. I noticed there was a bicycle parked in front of the *Blockbuster* and it was awfully late for a person on a bike to be peddling around. In fact I believe the *Blockbuster* was closed.

I waited a little while longer, waiting for someone to claim the bike, until I decided it was a '*Blockbuster* night'. I made my way down the slope I had perched upon directly to the bicycle. I stepped up to the vehicle, pulled it from the bike rack and took off down the street. It was a mountain bike having to be five or more years in age, a bit closer to or more.

I pedaled around in that vicinity to see if anyone would come out to claim the two-wheeler. No one appeared, so I traveled down the road to an empty parking lot. I did some circles around the lot before a *Denny's* caught my eye. I hadn't had anything to eat on this day making a chew and screw, which I had perfected, in order. I cruised on down to the *Denny's* ordered, ate, and left, hopping on the bike and taking-off.

As I distanced myself from the restaurant I made a joke to myself that kept going on. I told myself, 'I8'. I then went on to, 'I8B4'. I ran this through my mind a few times before adding, 'I8B42'. These messages put a smile to my face. My final line was, 'U8B42'. This grabbed my attention for a good period of time as I pulled into some kind of park with picnic tables under a roof. I parked the bike laid down on one of the tables and fell asleep.

The morning flooded southern Illinois with a bright and warm sun. I was back on the bike riding up and down the streets, preparing what to say when I went door to door. I was stuck between two. One of them I would say I was collecting for the church to help stop the homeless problem, while the other one would say I was collecting for the Chi Phi Fraternity to help stop homelessness.

Once I felt it was late enough in the day I pedaled out into what looked to be a pretty affluent neighborhood. I started with the church as my supporter and collected some change. Roughly five to six houses into my collecting a man interrupted. He drove by and told me to get out of the neighborhood or he would call the cops. I listen to the man's threat, but thought it would be O.K. if I stopped at the houses on the way out.

The next thing I know a police car pulls up and asked what I was doing, what my name was…etc. As the officer ran me the drill, a woman from the neighborhood drove by and contributed $20. The officer kindly told me to leave the neighborhood and let me go. The cop then pulled away and I pedaled back into town.

There was a pizza place, *Godfather Pizza*, in Carbondale advertising on their sign a pizza buffet for X amount of dollars of which I now had. I took my twenty plus dollars to the pizza place and ate until I couldn't eat anymore. I felt good to be able to pay the tab. I paid then took the bike for a spin around the city of Carbondale as I made plans to head to the University of Indiana and the Chi Phi chapter at the school. I would be able to travel at a much greater rate with the bike.

The sun had begun to set as I began riding westward, at an easy clip to maintain. I pedaled and pedaled into the night hours. The most difficult part of the riding was the lack of lighting and the repetitive motion of pedaling which became hypnotic. The motion became so hypnotic I must have been sleep pedaling like sleep walking, because I was awaken on the bike in the middle of the road by a Mack trucks horn. As the truck beard down on me I casually turned the handlebars making my way to the side of the road. I can't begin to explain the lack of feeling I had when I turned to the side of the road. I was numb. There was no shock just a motion to the side of the road as a huge truck let me know I was still on the bike in the center of the road, I was out. I could have fallen of the bike injured myself in the center of the road and hit by the truck or if he didn't see me in the road he could have killed me. That was definitely the closest I had been to death on this entire pilgrimage.

I was scared straight once I had time to register what happened. Riding a little further into the night I came across a *Home Depot*. I saw the collection of sheds on display in the front of the store thinking I may be able to find shelter. I parked the bike in the back of one of the sheds and lay down in side the shed for a nights rest.

The following morning I was awaken abruptly by a *Home Depot* employee. I know I scared him by his reaction. He went running off to get someone else. I was also startled, but made it to my feet quickly grabbing the bike and pedaling off. I believe I woke up in the town of Marion that morning.

I chose to ride on the back roads away from high traffic. As midday presented itself with a high sun, I stopped at a convenient store to get a few things to eat with the left over money I had. I bought a bag of bagels, peanut butter and a big jug of lemonade. I sat and ate on the side of the store, filling up with what I was able to buy.

From there I took off headed for the next town. I took the jug of lemonade with me. I dropped it once, but most of the liquid stayed in the container. I remember seeing the next town as I rolled further and further. I could see it from a distance, but when I arrived there wasn't much there, so I continued riding. As I moved along a strange theory crossed my mind. If humans had ever received communications with an alien, how would size or a measurement be established when measurements are relative? For instance alien life may understand the break down of an inch and a foot as far as how many lines make up what, but there foot could be the size of one of our yards or smaller than our inch. It was then I looked back at all I had endured and came up with the theory I was being used to size the planet. I had traveled by, boat (Block Island Ferry), plane to Venezuela, train to Missouri, bus to Penn State and South Carolina, swimming in Venezuela and walking all around. I put belief in the notion I was being used as a barometer to scale the planet in an experiment being run by several different cell or test Universes interested in the human life form and the properties of our planet. I thought this was being done through the amount of time it took to travel X distance at Y speed as well as the rate my heart pumped to size humans.

There was another experiment my troubled mind concocted. I was now traveling through a state with a Big Ten School in it, the University of Illinois, and I had traveled primarily in Big Ten Country with the exception of my stay in Missouri. Excluding Missouri from this exercise and perhaps my visit there was only to cross the threshold to the west in a different experiment. I began to put together a *Wizard of Oz* for the Big Ten mascots. Of course I'll begin with the obvious representative as the Lion, the Nittany Lion from my Penn State. As for the Tin man, the Purdue Boilermaker was an easy choice. Casting the Scarecrow was a little more difficult. I was stuck choosing between the Spartan of Michigan State and Chief Illinowek of the University of Illinois. After some debate I elected to go with Chief Illinowek. For Dorothy I went with a Hoosier from Indiana University, in which I was targeting a visit. I even went as far as to make the Michigan Wolverine Toto. For the Wizard, the nut, a Buckeye, at the University of Ohio State would fill the spot in my fantasy. What I deducted from this experiment was Chief Illinowek, the Scarecrow, may have a hatchet, but the only character in the Wizard of Oz was the Tin man, Boilermaker carried an ax. From this I gathered the Tin man stole the Scarecrows ax, which may explain how Oz got so out of whack.

I continued traveling coming up to a good pitch in the road. It was a tough climb and as I pumped my legs with more and more strength, I could see lightening in the distance and the skies threatening. I climbed the hill, which seemed to go on and on until I found the summit. The sky grew darker as I continued to hope it would be a quick afternoon thunderstorm. Good fortune then produced a haven. A canopy at a park was in my reach. Just as I made my way under the shelter the heavens opened and the rain and lightening began pounding down. I flipped some of the picnic tables on there sides to block the rain.

While I weathered the storm a police car pulled up and offered a helping hand and I took it. We got the bike and put it in the trunk. He took me back to the police station. At the station the officers were nice enough to give me something to eat. Since I was in a police station I gave them my Marcus Allen O.J. Simpson theory, of which I got no response. Once the time had passed I was given a mat to lay down on in one of the rooms with a window for visitors, so I could sleep.

The next morning I was treated to some food and sent on my way. The only bad thing about this experience was I had to backtrack the long stretch of road from the police station to the point I had advanced in the previous day. I mounted the bike and took on the hill for a second time. I traveled down back roads for miles and miles until dusk when I arrived in Franklin. I road up and down the strip a few times noticing a *Pizza Hut* I could eat at. Again, I was out of money, but knew I could eat and get out without paying. I parked the bike a few blocks away so they wouldn't know I was on bike when I left.

My waitress was the prettiest young thing. I wanted to tell her what I was up to. Maybe she could help me, but I didn't. I ordered the spaghetti, something that probably doesn't happen to often at *Pizza Hut*. After eating I visited the restroom thinking this could be a good B-line out of the building. When I came out the girls working there where waiting for me to pay my bill because they where closing. I just kept walking to the door, which was locked when I got to it, but they had left the key in the dead bolt, so I turned the key and let myself out. I ran down the back road to the bike then hopped on making my way to a large parking lot.

I proceeded to do the bike tricks that I knew as a boy. I road some wheelies and did some bunny hops. It was also at this time, for the first time, I considered the other Massajah to be a women like a queen of government. I tagged the position as the Massajahess. I liked the idea of a women holding such a high position, demonstrating the advances women have made. I was now in search of the Massajahess. This lasted for a few hours before I took off into what had to be the morning hours of the night.

I stopped at a VFW on my way for some rest. Again I lay on a picnic table, but found little shuteye, due to the passing cars. When sunlight filled the sky I got back on the bike and road eastward. That morning I encountered a dog. The dog would chase me and I would slow down when he began to slow. I played this game back and forth with the dog for a stretch of three to four miles before he finally quit chasing.

As I road further I got rid of my shoes, leaving them on the side of the road. I was also looking into back yard for clothes on the line, but encountered none. I pulled into a small town not far from where I through my shoes to the curb. I stopped at a *McDonalds* drive through asking for any food they may be throwing out, but they offered none. I then took myself across the street to a super market where I was dodging the morning raindrops under the overhang of the building. That's when a pear of men came from the market. They had there lunch in hand in Styrofoam containers. One of them sparked up a conversation with me. I gave him my story and he gave me his lunch. It was chicken and rice. He not only did this, but he went back to his house and brought me a pear of jeans, a pear of shoes and a Desert Storm shirt/coat. I was more than thankful and started back down the road, as he had left.

I continued my riding until I came to the town of Carmi. Once I was in the town I stopped at a convenient store where I chose to beg for a ride, as I had vowed not to beg for change or hitch for a ride, I combined the two. A couple was more than willing and asked where I was going and I told them Bloomington, Indiana. They told me they would get me to Evansville, Indiana and try to get me a ride from there.

AN AMERICAN MESSIAH

When we arrived in Evansville the people who helped me went to a church to see if they would buy me a bus ticket to the University of Indiana. The woman running the church took me to the bus station and paid for a ticket to Bloomington. In no time I was on the bus to the University of Indiana.

There where several stops in Indiana on the way to Bloomington. I napped throw the majority of the ride. After a couple of hours my stop at the University of Indiana came up and I got off the bus. As usual I found myself wondering aimlessly attempting to reach a destination. I found my way up one end of campus. Entering into the vicinity of the University wearing the Desert Storm garment was an honor and also symbolic of the long dragged out battle I had endured over the past several months. I felt as if my mission had been given to me when I enlisted in the National Guard back in 1997 and was finally coming to an end.

As I said it was an honor to wear the top of the Desert Storm uniform, but at the same time I couldn't keep wearing something I wasn't a part of. When I went to freshen up in an Italian restaurant's restroom I hung the garment up and left it there. From there I asked around where I could find the Chi Phi Fraternity. I began by walking down a strip of Fraternities. Like Penn State they had a good number of houses. I had to ask again for the Chi Phi house, because I couldn't find it on the strip. Finally someone was able to give me the directions to the house.

It was a descent house, but of course, I held the Penn State Chapter as the better of the two. I was greeted with a worm enough reception. The brothers who where staying at the house for the summer where eager to see how they could help me. I didn't really give them a direct answer of how they could help, but they showed me to their TV room. They showed an interest in me for a while but left me alone to relax.

After a short nap I headed out to see if I could find something to eat. Not to look a gift horse in the mouth, but the shoes I had received from the kind gentleman who also gave me the Desert Storm garment and jeans, where to small and full of foot powder. Once I came across a shopping district supporting by the University I spotted a *Target* store. I had my mind set on one thing and was to get a pear of shoes. I even took off the pear of shoes I had, so no evidence would be left behind. I entered the *Target* with no shoes on. It took me a few minutes before I located the shoe section. The wide selection of sandals captured my attention and I gravitated to a pear. I broke the thin plastic thread holding them in a pear. I put the sandals on and commenced upon a stroll around the store to see if anyone noticed. I walked a big loop around the store before starting toward the door. There was a young lady making her way to the door and for the first time I was looking at a woman as a Massajahess. My mind was telling me she was a diversion as I headed for the door maybe five yards behind. I escaped through the door and lost track of her on the way. I continued walking through the parking lot without a poseur, I was sure I got away with it once I was a good distance from the store.

I by past diner and bumped into the football stadium, which was in a fear proximity to the Chi Phi. I walked around the structure looking to get in. After considering hopping a high fence I continued around the stadium. I was able to locate a garage door that wasn't closed all the way, open maybe two feet. I was able to make my way under the door to gain entrance. Once I navigated through the stadium I was able to occupy one of the bleacher seats. I sat for a while wondering if I could still play football. I knew I hadn't used up any of my eligibility and made note Chris Wenky won the Heisman Trophy at Florida State University, I believe at the age of 24. As I sat what had to be a player popped into the stadium and began running the stairs. I had to respect the fact he was putting in extra work. I left before he did.

It was night at this time, how late I couldn't quite say. Again I wandered aimlessly exploring the Bloomington and University territory. Even at this early stage of my stay I was able to determine one side of campus from the other. That early evening I found my way to a bar, the *Upstairs*. I made my way up the stairs and found the bar was mostly empty, but there where two girls playing dart. I hadn't had much time to think about girls. I engaged in conversation with the two. The conversation was little and they ended up meeting another group of people there. They left with the group, but it was nice just to see and talk to some young ladies.

From there I found my way back to the Fraternity and crashed in the TV room. I had a good night sleep on the couch, before heading on to campus, some how I came in contact with a map. I wanted to find the Admissions office. I was able to find the building and was given an application and direction to go to the Arts and Science building for more details and help. When I got there I was faced with a secretary who tried to send me packing, but I persevered and was able to meet with someone. I met with a man roughly in his fifties. The only thing I recall about the conversation was my desire to play football if I could. I also volunteered I would also like to help out by coaching, if possible. I also tried to explain a new offense I had formulated using two quarterbacks. It was somewhere around there he told me he had an appointment to get to and he got up and left.

I had some conversation with the secretary before I left. From there I headed to the shopping area I found the day before. I was looking for a place to eat. Something I hadn't done in some time. It didn't take me long to found a place. One of my favorite places was in clear sight, a *Pizza Hut*. I did my usual thing. I had some pizza for lunch and then passed through the door without paying the bill. Again no one perused me and I was free and clear.

From there I visited the Athletic Department to see if I could talk to anyone about playing or coaching football. As I went down the stairs to the football department I encounter to large fellows at the base of the stairs. I asked them for some help. I told them I wanted to play or coach football. I'm pretty sure they told me I couldn't play because I had graduated from a school and would have to be in a Masters program to coach. I left somewhat defeated.

From there I explored more of campus. Making my way down the street lined with Fraternities the thought came to mind to form a football league made up of Fraternities. I imagined two levels. A level for each campus where Fraternities would play one another and another that would represent the University a Greek player attended. The team would be like an All Star team from the Fraternities. A players Fraternity letters could be displayed on the uniform. Queen Elizabeth entered my fantasy as a fan from a previous life in this system. I recall giving the name to this league. I came up with the Fraternity and University Collision Association and the Sorority and University Collision Association. Using the initials one comes up with FUCA and SUCA. The Queen as a young college age fan was hollering over and over again, "You FUCA's and SUCA's". She was into it and it made an embellishment on my mind.

I went up to a new level with a Pro League after college where a player would automatically go to the team with his Greek letters. It would work better than the draft because players from one campus or Fraternity to another would produce different talent levels. This may also be a better way for a young man to find his way through the football rains and they would have total loyalty to there letters. I even thought maybe this league could be the team for a MegaPlex.

Night came quickly and I found myself in a different bar. There was a live band and I listened for a good while. There was a girl who sat against a wall again peaking my interest as a Massajahess candidate. I remember she had a long sundress on with running sneakers. I introduced myself after some time. She wasn't much of a chatterbox and left to her boyfriend after a few minutes. I didn't stay too much longer after that.

I found myself back on the Fraternity couch for another nights rest. The next day once I woke up, the Chi Phi brothers at the chapter informed me they wanted me to leave. After a few moment to let it sink in I did leave. Even stranger the brothers called the police on me. The police were at the front of the house when I exited. I knew the police had nothing on me, but one of the cops told me I could never step foot on the campus again. The next thing I did after leaving the Fraternity was walk all around campus in defiance, knowing he had no idea whether I was on campus or not.

I guess the brothers had a problem with me not giving them a hint of what kind of help I needed. Maybe they had begun to think I wasn't a Chi Phi brother and just some guy off the street looking to rest.

That afternoon produced a beautiful rainbow appeared after a brief shower. I spent time in and out of campus shops and the Mall, which was much further up the road. This behavior of perusing stores took me into the night, where I found myself back in the *Upstairs*. I spent a good amount of time there, which once again was almost empty. Toward the end of the night there was a group of guys who asked if I wanted to go hang with them.

I was taken back to their apartment where after a while their partying slowed and I took up residency on a couch. Just as I began falling asleep, they told me to leave. I didn't make it far I tried staying inside by resting on the stairs in the stairwell. They came down the stairwell finding me hanging around and told me to leave, so I did.

That's when I found a 24-hour restaurant toward the base of campus. I wasn't going to sleep, so I may as well have something to eat. I sat down ordered from the menu and ate. Not only did I eat I had a few cups of coffee before making my way out. Again I was free and clear. I found a shopping gallery with a hall way that was open at night. I just kind of moved around going in and out of that gallery until dawn.

The morning gave me some energy as the sun gives a boost to ones psyche. I plodded through the morning until I remembered the church I had noticed just a skip from the stadium. I went there looking for some help. When I made my way in on the first floor there was no one around. I looked around and noticed a sliding glass door to a sunroom. I peaked in before opening the door. There were a lot of things in boxes. Generally the church was storing items in this part of the church. I found this might be a good place to get some sleep, as blinds where on the windows, there was a couch, and it seemed like this portion of the church was forgotten. I took some boxes off the couch, then lay down and got some sleep.

When I woke up it was night. I had no idea of what time it was. I thought to go to a place I had been to earlier, the *Upstairs*. The bartender greeted me. He informed me I couldn't hang around there anymore. He gave the reason the guys I had left with a night ago told him I was strange.

I left in dismay. I sat outside the bar telling people not to go into the 'Upstairs Queers!' After a while I left going back to the 24-hour restaurant. Once again I was able to order food and leave without any money. Once the night was into its wee hours, I spotted a shirt in a window I coveted. My clothes where tattered and I had once again made shorts out of the jeans, but that was back when I first got to Bloomington. I was in need of some new clothes.

The sun splashed itself around the University, again giving a little life into a person that didn't sleep. My plan for this shirt was to casually browse around the store and then as I was leaving grab a shirt from the rack and start running. Something stopped me. I couldn't go through with it. That morning I made it to the Mall where I found a traveling carnival. My first thought was to see where they where going next and if I could somehow get a ride. I looked around the rides for someone to talk to. Someone finally noticed my presents between the rides. Though I wanted a ride, somehow our conversation turned to me helping tear down the rides. I believe I was offered $35. I had nothing else to do and $35 seemed like a lot to me, so I accepted. He told me they would be tearing down in two days.

From there I sat down at a Mexican restaurant and ate, but I felt bad for my waitress and waited in my seat until I asked to see her manager. He came out and I explained I would be able to pay in two or three days. He accepted my explanation and I was on my way.

After I went into the Mall to look around. Something came to my mind. I thought maybe I could somehow get my hands on a tent and go camp in the Hoosier Park. I thought I could pay for it after helping the carnival or maybe grab one and run out of the store. The store I found tents in was *Sears*.

Again I didn't do much until the night squashed away the sun. This time I wasn't going to be left out in the cold. I went right to the church where I went to sleep. The next morning came and I left without any notice what so ever. I judged that it was early morning due to the dew on the grass. I can't remember where I spent the morning, but I do know I had in my head I was hunting and gathering and where would I go in today's society to hunt and gather. My logic took me to the Super Market. Once I had found the market and the bounty of food there I began putting together a diet without the use of an oven. I thought sandwiches, but bread needs to be cooked. I then turned to apples pears, peaches, potatoes, and peppers. I thought one could cut them in half and put meats in the center. During this process I grabbed a sports bar and soda to eat. I finished both as I continued with this diet.

The next thing I know three police officers came into the market and escorted me out. They stuffed me in the back of a police car and rushed me, as only police can rush, to the station. Once I was fingerprinted my mug shot and personal information was taken I exchanged my tattered clothes for the orange prison uniform. When processing was completed three or four other men along with myself formed a chain gang with the Bloomington courtroom as our destination. One at a time we faced Judge Welsh. When my time came I found a small discrepancy in the accusation against me. The Super Market alleged I consumed a sports bar and soda, but also included something about a toy football. I made the error clear and the toy football was thrown out. Judge Welsh also asked me to fill my profession in on my personal bio. I was creative with this. My first thought was to fill in Massajah, but thinking quickly I entered 'Unpaid Government Official'. I can't be sure if he looked it over or not or even his reaction. As I continued facing the Judge he asked me my plea and I pled guilty. As I left the floor I told myself aloud, "I would plead guilty to just about anything at this time". This is the way I felt as my ordeal over the past several months begun to wear on me. Judge Welsh heard this and entered my plea as innocent. It sounded good coming from the Judge, but from there I was taken to a single cell of my own.

The cell had four walls with a door not bars. The door had a thin window on its right side, roughly four inches wide and three feet in height. The only view was of the nurses' office, but that could only be seen at an angle. A metal sink and john accompanied a metal cart fixed to the wall to put ones mat on and sleep. With that said, the toughest thing was I was in lockdown 24 hours a day. The only interaction I had was when my meals came through the slot in the door. The only time I was let out of the cell was for showering. There was a camera in one corner of the cell and lights for the day, which where shut off at night. I guess I landed my way on to isolation. A large drawing of some kind of lepracon or cartoon character was sketched on one of the walls in pencil. A Confederate flag may have also graced a wall in pencil.

My first day or so I had images of movie star Christopher Walkin, Purdue basketball coach Gene Caddie, comedian Andrew 'Dice' Clay, actor James Gandalphini 'Tony Soprano', and the women who gave me $20 when I went canning for the Homeless. They occupied my fantasy projected on the right cell wall. These characters kept me company. With the exception of my $20 lady, who I could vaguely make out saying, "brimstone", over and over again, for what ever reason, the celebrities would be muffled by the sound of the vent coming into the cell. They just occupied my thoughts through the first few days.

I made my holding tank homier by laying my cotton sheet over the hard cement. One guard told me he liked what I had done, while a woman guard wanted me to take it of the floor. I told her another guard liked the move and she was over compensating because she was a woman. After that exchange she left me alone.

Somewhere along the line I started keeping my cups and bowls along with a spoon or fork. I started to make small water fountains. I would use the fork to punch a hole or a few holes in the base, not bottom of the cup. I placed a cup face down in a bowl, than another cup, with holes in its base, was seated on the first cup. I would then fill the top cup with water amusing myself with the water slowly flowing from the holes in the cup into the bowl. I did this repeatedly and at one point thought it may be possible to keep track of time with the devise. That quickly ended as watching water travel through became boring.

The drawings on the walls became an irritant, so I got my bar of soap some water along with some forks and rubbed the illustrations from the walls. This was an undertaking taking more than a day. As I scraped the pencil from the walls with my forks and soap I couldn't help but feel I was some how washing away the crimes and sins from the inmates who defaced the cell.

Whenever I wanted privacy from the guards walking passed my cell I would wet the soap, rub a small spot of the soap on the top of each side of the window and glue a long piece of toilet paper to the spots, which would cover the window. At times someone would come right away to have me take it down, while other times it hung for a good amount of time.

In my best estimation I was isolated in the cell anywhere from five to eight days, until one day I was taken from the newly cleaned holding tank. I was taken and dressed back into my street clothes, but remained cuffed. I was put in the back off a prison transportation van, which I was chained to. The back of the van I road in was gutted and furbished with metal walls and a small narrow bench for criminals to sit.

I was taken to a hospital. I wasn't only taken to a hospital but I was taken to the mental health wing. This was a small unit when compared to Butler Hospital. It was basically a hallway with maybe six rooms, a lounge area and a medical room.

My first guess was they found my mental health record, but they made no mention of Rhode Island. Not only that they never began to medicate me, but from my past experiences with the mental health community I thought I might be there a while.

A girl or young woman was also staying in this wing. I can remember her being distraught and looking for help. I consoled her with a hug to try and stop her tears. This helped and she became subdued. I was there for as a very short while, but felt maybe I was supposed to be there to help this young person deal with her troubles.

After a few days the cuffs where put back on and I was taken back to the Bloomington Jail. Back into the orange suit, but this time I was main streamed. With my hands full from the mat, sheets and other items, I was taken to a cell in a cellblock. I started in the lower bunk desiring the top bunk, because it had a window to look out of. My cellmate was around the same age as I.

The cellblock had two levels to it, with eight to ten cells on each level. Each cell had a door similar to the door in my isolated cell. The shower was in the back section of the cellblock. The most drastic difference between my confinement and this cellblock was the cellblocks doors where open all day with the exception of the 3 o'clock hour, from what I remember. The inmates would be locked down for that period of time.

Unlike my stay in the Jonesboro County Jail, this introduction into the community was hassle free. There where a lot of cards played and on occasion I would join in on a game. The game of choice again was Spades, but I refrained from trying to teach High, Low, Jack this time around. Each morning we would wake up for breakfast and the Country Music channel. Finding a table to eat was never difficult. By no means was this a band of happy campers. One inmate bloodied another prisoners face pretty well in a fight. In fact there was a little guy in the block who looked to be having a great time laughing and smiling all the time, which aggravated the hell out of me. A little guy like him should be scared for his life, so I threatened asking, "What's stopping me from smashing your face into the wall?" He took his stay a little more serious from that point on.

Though I spent most of my stay outside of my cell mingling with the other criminals, some of the time I did rest on my bunk. I spent some time wondering who came up with idea of putting your hands together in prayer. I received a visual of people praying with their hands pointed up only to keep them together pointing them down at a large pool of water and diving in. My condition allowed me to come up with the concept the people where praying so they wouldn't have to reverse their hands and plunge into the water. I figured the water would indicate how much pressure an individual could endure by the depth they could achieve. When the pressure of the depth was to great to continue the subject would be taken from the water to the shore. At that point I entered one form of a Devil who would nurse each human being back to strength just my flying and hovering over them. Visions of this winged Devil and the entire process engaged my thoughts hear and there for a day or two. I could see my friend Jesus withstanding the lowest depths of this experiment. I also imagined myself chasing him down. I concluded the water was holy water and they where praying to God not to have them dive into the holy water. At least this is what my troubled mind came up with for why people pray with there hands up, they didn't want to start the diving motion into the water.

Again as in my last detainment in Illinois, Jail is pretty boring for the most part. The same routine is kept day-to-day, week-to-week, and month-to-month with out much change. Though my cellmate was let go and I was able to capture the top bunk. This time I had a huge man sharing the cell. He was large as in heavy and he had to take breathing treatments now and again.

They handed out psychiatric medication every night before bed and I was happily excluded from the treatments. One of the nurses who handed out the meds was young, cute and just about my age. The thought she was a Massajahess entered my mind, but for her to seize this position she would need to somehow get me out of Jail. From time to time I would see her hand out the medication with no indication she was playing along and she was dismissed in my mind.

I continued to think more about the Massajahess and how a woman would hold such a high position. I worked out a game a Massajahess and Massajah could use to unite the two while at the same time stay unmarried. I do consider marriage to be a mix of religion and government. I have learned not to mix religion and government and devised a way to be unified without the tangling of the two. I have no problem with having a religious ceremony, but one also registers their marriage with the government. If everyone stopped filing with the government divorce would be virtually none existent. A person could go there separate way when ever they chose. Back to the Massajahess, I would have a million ceremonies marrying who ever as long as I didn't register with the government. With that, the game I came up with to unify the Massajah and Massajahess would be to change their names to the exact same name and I have one already thought up. Antaeus Vanitas sounds both masculine and feminine enough depending how one pronounces it. They would become almost the same person.

The free time had my mind looking for another powerful position going on the chessboard with God as the Bishop or religious piece and the Devil as the business minded Rook position. After a struggle of who would be the government piece, the answer came to mind. I could put a King in between them as the government minded knight. This made good sense to me and I noticed another way to link them. Devil has five letters in it, King has four letters in it, and God has three. These powerful positions descended in the number of characters that made up their names, as one got closer to the center spots of Queen and King on the board. I took this logic and made the Queen a 'US', as in United States or us as in the two of us together. Finishing what became what I called a Powermid, I made the logical choice of 'I', as in the Roman numeral one or I as in I am the most powerful one on the board. I find these Powermids to add more structure and order to a Kingdom I created another Powermid I can remember for the Aides Virus, which I will display in Powermid form below. Again I'm only playing:

I	+
US	VD
GOD	HIV
KING	AIDS
DEVIL	BLOOD

As days past I made a board for a female dominated Kingdom. I used the Queen as the King and the Queens partner a Moon. I chose a Moon to stay uniform with the double lettered 'ee' in Queen. For the Bishop I came up with a Book, who also has the double 'oo' in it. Next spot would be the knight for whom I named a Cook, keeping with the 'oo' motif. The Rook would be replaced by the Loose. All the pawns would be regarded as Looks.

My new cellmate lasted maybe five to six days before he was

shipped out. Another jailbird found his way into my cell, another young guy. I expected this long stay after the time I spent in Jail a couple of weeks before this visit. Though most of the days where routine there were a few ways to get out of the cellblock. For one I was able to get out for a haircut. I also took advantage of the time provided to go to the library. The library was small, but I got a few history books to look at. When I say history books, I mean third grade level reading with mostly pictures. The final way to get out of the cellblock would be to go to mass or church. I enjoyed church for nothing else, but the fact the female criminals also joined the flock. A few were pretty good lookers. Other than that one would have to get bloodied in need of medical assistance to leave.

There was a car accident outside my window one day, which gave a little bit of excitement to the day. The car somehow swerved off the road into a tree. I thought this might have been a way to inconspicuously draw attention to my location to any on lookers who may care about this test subject.

A few weeks had passed and I saw the same faces day after day. It came to my mind one particular day maybe I should try to get the other inmates to form a crime family. A gang of men from jail to establish a crime ring. It was a passing thought that got interrupted one day. I was finally called to see the Judge.

After around 40 or so days I was put in front of the Judge, a woman judge whose name eludes me. After taking a quick look at my case she declared I had served my sentence and would be free to go. I was taken back down to get my street clothes. Then I was guided to the exit of the building, which came out into a waiting room. I stayed in the room a while before leaving. I had nowhere to be. After maybe 15 to 20 minutes I began to stretch and warm up. I chose to get down in a sprinters stance and run from the jail as fast as I could and that's what I did. The door opened and I went sprinting out, throw some streets before finally getting winded and stopping.

I was now a freeman. I took some time to gather myself, walking with no particular destination. The day went by quickly and I found myself seated by a young lady in front of a store. I exchanged words with her making an attempt to have her maybe ask if she could help me. I did mention to her I didn't know where I was staying, because I just got out of jail. I mentioned to her I was an artist and asked if she would like a portrait of herself. She handed over a notebook and I began to sketch, but the friends she was waiting for to pick her up arrived and she took off.

Night found its way into Bloomington and I again began to walk with no particular purpose. The dark of night stood still as time continued to eat into the p.m. hours. Somehow it came to mind I wanted to celebrate my freedom with a cigar. The only place I could find open was a drug store. I went in and looked around until I found an assortment of cigars. They all came in packs and I decided I wanted a pack. I casually put a pack in my back pocket and left the store. Again I had no pursuers and was free and clear. I picked up a pack of matches somewhere along the line and lit one up. I smoked and made my way down the street until I found myself in a dance club. I sat down puffing away at a cigar as the bar began to close. I was forced to the street with the rest of the crowd. I didn't really mingle, but I did look around and blend into the crowd on the street until the crowd dwindled down to almost nothing.

I lit another cigar and then another after that. The cigars burned away like the hours in the night. By morning I was fresh out of cigars and walking up the side of campus. My short had begun to literally come undone and I needed some clothes to replace my weathered outfit.

Early that morning before any shops had opened I came across a sign at a college bookstore reading, "Buy one get two free!" I took a seat in front of the store with full intention to get some clothes out of a store giving the majority of the clothes away. I remember sitting there that morning literally cracking myself up with the fact this store was having a 'buy one get two free' sale.

When the store opened I didn't cross the street and jump right in. I waited for some time to elapse and a flow to the day to start. When I found it was time I went into the store and spotted the clothes, but looked all over the building just to make it look like I was shopping. When I thought it was time I grabbed a pear of shorts, a shirt, and a visor. I went into the changing room leaving my old clothes behind and jumped into the new items I had selected. I exited quickly, but grabbed a free drink they offered before making my way out the door and around the building.

I thought I was safe after I had cleared the parking lot in back of the bookstore, but someone flagged me down and the owner came running toward me. I stopped and waited for him. He told me I had to go back and change into my old clothes or he would call the police. As the words came from his mouth a cop car started it's way down the street and believe it or not it was me who flagged the officer down. He stopped and the storeowner pled his case. I didn't say two words until the cop told me to through my drink down, which I replied, "I'll place it down." I began putting the cup down on the sidewalk when the cop attacked me.

I don't know exactly what he was attempting to do, but he did a poor job at best. All I did was defend myself from his attacks. During this skirmish the cop was able to call for back up. He continued to attack me even resorting to pepper spray, but his attacks where futile. He kept on trying and he was unable to get me rounded up until another officer came running at me and tackled me to the grass. I was then cuffed and put in the back of one of the cars.

As they took me to the jail I was shouting at the top of my lunges they 'sucked'. I continued to call them losers and other names, but "You suck!", was my favorite choice of words. They let me stew in the back of the car once we where in the building. I continued to shout at them from the vehicle. After some time they brought me in and I let them know they sucked on the way. When I first entered the building into the small intake room an officer asked me what I was on, looking for a drug. I wasn't on any so I told him H2O.

From there I was taken into a holding tank, where for some reason I dragged Bill Clinton into the mix shouting he was caught in between the Bush's as we passed over the Millennium. That and the fact they all sucked was my belligerent cry. I was in the holding tank with a few other guys for quite a while before and they where annoyed with my banter, but did nothing to shut me up.

From there I was re-fingerprinted and given an orange uniform. I was supplied with the mat, sheets and other items and brought back to the cellblock I was in a day ago. From my cell I used the intercom, there was one in each cell, to call down to the guards to tell them they sucked. I did this a few times from my sell and a couple of times from other cells.

I cooled off a little as the day persisted. My roommate was a very young tall but thin individual. When they called me to do a TB test I told them I had one on my last visit look it up. Eventually they got a guard to get me and take me to the nurses' office. He told me to take a seat outside the office, but I refused letting him know I would rather stand. Again he demanded I sit and again I told him I wanted to stand. He told me one more time and before I could tell him I wanted to... he had me around the neck forcing me to sit, but as he did I got some leverage with a step too the side and stood up just a hair before he forced my head of the wall and on to the floor. I was out for at least a few seconds before I awoke up with him telling me to get my hand behind my back. I couldn't move them, they where beneath me. His weight along with mine was on top of them. He then allowed me to move around a little to get my arms around my back.

At this time he sat me down and I broke down in tears, mentioning I had Woodrow Wilson's League of Nations on my mind. This fell on deaf ears of course and the TB test was administered, but my residency in the prison was changed. I was taken to a small cell with five other men. There where two cells both with bunks and two cart on the outside of those cells. I was assigned an outside cart. When I entered the small cellblock I sat down and kept my back to the other inmates, because I could feel some damage done to my eye and my cheek from the blow to the floor. I didn't want them to see what had happened. Eventually I faced them. It was in this cellblock I learned how to play solitary. There was a guy a few years younger than I was who ran the block. He was good humored and no one seemed to mind.

Like the other cellblocks not a whole lot happens, its all time with the same walls. I do have to admit out of all the criminals I had met one took the cake. Bob was in this cellblock with us and well Bob was the sickest guy I came across. My buddy Bob's parents owned a funeral home and well Bob had a problem with having intercourse with the dead bodies. Bob wins the totally sick bastard contest. How does one actually punish a warped individual like him? Talking to him one would never imagine his crime until he tells it.

I was in this cellblock for approximately six to eight days before an epiphany. Over the intercom came a voice asking if I knew a Ted so and so. I was shocked and replied back, "Yes?" The voice then said, "You have mail." The letter arrived shortly after the inquiry. I opened it right away.

I have known Ted since I was one or two years old. We started on the same street when we where very young. I moved away at about five years old and Ted and his family moved across the street from that house. Ted may have moved from there while we where about 11 or 12 to Pawtuxet, Rhode Island, but I visited on occasion. During high school he moved back to West Warwick and was a member of our 1990 football Championship Team. I saw him here and there through the next few years as I was away at Penn State and I do believe he went to the University of Montana. Ted is my longest standing friend and really one of the truly better friends I have. To know Ted is like knowing a comedian.

I have to reflect back on the same gender marriages. This is how it is intended to work in my mind, a way to get out of mischief, not have sex with one another. I felt in an odd way this was an example of a good relationship, built over years coming to a partners' aid.

Ted's letter mentioned he was happy to get in touch and he had some work I could do for him. I'm not exactly sure if I called him from a number in his letter or if he contacted Judge Welsh, or Ted gave me a call in the cellblock. I do remember Judge Welsh meeting with me telling me I could either serve two years for resisting arrest or go back to Rhode Island to face the mental health community. The prison had already started to medicate me so the easy choice was to go back to Rhode Island. During the meeting I think I scared Judge Welsh out of his seat when I told him I walked my fine line between genius and insanity when I walked along the Mississippi River. Missouri was 'misery' and Illinois was 'ill and annoying' or 'illness annoying'. I followed that by telling him it was all 'sick and logical' which rhymes or sounds like psychological.

I also spoke with Ted over the phone a couple of times. It was in these conversations and the cooperation of Judge Welsh we formulated a plan to get me back to Rhode Island. After a few days of planning and getting the details ironed out, Ted would fly out to Indiana and I would be put into his custody.

First I had to face the Judge in court to make everything official. Ted would meet me in the airport later that day. When I was faced with Judge Welsh he gave me the opportunity to drop one of the charges against me, the theft of retail or the resisting arrest. I knew right away to lose the resisting arrest. After that he asked if I had anything to say and I said, 'I apologize for my antics."

AN AMERICAN MESSIAH

From the courtroom I was whisked away to get dressed back into my street clothes, but there where none. The storeowner took the clothes I wore out of the bookstore and I left my old clothes in the bookstore. The guard quickly found me a pear of shorts, from where ever, and a shirt, I still had the sandals from *Target*. I was then loaded into the back of the van transporting me to the hospital. I was kept locked up throw out the drive, which took some time. I believe we where to rendezvous in the Indianapolis airport.

We finally got to the airport and I remained in cuffs, as I was escorted through the building. I waited in chains until Ted arrived. I can recall him coming around the corner carefully trying to pick me out of the crowd. Once Ted was there to take over the cuffs where taken off.

I remember we got a bight to eat and spent some time outside the airport getting reacquainted. I tried to explain my craps strategy, but he wasn't that familiar with the game. I must have looked strange to him, I was wearing the phew man chew mustache and long side burns, nothing I had sported back in West Warwick. We eventually boarded the plain, taking off for home.

CHAPTER 20

Ted explained to me, on the plane ride, there wouldn't be anyone greeting me at the airport, due to the documented distain for my father. I would stay with him when we arrived. The ride seemed to go by quickly and we found ourselves passing through the T.F. Green Airport terminal. Ted had parked his car in one of the lots, which we found quickly, we then made off for Ted's apartment. When we got there I met his girlfriend Heather and was given a pear of shorts and shirt to replace the out fit I was wearing.

They where both very welcoming, but I was unable to sleep that night, on the couch, and woke Ted up to see if there where any convenient stores or anything of that kind I could stretch my legs to, for a drink or snack. He got himself out of bed, gave me a few bucks and directed me just down the street to a *Dunkin Donuts*. I took the money and made my way to the donut shop. I believe I had a honey bun and a soda, nothing like I would have found locked up. I sat and collected myself as I began to realize I was back in Rhode Island.

I made my way back to the first floor of a duplex Ted and Heather resided and crashed on the couch. The next morning as my good friend and I traveled in his car he asked me if there was anything I wanted? There was. I wanted another back of those cigars I had smoked after being released in Indiana. Ted obliged my request and we picked up a pack at the drug store. From there we had my first appointment with the mental health community. I did have the fear I would end up back in Butler Hospital, but Ted assured me the people at the Mental Health Care Center just wanted to meet with me.

Ted accompanied me on the initial visit, from the waiting room to the encounter with a case manager. She did her best to give an observation, but I was filled with so much energy and mania I gave long winded answers along with two interruptions where I had to visit the restroom. I was surprised there was no attempt at reconciliation with my family. Ted was true to his word; I left the Center the same way I arrived with no sign of Butler Hospital or my parents.

From there Ted dropped me off at a Motel in North Kingston and handed me $50. He had to get to work and figured I could handle myself at this point. After taking a quick nap in my room I made my way out for some lunch. There was a *Pizza Hut* down the road and that's where I ate. After eating I actually had money to pay for the bill. There were a few stores across from the *Pizza Hut* and I poked in and out of them just to kill time. Following my casual shopping I smoked a few cigars and headed back to my room.

Once in the room I found myself on the bed flipping through the channels until I eventually dosed off. Ted interrupted my slumber with a knock on the door. He was checking up on me, making curtain I was doing O.K. It may have been this meeting that he mentioned meeting with my family the next day. After all I had experienced, I had little gripe with my family and indicated it would be fine. He then took off for the night, but not before telling me he would meet up with me in the morning.

That night I picked up some more cigars because I had smoked my way through the pack I had. From there I went to a bar I had visited in the past. *The Red Rock* is a nice establishment to drink, eat or just play pool. They have three tables and I believe the pool was free that night. I meet some people as I played pool and smoked my cigars. I also drank for the first time in several months. In fact I spent the remainder of my money on drinks, as I felt entitled to some frivolous over indulging behavior. It was the best time I had had in many moons.

When the night ended and I found my way back to the Motel I was out in a matter of minutes. The next morning Ted woke me up with another knock at the door. We checked me out and Ted confirmed we would meet with my parents later that day. In fact Ted told me he would pick me up at 5 pm at the *McDonalds* in the shopping plaza I had poked around in.

I spent a lot of time kind of looking around here to there from store to store. The anticipation of five o'clock had time pass comparable to a jail cell. I waited and waited for Ted at the *McDonalds* before growing so inpatient I began to walk home. I figured Ted would see me walking when he came to pick me up, but I saw no sign of Ted.

This seemed like a last her raw, once again walking mile after mile, with the only difference being I knew exactly where I was and where I was going. After roughly seven miles of walking I strolled up to my house.

The only person home when I arrived was my mother. It was an awkward situation and I can say with a good level of certainty my mother gave me a hug to welcome me home. As I stated we where both at loses for words, until my mother filled me in that her father, my grandfather had died while I was gone. The news came as somewhat of a surprise, but in the same token he was in his 80's. I think the best thing I can say for this man is he was never trying to be something he wasn't. He was a grandfather to many children and will always be my grandfather above all else in my mind. I say this with the utmost admiration for the good, always happy man he was.

Ted showed up shortly after, most probably with relief to see I had made it home and hadn't taken off on him. My father did come home to see me, but it doesn't make the same memory as the first person to greet me, my mother. I could see she had been through a lot between her father's death and my long absence.

In the following days I met with Dr. Koyfman and began a medication program. Again we stared clear of a hospitalization at Butler and I was allowed to cooperate with my doctor's course of action. I had been under the impression I would have to find work until Dr. Koyfman told me she thought it would be best if I filed for disability, so I did as my doctor ordered and applied for disability. In the mean time I was placed on a state program that picked up my medication costs and provided a $200 per month allowance.

The $200 a month wasn't much to live off of, but I had few expenses. Most of the money went toward my *Havana Tampa* cigars. I was able to travel on my own in the aging Pontiac Grand Am I road in before I left. I headed to the beach a few times before the close of summer. I can recall lying on the beach running sand through my fingers enjoying my newly found freedom.

My brother's wife Stephanie had her second son Lucas just a few days before I returned to Rhode Island. I recall she had announced she was pregnant just before I took off. It took me a few days to a week before I made it around to see the little one; I was still getting acquainted with the people I knew before I departed.

One of the things I did early in establishing myself was getting my hands on the document stating my name change. My father took me to an office across from the states capital building to obtain the legal document altering my name from David Michael Garcia to David Michael. From there I went to the DMV to get a new license with my new name on it. That was that, easily enough my name was now David Michael. I also filled out the disability documents with my new name.

Now that the ball had started to roll I began meeting with my old friends Ed, Wally, Ray and John. One night my friend Ed, who had bought a home while I was away, had a cook out. It was a good night where I got to mingle with my old friends. I ingratiated myself more and more with my friends as the days past. One night I was at the *Crompton Vets* with most likely Ray and Wally when Jim, the President of the West Warwick Youth Football League, which practiced on the baseball fields adjacent to the Vets and housed the leagues equipment in the basement of the watering hole, was commenting the league needed a coach for the oldest division, Varsity (ages 12 and 13). I had been formulating plays for my new offence with two quarterbacks when I had nothing to do and jumped at the chance to try it out. I felt the older age level may be able to understand the plays. I told Jim I would be happy to help out.

When it came down to it I was bumped to an assistant coach with another coach Gary, the head coaching position was held onto by an individual named Todd. Somehow the league thought it was better to keep Todd as the head coach even though he would miss the practices at the beginning of the week, because he was teaching in Vermont. It was a difficult situation to be put into, to run a team without being the head coach, but Gary and I did the best we could. I have to admit Gary's out spoken and almost drill sergeant approach cased some waves, but again we where doing the best we could without the head coach at the practices. I never did get the chance to put any of my plays into the playbook.

I still had my days free, practice was 6 to 8 at night. With that free time I either made a trip to the beach or sketched into a pad items in my back yard. My father, who I had no anger toward, must have noticed my sketching in the yard because one day he brought home an easel, a few canvases, brushes and paints. My very first piece consisted of the nine planets in our solar system as their symbols and the sun running along the top. For my first painting it came out all right.

Through out these events I stayed in contact with Ted. Ted and his father Denis ran a program to educate persons without jobs computer skills they would need to find work in today's computer savvy job market. They where expanding into West Warwick and I helped out with a little bit of painting one night. I would also enroll in the class once the West Warwick *Opportunity Recourse* facility was ready. All of my computer experience and knowledge had been with the Apple or Macintosh computers. This class was my introduction into the word of IBM computers. I believe Apple only holds ten percent of the market, so this learning experience with IBM computers would put me in the 90 percent of computer users.

I was also faced with the debt I had accumulated before going to Venezuela and the center of the U.S. After meeting with a state supplied lawyer, I elected to pursue bankruptcy. I found a bankruptcy attorney in the Providence Journal who charged $200 to complete the process. My father was diligent enough to save all the collection letters I had got in the mail, which I was able to compile a list of creditors I owed money to for the lawyer. From there I would have to wait for a court date.

It was a day-to-day process, but the medications I agreed to take began slowly closing the door to my wild fantasy. This and my reluctance to share my Massajah theories, knowing people would find my comments strange, over the top and a sign I needed more intervention or medication, so I shelved my long battle across Missouri, Illinois, and Indian as well as Venezuela. It quickly became a distant memory, fading and numbed by the medication.

Then one tragic morning I was awoken by my father, with excited cries of, "We're being bombed! We're being bombed!" Awakening from the daze of sleep, my very first thought was to retaliate, even before I got out of bed to see the smoke billowing out of one of the Twin Towers. My father and the television got me up to speed before I witnessed another plane jab itself into the second tower. Not long after that one tower collapsed and then the other. As I watched New York City become a disaster area and people fled for their lives, I felt somewhat derelict. While I was filled with images and thoughts over

The previous several months not a single significant terrorist act was carried out, but quickly after I submitted to the mental health community and my mental activity was being reduced to a more "normal" pace there was an attack on the United States of the likes never seen before. I felt a guilt and a helplessness, a helplessness shared by any man, woman or child who witnessed this senseless act.

Earth would later get familiar with Al Queta and Assam a BenLoden, the cowards who plotted these sinister ideas. A plane was also found crashed in Pennsylvania and another target was stricken with a plane being used as a missile, that being the Pentagon. One of the wings of the Pentagon took a severe blow, but nothing can compare to the mayhem, confusion, or fair that draped the collapsing towers in New York City. Our lives would be changed from this event, but Patriotism and healing persisted through the months and years that followed.

Though 9-11 held us all hostages to fear, the 'normal' routine of daily life began to heal and refocus most of us. I continued taking Ted's class and did learn a lot about what the machine could do. One of his sisters Shelly was also taking the class with a friend of hers Ellen. Shelly and the rest of Ted's family - mother Mary Ellen, and two sisters Heather and Tony- have known me since I was one or two. Ted is the youngest in his family and Shelly was a few years older. I admit to taking advantage of the fact Ted and his father Denis ran the class by sometimes coming late and other times leaving after lunch. The class was useful to me and gave me a good platform to work with the IBM at a later date.

At just about the halfway point my Youth Football team had been held winless and it was a tough thing to undergo when I was more familiar with winning. I do blame the fact the head coach was commuting from New Hampshire or Vermont and missing one or more practices a week. It was the ultimate mind readers position.

I continued to learn how to paint with the brushes, canvases, and paints my father got me. Ted asked if I would paint him a Tom Landry (former Dallas Cowboy Coach). How could I say no to Ted. I struggled with the first canvas and took it off the easel for another try. The second version came out much better, but still carried only a fear resemblance at best. Ted was pleased with it and that's all that mattered. A few weeks later I would graduate from the Computer class. I was given a Certificated and a pen set on commencement day.

My other close friends Ed, Wally, John and Ray where there for a good time. They all had jobs so I saw them more sparingly than Ted, but they where around for a good time. 9-11 was a subject of conversation almost every time we got together if not every time.

My Havana Tampa cigars had me hooked. I budgeted almost all of the $200 a month toward the cigars. They acted as a simple pleasure.

In October I was awarded with disability payments. I would receive a $600 check once a month and I received a retroactive check of $8,000. The first thing I bought with the check was an Illustrator program for the family computer. I wanted this program, because I had an idea for a children's book. The concept was to write a book that would work with the inter net or a way to introduce kids to the inter net. The story I knew best was *Jack and the Bean Stalk*. My plan for this story was to have a child follow the story in the book until Jack went up the Bean Stalk. The story would then be played out on an inter net site. At the end when Jack comes down the Stalk the story would return to the book. Now that I had the Illustrator program I went to work.

Shortly after the date for my bankruptcy hearing came up. I can remember waiting for my turn to come. This took place in an office building in Providence and if one wasn't told what went on there they probably couldn't guess. After some time with my lawyer my turn did come up. There was a gentleman behind a pretty ordinary desk hearing cases. I answered every question I was asked. When asked how I accumulated my debt, I told him I tried to start a business and it didn't work out and I was using my credit cards to survive. I also showed I was now collecting disability and didn't have the means to pay it back. He quickly determined my case was good enough to go through bankruptcy.

It was a big relief to get all those bills off of me. The only bill I had left was my student loans and Dr. Koyfman indicated I had a health issue and a hard ship case that could erase my student loans. This process took only a few weeks to complete and I was also released from my student loans.

As the Youth Football team began to finish up the season, I began to paint a self-portrait. The big difference in this piece from my earlier attempts would be the brush I had selected from *A.C. Moore*. I chose a brush with a thin head to it. The number on the brush was zero. It gave me more control and a more delicate delivery to the canvas. This was a huge leap in my painting advancement and I would use only a zero brush on everything I painted, no matter how large the canvas. I believe I finished my portrait before the kids finished the football season. They wound up with out a single win. That should explain the entire season.

Another instance of good fortune in which I was the beneficiary of, was the aging and slowing of my Grandmother Garcia. Of course I wish wellness and health to the woman, but she had begun having trouble remembering where she was from time to time and it was decided to take her car keys away. I became the new owner of her Ford Taurus. With the car came the obligation of taking my grandmother to doctor visits and any other place she might want to travel. This was a huge up grade from the rusty old Pontiac Grand Am I was riding in.

Sometime in November I began hanging out at a friends' tattoo studio, *Forbidden Flesh*. I had known the owner Denis from the high school championship football teams. Other than illustrating the *Jack and the Bean Stalk* I had very little to do and found myself at the shop a day here another day there. It gave me something to do in the afternoon.

This became my routine for a while. Something worth mentioning as the holidays approached. My Raiders where victimized by the local Patriots on a play in the last few minutes of a snow filled game. The Patriots quarterback Tom Brady fumbled the ball over to the Raiders in the closing minutes of play, but the fumble was over ruled after replay. The official declared the quarterback, Brady, had possession of the football under the NFL 'Tuck Rule". The Pats got the ball back and scored a touchdown to beat my Raiders. This was the year the Raiders could have won the Super Bowl. Instead I heard it from my friends.

Christmas was uneventful and I have little to know memory of the occasion. New Years on the other hand I do remember. My friend Ed hosted a party at his house. Other than Ted all my friends where at the party. It was a good time and stands as one of my better New Years. One moment I can't forget is my friend Wally proposing to his then girlfriend Shannon as the year turned.

A few weeks after this celebration the New England Patriots won the Super Bowl defeating the St. Louis Rams. I never thought I would see the day where the Patriots won the championship. They where so bad for so long, but if one were to ask me they started contending when they changed their uniforms. Maybe they just had bad uniforms over the years. I would have rather seen the Raider take the title, but it was nice to see a hometown team win. It puts everyone in a better mood.

My treatment continued and I was considered stable for the most part. The medication had not only worn down my overly manic mental state, but had slowly slowed down my metabolism to the point I had gained a fair amount of weight. This is something I encountered in the past while taking Risperdal, but I didn't allow it to bother me as I went along with my doctors' wishes. My treatment at the Mental Health Center also continued with visits to my Case Manager Jacky, whom I was also seeing before I left the state.

I illustrated my *Jack and the Bean Stalk* book idea slowly but surely. It was more difficult to get things going than I anticipated. I know I had outlined roughly 50 pages for the story, which meant 50 or so fully illustrated pages. I shared what I was doing with Ted who was now keeping his office in the Pawtucket branch of *Opportunity Resources*. I had gotten Ted to, somehow, get the inter net portion of the story onto the inter net. Though I worked on the book constantly each day or two, I made only small advances in the progress of each page.

I made almost daily stops at my friend Denis's tattoo shop, *Forbidden Flesh*, to have some people to bounce things off. There was almost always someone to B.S. with. There was a whole lot of Xbox or PlayStation going on, mostly Madden football. It was also a good environment to show off my art.

My painting continued through the winter and I painted a seen across from the Pawtucket *Opportunity Resource* office. I had taken a digital photo of the landscape just to the left of famous Slater Mill. Again I selected a zero brushes from *A.C. Moore*. I mention *A.C. Moore*, because each week they offer a 40% Q-pond in the paper good toward anything in the store, not on sale. I began putting my Penn State education to use with what I learned in color theory and started paint with only the colors red, yellow, and blue. I could get all my colors and black with those three colors by mixing them and worked with white to tone down a color. I used this method when painting my first real piece, the landscape across from Ted's office and when it was finished I framed it and gave it to him. I would continue painting with more confidence after this work.

The early spring found me smoking not only my Havana Tampa cigars but also the smoking of a joint from time to time, mostly alone, but I had nothing to do and Mary-Jane helped past the time. As winter began to brake and spring filled the air I found myself burning J's in the park. I admit I couldn't paint or illustrate the book while under the effects, so I wouldn't mix the two, but again I had no obligations and there was a little escapism that came with the buzz. This behavior continued without anyone, from my family to my friends or even the people from the mental wellness community noticing.

I continued smoking cigars and pot along with painting, illustrating the book, visiting the tattoo shop, and visiting my doctor and case manager through the spring and into the summer months of 2002 as a kind of routine. Sometime in the early summer I completed the *Jack and the Bean Stalk* illustrations and sent it out to two children's book publishers.

Around that same time my weight had gotten to a point where I felt I had to do something about it. I signed up in a gym to work out and started a strict diet of a glass of orange juice for breakfast, a sandwich for lunch with no chips or snack items, and two cans of tuna each night for dinner. I would have a bag of popcorn at night for a snack along with a Gator Aid, which I was surprised, had low calories for the taste. I dropped weight at a good pace as the summer carried on into August.

With August came the kick off to Youth Football practices and I signed up for another year. We had a lot of kids returning, which fueled optimism that those players had matured and had grown and would be more confident playing at the same level again. Again the team was faced with the head coach living in New Hampshire or Vermont, missing at least one of the three practices per week. The season began with several assistant coaches, but none of them attended practices with any consistency and I found myself to be the only coach to attend every practice that season. The season started of much better with a win or two in the earlier part of the schedule.

Jack and the Bean Stalk came back returned from one of the publishers with the message they would print the book if I paid for it. This wasn't a good deal for me, because Ted couldn't find a way to get page after page to follow on the inter net, so I was hoping the publisher would like the concept enough to invest into getting the inter net portion of the story up. The second publishers came back with a simple 'no', mainly due to the fact I put an inter net address in the book which linked to a company unrelated to the book, they did comment on the address.

It was a set back receiving two thumbs down, but I was making strides with my weight and was slowly gaining strength in the gym. I had gone to school with the gym owner, Mike. He is a little guy, probably about five feet tall, but he is strong for his size. It's just a bit comical to see such a short individual own a gym that produces large men.

As the Youth Football season came to an end, we found ourselves tied for the final play-off spot. We won a game to break the tie, on a Wednesday and lost Sunday in the same week, with little rest, to the number one team in the play-offs. It was a good season considering the previous years debacle, but I told myself I wouldn't come back for another season. I felt under valued for the amount of football and winning I had attained in the past.

The winter came blowing in again through New England, putting another freeze to the region. The Holidays came and went without any memorable moments. If my memory serves me correctly I even stayed home for New Years. Though I did make the decision to get into Real Estate as I watched my father make some good money along with a lot of free time to do as he wished. The decision to pursue a Real Estate license also affected my pot smoking. I quit smoking herb, in order to fully concentrate and focus my energies on the profession.

CHAPTER 21

2003 began with a renewed optimism for my future. I had been considered stable for quite sometime and was looking forward to the possibility of returning to the work force in the form of Real Estate. The beginning of the year also featured a visit to the Super Bowl by my beloved Oakland Raiders. Unfortunately they fell victim to the John Gruden (former Raiders coach) lead Tampa Bay Buccaneers. I'm one to believe the distraction of the Raiders ProBowl center going AWOL caused the team to loose focus on the game, but I got a lot of enjoyment out of their season, which fans for other teams can't say.

I began Real Estate classes hosted by *Coldwell Banker*, the company my father was now a Broker for. The class was made up of approximately 20 students eager to get their licenses. One of those candidates was my friend Eddy. The class covered the contents of a thick yellow Real Estate book. Each class would be a review of three or so chapters assigned from the previous class. The classes met nights twice a week from what I remember.

Some time during the period of classes I felt ill. It wasn't a day we had class, but just the same I didn't feel well. It was this sick feeling that lead me to quit the habit of smoking Havana Tampa cigars. From then on I only smoked the occasional traditional cigar.

Along with the class I had been working on a letter since the end of the Penn State football season to send to the legendary coach Joe Paterno. It gave a brief history of my football resume, and then moved into my double quarterback offence. To simplify what I had in mind, one QB would be in a deep shotgun position and the other would line up under center. For a full backfield I would have two split fullbacks at a running back depth. The design behind this offense is to take advantage of the prototype running/rocket arm QB's emerging in the game as a deep quarterback, with a signal calling pocket passer under center, in an attempt to get the best of both worlds. The QB under center can always go in motion to make a lane for a shotgun snap to the deep QB. The deep QB has the same opportunity to leave his spot by going in motion or moving in a change in formation. This is the idea in a single paragraph, but once one begins to move the players around a defense should have problems with match-ups. I dubbed the formation the split-I, for the QB's in an I-formation and the split set of the fullbacks. The fullbacks don't necessarily have to come from the fullback mold. I sent the brief football theory to Joe Paterno for his opinion and thoughts.

As 9-11 was a tragic date the globe morns, a tragedy at a truly local level gripped West Warwick, thrusting the small town to the national news. On February 21, 2003 the *Station Night Club* was engulfed in flames taking the lives of 100 concert attendees. This club stood less than a mile from my house and I pass the site of club daily, but months if not a year before the fire I began traveling past the club and up the hill whose foot started roughly in front of the club. Taking a left onto the street abutting the watering holes parking lot was a shorter rout home. I was taking this unnatural direction home, up the hill, in order to avoid driving passed my former High School Sweet Heart Michele's house. The house she lived in, as a youth was becoming a daily reminder of her as I drove by, when I was truly trying to put our relationship in the past. I offer this only because I consider the daily habitually unnatural behavior to be a contributor to the horrific fire. Not the igniter, but perhaps a vapor, which fueled the flames. Ultimately I believe bad karma and unsafe pyrotechnics reduced the establishment to ashes, though there is an amount of guilt I feel. I realize taking an alternate rout seems like it would have little to no effect on such a disaster and can be filed away as a coincidence, my mind does make a none pleasurable connection from time to time.

On one of the following days I was in a sub shop getting lunch while a reporter for one of the local news channels was finishing her lunch. While I waited for my sandwich to be made I couldn't help but talk to the reporter. As we exchanged conversation on the nightclub tragedy, she asked if I wanted to be interviewed. That was my goal when I struck the conversation. She asked me a few question regarding the fire and one of my answers made the news that evening. I appeared only as a voice over the video they showed of the line of cars stretching along the road trying to get a glimpse at the event. I was commenting on how I thought there wasn't much to see and people should refrain from visiting.

It wasn't long, just a few weeks, before Eddy and I finished the Real Estate classes and would need to review and study the information we had covered for the RE exam. While I studied page after page of the Real Estate book, day after day, I was engulfed in the debate on what to do with Iraq. The thing I found most ridiculous was the U.N.'s involvement in the debates. For one Iraq had a representative for his country sitting in on the U.N. day after day, as Colon Powel was making accusations of weapons of mass destruction in Iraq's possession. I often wondered why Colon Powel didn't just have one on one conversation with this individual or why couldn't this Iraqi delegate be traced or followed back to Sedum. Secondly, after the U.N. voted not to attack Iraq the United States did any way. I have to say I like the fact we thumbed our nose at the U.N. and proved in my mind, the existence of the U.N. was totally dependant on the U.S.A. On the other hand when the U.S. began to invade or attach Iraq I was disturbed. I make the same case over and over again. One life taken in war is too many. One doesn't know if a fallen soldier was to been the father or mother of a child who was to find the vaccine or find a better treatment for cancer or even a cure. Life is too precious squander on contests of who can kill better. I'm truly disappointed in the fact the W. Bush administration couldn't prevent war. I do believe in this day and age our leaders should prevent wars not begin them. Don't get me wrong when it's time to kick ass I'm all for it, but this was a preventable waist of thousands of human lives. I'm not just blasting the war without my own solution to the conflict. Early on I used the concept of rebuilding after a war and started with the thought. I suggested Iraqi's could be shuttled to sights away from the major cities to develop new modern cities, competing with the current Iraqi leadership for the hearts of the people. The military would be called on as Iraqi civilians, Americans and U.N. delegations build new modern structures, to defend not attack, the area. This would be a long project, but so is the wasteful undertaking of killing as many people as it takes to get 'freedom', because I do ask how many lives is to many.

The only positive I gained from the war was the exposure to the Moslem religion. This exposure leads me to soften on the position of a titled Jew. Originally I used the title in an attempt to recognize religions other than Christianity and also create a rival for the Pope. The thing I don't see or I am ignorant of in other religions are a high-ranking holy man which represents other extremely popular religions through out the globe. My thoughts and theories are more or less suggestions to be adapted, and or can evolve over time. For example I've also been exposed to the head of Buddhist faith, the Dalai Lama, may also be able to fill the seat opposite a Pope.

As the attacks on Iraq began I was readying myself for the Real Estate Licensing Test. There are two parts to the licensing exam. The thick yellow book covered the national test and a stack of state laws are mailed for one to study. The first time I took the exam I passed the National test and failed the state test. Again I took the state part of the exam and failed, but on my third try I passed the state test. I guess the third times the charmer.

Spring began making its presents felt as April and the war continued, even though no weapons of mass destruction where found in Iraq. The mail produced a letter from Joe Paterno. It contained a one-line thank you for sharing my thoughts. I was pleased with the response, even if it wasn't truly him who composed the line. Even with the arrival of this letter my focus was on Real Estate and getting started. I was introduced to the *Coldwell Banker* office in Coventry, Rhode Island early that month, but the starting date for my training had to be delayed.

My parents where taking the entire family on a cruise through the western Caribbean, which included my mother and father, my brother and his wife and their two kids, my sister and myself. It was my first cruise and I very much enjoyed the week out to sea, as well as, the tropical stops on the way and I highly recommend such a vacation to anyone. The thing I remember most about the trip was the amount of food available, especially at the buffet. It was a pleasant voyage, one that actually lived up to the hype.

When we returned I began my Fast Start training *Coldwell Banker* provides for its new people. My friend Eddy also started these classes, but his attendance became spotty until he stopped showing up. The training classes consisted of a full day of information over a few weeks time. I was still in Fast Start when I received my first listing of a house. I was lucky enough to receive a phone call during the

Coventry offices opportunity time, which I had picked up on one of the days I wasn't in the training classes. I made an appointment to see the home in Exeter and my father helped me land the listing. He did the heavy lifting with the presentation and I was an observer, but the listing was placed under my name.

I recall making phone calls during our breaks in the Fast Start classes to set up showings for the Colonial style house. I also had a buyer for a Condo in West Warwick, when my dad sent me on appointment to show the Condo. The individual interested in purchasing the unit was a guy roughly my age. Another young guy, Mike, who also worked out of the Coventry office, listed this Condo and we worked on the deal together. Unfortunately the deal fell apart on three separate occasions before Mike and I gave up on the transaction. The problem with the deal was my buyer couldn't get the financing he was promised by the Mortgage Company that per-approved him.

Back in Fast Start we where directed to make five phone calls simply letting five people we knew know we where starting a career in Real Estate. I contacted five, one of which was an assistant coach with me in the Youth Football League, Matt. This call planted a seed, which would be cultivated at a later date.

During one class, we were somehow asked what are hobbies where and what we did in our free time? It was an easy answer fore me. When my turn to volunteer my interests I stated that I painted, fine arts painting and weight trained. This caught the attention of one of the female students in the class and she approached me the next break inquiring about my art, because she was on an arts committee in New Port. By this time I had taken digital photos of my works, printed the samples and bound them in sleeves. I keep the book in my car for just such an occasion to show off and offered the examples for her to look at. Her name was Lisa and she was impressed enough to ask if I could bring one of my pieces to show her. The next time the class met I brought the landscape from Pawtucket.

Lisa and I started a relationship, which lasted over the course of a few weeks. She was older than I was. At the time I was 30 and she was in her early 40's, but that's not the reason we didn't last. We had fun together, we went to a play, attended an art exhibit, ate at several different restaurants around Kent County (town including West

Warwick), as well as, New Port. The reason we didn't see each other longer was that fact I stopped calling her, just to see if or when she would call me, but she never did.

The home I had listed in Exeter kept me occupied and a potential buyer made an offer on the house, but only if it was possible to put an in ground pool in. I had to do the legwork in the Exeter town hall to see where the septic tank was in the yard. It was quite an experience rummaging through the boxes of plats and lots only to discover the septic tank sat where the buyers wanted to put the pool and the deal fell through.

Summer produced a buyer for the home. My father was able to procure a qualified and ready buyer for the colonial, but he shaved a point, which did upset me. I got over it and my first house was sold with obvious help from my father.

The summer also saw my Manager, Coreen, through a Labadoozy party at her house. This party theme comes from the Island of Labadie, which is one of the stops on the cruise I went on and oddly enough Coreen had gone on at a different time. At the party I encountered another agent from the office, Maria. She was also an artist and for a second time I pulled my samples from my car to display. Like Lisa, Maria was a bit older than I. Again I had just turned 30 that May and she was in her mid to late 40's, but the age hurdle didn't keep us from getting together.

July 4th I went to Oakland Beach in Warwick to try and get some shots of the fire works. The web site I went on to find fire works for the night accidentally listed Oakland Beach for the 4th. The only fire works I saw where somewhere across the bay and to far away to get a descent shot. What salvaged the night was my meeting of a man called 'Red'. He was in his 60's or 70's and was walking around without his shirt on revealing his tattoo of the Statue of Liberty on his chest. I couldn't resist taking a photo of this colorful character to paint later. I asked if I could take a few shots of him and his friend and he allowed me to. He made my night and this picture would go into my files to paint at a later date.

In the gym I came across a friend of mine and a player on both the 1989 and 1990 championship football teams, Tom, who told me he was going to be the head coach for the Youth Football team I had helped coach. Somehow I was sucked back in, mostly because I thought Tommy could use my help. I knew he didn't know what to expect. He took the job seriously, we met a few time to make plans for the up coming season. Once August came around and practices started I knew he had to be surprised at the lack of enthusiasm from the mostly 13 and 14 year olds. His nephew was on the team and Tom let a lot ride on his nephew's success at quarterback.

When I came to coach in the Youth Football League, Matt, one of the five people I call to let them know I was starting in Real Estate, informed me he would be moving and remembered the call I had made to him, which led him to obtain my services. They, him and his wife Ginnie, asked me to find them a house a well as list their home. We met before practices to start things off and get better acclimated with each other. This would be the first time I worked solo on a transaction or transactions, as would be the case.

Maria stopped by at one of the practices to check out what I was up to. We had good times together. I recall golfing on an occasion, she cooked me diner a few times and we ate in her yard under grape vines, went out to clubs, attended a Red Sox game, but most of the time I would visit her apartment to spend time together.

August practices and the obstacles leading up the season, like tag day and weigh-ins where events I could give a heads up to, but the actual playing of games where a totally different topic. The season started with loses, which had to wake Tom up, I know he said he intended on winning every game that season and I somewhat told him to keep his optimism guarded. The team didn't only lose the first few games, but they lost me as a coach. I was getting busier with work, I wasn't really needed and I really couldn't take another season of loosing, so I let Tom know I was leaving the team. I believe the team lost all their games that year.

Once I severed my obligation to Tom and to the football squad I focused my full attention on Matt and Ginnie desire to move into a bigger home. We began our search for homes before listing his. We started with a home in West Warwick, which had been on the market for a while. Matt had been interested in the home for some time before the price was dropped enough for us to make an offer. It was a low offer, which was rejected, so the scope of our search grew.

Along with the work I was doing with Matt and Ginnie, my manager Coreen gave me an opportunity for another client. It was a referral from an out of state agent. I was able to list the gentleman's investment. He had a cape to sell, which was being sold separate from the apartments in the back of the house, which shared the lot. Most of the inquiries I received asked about the apartments in back, which where not for sale. Philip, the person selling this investment property was a huge maybe 6'4"or better and built like a tight end. He had to be in his early 40's and wanted to make two lots out of the one, separating the cape from the apartments in the rear. He really desired selling the cape in order to pay off the mortgage and retain the six units in back, free and clear of a mortgage.

It was around this time, late August to early September, I went to refill my medication when the *CVS Pharmacy* in East Greenwich changed my prescription without consulting my doctor or myself, to a cheaper generic brand. The drug I was on, up until that point, was Lithobid, a designer drug. The pharmacy chose to fill the bottle with a generic Lithium drug. The pharmacy told me my doctor didn't specify I needed Lithobid, so they made the switch. I was quite upset and called my case manager Jackie to complain. She called the *CVS* in East Greenwich and they fill my prescription with Lithobid.

That remedied the problem until the next time I went to fill my prescription. This time I went to a *CVS* in Cranston, because the other pharmacy had left me with a bad taste in my mouth. Once again I was given the generic Lithium drug because it cost less. This second instance had me even more upset and I called for an appointment to see my case manager. Jackie and Dr. Koyfman convinced me the generic drug would be just as effective as the Lithobid. I accepted what they told me, but not before letting them know I wasn't happy about the change and I would be filing a complaint against *CVS* with the *Department of Business Regulations*. That week I filled out the complaint forms and sent them into the DBR.

In high insight, I believe it was at this time my mind began to reach for the closed door that had my mania caged. I was considered stable up until this point, but I believe I began to slip after the switch. It was a slow steady slide back into mania.

I listed Matt and Ginnies home on the last day of September. I came across a boundary dispute with one of their neighbors. An aging woman living next door had filled a complaint with a lawyer, but the title was free of any leans, as the woman never followed through. She was looking for a cash settlement, which never happened. We found a house for them in North Kingstown just after putting their home on the market. We where somewhat under the gun to sell their house now that they had gone under contracts on the North Kingstown home, but he did make the purchase subject to the sale of their home.

When a buyer and a seller agree on a price and conditions, they sign a purchase and sales agreement. From the time of the signing or excision the buyer has 10 days to carry out inspections. I know this now, but after Matt and Ginnie came to terms on the house in North Kingstown I had no idea of the 10 days to conduct inspections. During the 10 days, some where around the 5th of 6th day, Columbus Day came around. It marks the anniversary of my first hospitalization. The night leading up to the holiday I spent time at the *Foxy Lady* before they closed. I then traveled to the *Foxwoods Casino* for a little gambling. It was then early evening when I returned to Providence to visit Butler Hospital. I didn't go to check in, rather I went their as David Michael to ask if David Garcia had been checked into the facility. The guard at the front desk was an old man and told me he hadn't after checking his list. From there I went to a *Starbucks* in Warwick for a drink. My celebration of Columbus Day, which started earlier that morning at the *Foxy Lady*, continued as I made my way to the *Providence Place Mall*. While cruising around the Mall I was stopped by a woman who asked if I would be part of a survey for $5. I had nothing to loose so I accepted her offer. After an attempt at a survey on bottled water I was taken to do a survey with cleaning products. It didn't take long I just had to pick out the products I had seen before. The company *Performance Plus* gave me a $5 bill and asked me to come back for a music survey fore $60. Again I accepted the date, which was two weeks in the distance, but it was sixty bucks.

Later in the day my mind was consumed with football, more than likely due to the fact it was football season. I was think about the offence I had come up with and was thinking along the lines on how sports evolve in style and some times the same game can be played differently. Again I was thinking football and the small differences the Canadian league had, when compared to the NFL. The Canadian 120-yard by 60-yard field with 20-yard deep end zones, justified my thinking, for new playing dimensions and design. I came up with a 100-yard circle, with hash marks of 50 yards apart, which would run down the field and line up with the edge of the end zones, which would be found out side the circle. I would also run a strip of hash marks straight through the center of the field to spot the ball on. The end zones would be 50 yards wide and 10 yards deep from the middle of the end zone, but the end zones goal line would hug the circle, creating a goal line that lies partly in the backfield. This would lead to the rule; the offense can't line up in the end zone, so they need to line up along the end zone and the defense can't line up beyond the ball.

Other changes I would implement would be no more kicking. The offence always goes for it on 4th down, because the receiving team would get position wherever the ball lands at the end of the play. Deep pass routes would be the norm. If the offensive player does come down with it it's a first down, but if the ball simply falls to the ground it takes on the rules of a punt in today's NFL. The long passes should lead to more scoring. A field goal try would come from an underhand throw from the backfield and a player would throw off instead of kick off to start play. Kicking's bad for football. Kickers aren't football players in my mind. In addition I would add two players to each side of the field due to the wider surface. I would also suggest the same 4 downs, but a team would have to go 15 yards for the first down. I would like a rule of four men in the backfield, lined up between the tackles and two men in the slot, with the ability to line up on the same side or on different sides. I also never said the men in the backfield couldn't go out for a pass after the snap. That was pretty much the end of my celebration of Columbus Day.

I began growing a Bolshevik style beard to try to add something new and different into the deal with Matt and Ginnie. The sellers agent gave me a ring the next day asking when we where going to conduct inspections, informing me of the 10 days. By this time it was near impossible to schedule the inspections. Matt didn't seem to be bothered and said he would have the house inspected at a later date for informational purposes only, waving the 10 days for inspection. I also still had to find a buyer for his property.

Though the calls I received on Philip's property, the cape, almost always, with a rear exception, asked if the apartments in the back where for sale? I had to tell investors they where not, but the cape was. I met with Phil a couple of times to talk over the survey needed to produce separate lots for the cape and apartments. The main obstacle was the driveway went to the back apartments, which would run through what would be the capes lot in front. We concocted a few scenarios for the boundary lines to avoid an easement on the property, but needed to speak with a surveyor to see what could be done.

Philip on an occasion mentioned to me he shot clay pigeons with a shotgun. The more and more I encountered Phil the more I liked him. He personified the strong silent type. I would have conversation with him where I would finish speaking and he would just sit there until I began to cover another topic. He made such an impression on me I strongly considered him to be a Visroi candidate, if I needed some one to fill the position on the spot. He was a big boy selling a toy. To me he was a man built like a building, like the chess piece of the rook.

At the gym I had gained a great deal of strength over the past year as well as losing the weight I wanted to, and kept the weight off because my doctor took me off of the drug putting the weight on. That drug was Haldol and Dr Koyfman had dropped the med from my regiment way back in February or March, but I continued taking the generic Lithium I was given. I was waiting to hear from the DBR, but heard nothing, while in the gym I thought there where people from *CVS* watching me. One day I did mumble something to one of them as I passed by. Something like, "So you think so?" The guy asked if I was talking to him and I said no I was talking to myself.

As I had plugged Philip into a possible Visroi spot I did the same with Mike the owner of the *Worlds Gym*. As a reminder, Mike was all of 5 feet tall. I really liked the size difference in the Visroi candidates, Mike and Phil. As Phil was like a building like a castle, Mike would reside in a castle. They went hand and hand in my mind.

Coreen was not only the manager for the Coventry office, but also the Narragansett office. Narragansett is a beach town sitting in the southern part of the state. I figured the houses went for more down there and I would like to try the area out. I asked her if I could transfer down there in the New Year and she gave it the O.K.

I wasn't keeping track of my finances and went through a good amount of money, but hadn't emptied the coughers just yet. I don't have the foggiest of what happened to my first commission check, but I did know I was going to the *Foxy Lady* a lot and was still seeing Maria, although she wasn't a huge drain on my wallet.

I attended the music survey for *Performance Plus* and got $60 to sit and listen to music for about two hours or so with about forty other people. They played a song for a few seconds; then played another, then another. We where furbished with a dial. Each went from 0 to 100 and we would have to judge each song with the dial. It was an easy 60 bucks and I was invited back for a DVD survey at a later date for another 60 bones.

My cousin John was getting married in Chicago late October and my family and I where invited, but I refused to travel by plane with the rest of my family, I declared it to be too risky. I opted to take the train and leaving for Chicago a few days a head of everyone else. Maria dropped me off at the train station. The train took its time, but I made it there ahead of everyone else. I rented a car and stayed at motels I came across on the way. One of the days before the wedding I met my cousin John, his fiancé, my cousin Ben, my Uncle Tony and his wife Isabel. After meeting them I went off on my own, as not to disturb any plans they may have had.

From there I visited a casino near by and stayed at another motel before the wedding. I met my family there, but for the first time I can remember I carried angst toward my family, with distinction to my father. It was a beautiful wedding and it appeared to go off without a hitch. Before I knew it I was back on the train headed to Rhode Island.

Maria picked me up at the station. Unfortunately on the way home she stated the fact she was much older than I was and she suggested we stop seeing one another. She was right and I agreed we should go our separate ways. Even though we had several years in between us we had a fun time together.

When I returned I found there was no money left in my account. At first I thought someone had to have gotten a hold of my debit card number and emptied the account until I saw my bank statement. There was a lot of nickel and dimming, but the trip to Chicago was the final culprit in the emptying of the account.

Anyhow the firewood for the winter had arrived and I insisted I would only stack the wood if my father gave me the $4,000 left over from my Disability Reward Check. He was holding it for me in one of his accounts. After a little bit of friction and questioning of where my money had gone, he cut me a check and I stacked all the firewood.

As the days in October approached the end of the month I

received, as all Realtors in the state did, a letter from the Rhode Island Association of Realtors (RIAR) listing positions to be filled by qualified candidates. I thought this would be a good opportunity to beef up my Real Estate background, if I could land a spot. Working against me was the fact it was noted two years experience was preferred. Along with the letter was something regarding Sub-agency. I took the time to write a letter concerning my views on Sub-agency and attached it to my sheet with the positions I would like to fill. I then hand delivered the envelop to the Kent Washington Board of Realtors office, where the contents where looked over on the spot. The woman who viewed my application and letter gave me the phone number of someone to call in RIAR. Her name was Monica. I spoke with Monica on issues concerning Real Estate and I began thinking I had an in, which gave me high hopes. In fact she mentioned a task force I could work on in the New Year.

On the first Sunday of September I conducted an Open House for Matt and Ginnies Raised Ranch. I had a turn out of about six couples, but there was one couple who stood out in my mind. They seem to look around the house with comfort and a serious eye. The following Monday I gave them a call and left a message on their machine asking them to call their agent if they where interested in the Raised Ranch. The next day their Realtor, Lori, gave me a call and later in the week we put together a deal for Matt and Ginnies house. That same week saw the house Matt and Ginnie reached agreements on in North Kingstown conducted inspection. Things where now coming together.

I attended the *Performance Plus* focus group on DVD's I was asked to sit in on for $60 in the Providence Place Mall. The Mall Is right next door to the State House and I have to mention Rhode Island has a beautiful and unique Capital Building, in fact it has the second largest free standing dome on earth. At least that's my understanding of the dome. Having frequented the Mall more frequently with the *Performance Plus* surveys a desire to some day work in the magnificent structure began to build. Not only did it begin to build I thought the State House would be the perfect venue for a wedding to take place. There is a balcony over looking the back lawn, to be filled with invitees, perfect for the exchange of vows, but first I would have to find the perfect bride, perhaps a Massajahess.

Going back to the DVD survey, I was taken into a room with

roughly six or seven other guys to talk about TV shows we would like to see on DVD. The one comment I remember making was I would love to see a Boston Red Sox World Series Championship on DVD. This is a few weeks after Aaron Boons home run dashing the Sox hopes of a championship to bits. After the focus group I was handed $60 cash.

One of these autumn nights I began to write. I began to write this book. The first page or so really took a good deal of time, as I had to over come the initial fear of writing and remembering all that had happened.

I not only began to pen this book, I also scribbled another letter to the Penn State Head Coach. I do mean scribble. Acting on an impulse I grabbed some lines paper, quickly authored five or more pages and faxed them to the football office. I used the fax number on the letterhead from the initial response I received from Joe Paterno. I still have the make shift letter which never received a response. In the letter I spell out I may be the next coach to fill his shoes. This crudely planned pursuit of a coaching career had manifested itself as a respectable position to fill a Massajah's resume, for just a short period of time.

The thought of the Massajah position had now worked its way back into my conscious. I felt being rung up the professional ladder could achieve a great deal of influence. Possible recognition as a Judge would certainly create a great deal of respect. My fantasy took me beyond an ordinary Judge, rather thirsting for a Supreme Court Justice. This to me would be the ultimate feather in my cap and I seriously pondered a return to school to get a law degree to start the chase. Taking the story line further I came up with a scenario to pad a Massajah's legend. From the position of Supreme Court Justice I would step down from the bench to run for President. These where passing thoughts as I also remembered my political parties.

I resorted back to the Freedom Party, which up linked to the Federalist, which morphed into the Phederalists, which served as the springboard to the Populists. I always looked at new parties with strange curiosity. Almost all the parties say they are grass roots, when they turn around and prop up a single candidate for Governor, a states highest position, or President, the nations highest title. What ever happened to the Mayors and local Representatives? I consider these to be lower achievable grass roots level positions to build on. With this I selected the Freedom Party in an attempt to cultivate a new political party.

I will share my hopes and views for the political party. First of all I like the Rhino as the parties political animal. I'll begin with the always-controversial subject of abortion. I have a strong belief in the right to life, to the point I will lecher: One doesn't know the potential of an unborn human. The life of a great scientist who may be destine to come up with an AIDS vaccine, or cure or better treatment for cancer. A great athlete may have been snuffed out, or an amazing artist will never hold a brush or actor. I truly believe humans destine for great things have already been snuffed out due to abortion. In fact I will now jump to the other side of the coin, because I feel a delectate topic like abortion needs understanding of both points of view. I do consider abortion to be necessary in our society to keep woman from harming themselves and their unborn child. Now I will give you my solution to the problem. As a pro-lifer I would insist that every woman asking for an abortion have three interviews with families wishing to adopt. If the woman can resist the desire of families that can't participate in such a gift on their own, the option of abortion will remain an option.

Second I push space exploration and travel and to the top of my agenda. I theories we as humans will find alternative fuels as well as remedies for illness throughout our galaxy. Answers do lie some where out there. I have to add the party and I recognize when humans first entered space, I believe, in the late 50' early 60's, humans made more than just a leap for mankind. For the first time in human existence we left the cell called earth, freeing us all from the planet that has held us captive over thousands of years. That's freedom. I'm such a proponent of space exploration I push for a federal holiday in July, I believe July 20, marking the first moon landing, holiday to celebrating exploration as we due on Columbus Day. If one says we can't have two holidays in July I ask them to look at the big two holidays of Christmas and New Years, which are in the same week. It's also much warmer in July than December and January.

I have a very different point of view on the funding of health care for everyone. I've kept this solution to myself until now. I've never really worked the numbers, but I believe in a drugs for drugs funding of health care. Keep an open and free mind when I suggest the legalization of drugs could generate enough money to back health care. That's right drugs for drugs. I don't offer this without reservation. First of all I believe in an age scale for drugs. I really struggle whether to make the legal age to smoke pot be 18 or 35. I do want it to stay away from young people, but 18 is roughly the age I could see getting ones hands on marijuana, I would suggest the age 35 be the age to purchase cocaine. Drugs like heroin I really don't like at any age, but 40 may be a prescribed age.

I have no room for other drugs like crack or meth. Another drug like acid or magic mushrooms may be 21 or 25. I do see all the profits going toward health care, but some may think taxation may be enough, but I prefer a strictly regulated drug culture. I believe crime will also go down, now that smuggling and dealing would be gone and the money to combat drug smuggling can be used elsewhere. I add that smoking and alcohol are two of the more filthy drugs out there. I offer the freedom to use drugs and get healthcare. I do prescribe places drugs are sold there be information and posters detailing the ill effects of drug use. Accompanying that I advocate media drives warning the negative effects coming with drug use. It would also be more visible if an individual had a drug problem do to the more tolerable stance. Such an individual's drug use wouldn't force them into a secret life of abuse.

As I suggested early on in this book sports should be considered as an alternative to war. War is another necessary evil I don't enjoy, but I do understand a superpower can't relegate it self as defenseless. War should be averted or prevented in this day and age of athletics and sports. These are our greatest men and women. Do battle freely and aggressively.

I am an isolationist and an expansionalist at the same time. The United States should look after the well being of their nation relying on it's own ingenuity and innovation. If other nations choose to join our cause I welcome them. The only occasion I do O.K. war is when the United States chooses to expand their boarders. I do strongly insist the U.S. can provide a better life for other struggling countries. In my mind the United States government should rule earth.

Guns are a tough topic. I'll put in my two cense as a person who doesn't own a gun. Bullets should somehow be more difficult to get a hold of, perhaps regulated in some way. I suggest an outrageous tax on bullets making them less accessible, perhaps as much as $5 to $10 on each individual bullet, maybe even more severe. I don't think guns can go away, I suggest a more difficult process to receive the honor, obligation, and conduct of owning a weapon. I fall on the freedom to bear arms at an expense.

Another topic in some circles is tax reform and I do believe reform is necessary. Earlier in this book I gave a tax plan with $1 on every ten dollars, $5 on every hundred dollars and so on... This plan actually is close to what happens once thousands of dollars are being taxed. I don't remember exactly when, but it dawned on me the only reason we still have coins and haven't evolved into only paper money is the fact we need the six or seven cense tax to pay on every dollar. I propose getting rid of coins and going with paper money only, by taxing 1 dollar for every ten dollars spent. This would make any item fewer than ten dollars taxed free. I realize there aren't many things out there less than ten bucks, but there are quite a few if one looks. I would still recommend a progressive tax that would go up to $5 on every hundred, $10 on every thousand, $15 on every ten thousand and so on. I still believe employees shouldn't be taxed, but the businesses they work for should. This would have to be calculated by how many employees and the revenue a business accumulated. I support people having more money in their pockets to spend rather than tax it out of them. I hope taxation reform could come from the business minded Visroi position, while working with the government to sort things out. My statement 'the only reason we haven't done away with change is the six or seven cense tax on a dollar' wasn't exactly true. Such items as stamps, photo copies, paper and children's penny candy, as well as, other items fall beneath the dollar. I propose the addition of a paper half and quarter dollar or hiking the price of these items up to the dollar or even selling them in packs that push the value over the dollar mark.

That was a rough guideline of how I would like to shape the Freedom Party. What the party needs are members to discuss all the pertinent topics. It was late November when I made my first real move in the start of the Freedom Party. I went to the state capital, told the guard at the door I was there to see how I could get a party started and picked up directions to another office outside of the capital. For some reason I didn't trust the directions I was given, so I made a second visit to the capital. This time I would enter the building after smoking some pot. I'm not really sure when I started smoking again, but I wondered through the capital building with a buzz. I went to the same room as last time and they gave me the same information as before. I was just checking to make sure I was pointed in the right direction.

From there I did follow the directions to the office on the map I was provided. I received more literature there and was given the heads up, to register a party one needs to get x number of signatures, have a candidate in the Governors race get 5% of the vote or have a Presidential candidate get 5% of the vote. I put this information in a safe place until I needed it.

I still had my mind on Matt and Ginnie who where closing on both the home in North Kingstown and their home in West Warwick on December 18. The date came quickly as the holiday cheer made its presents felt. The day before the closing a football player from the past passed away. Otto Graham wore the numbers 14 and 60 for the Cleveland Browns. He quarterbacked 7 Championship teams and appeared in the championship game each of the years he played. He was someone I was exposed to as a youth during some football show and he stayed with me.

The next day, the day of the closings, I wore all black and let Matt know I was dressed as such in memory of Otto. The closings went by with out a problem. We had the first closing in the morning and the second in the afternoon. The lawyer in the afternoon was someone my father had used several times and I told him Joe was my father. The lawyer was somewhat a comic. I mentioned to him in conversation I was considering going back to school to pursue a law degree and he for some reason shot down the idea. I remember it because I commented my law career was already over. With that the closing went fine. With the closings going down I was now owed about $5000 between the two. Don't ask me how, but I was spending the $4000 I got for stacking the wood like water and the $5000 would be a welcome replenishment. The $5000 would come in two separate checks, because there was a different company representing the sell in the North Kingstown deal.

At the time I was looking for some male influence in my life and called the Mental Health Center asking if I could change my case manager and doctor, who where both women, to males. I talked to someone and voiced my request and he obliged the best he could at that point.

As Christmas approached I made the decision to only buy toys for the children involved, my brothers kids Zack and Lucas, and a nephew Nicholas. I got each of them three toys and a book. Each of them received their toys in a bag I had to stick the sides up on. They seemed to enjoy the toys, which is all that mattered. Another reason I bought toys only for the children was I spent all the money I had and was waiting for those two checks to come in.

I spent an awful lot of time driving from home to the office to check on my checks. Each afternoon I would make the drive to see if any checks had come in the mail. Each day I wasted gas until I had to search for coins in between the couch cushions to put gas in the car.

New Years came along and Denis was having a party at his tattoo shop. One of the checks came on New Years Eve, but the bank needed a day for it to clear. It ticked me off that I had to wait not one more day, but two more because the bank wasn't going to be open on New Years. I was out of luck, so I asked Denis if I could borrow $100 until my check cleared. He did willingly, knowing I had money on the way. I had a good time at my friend Denis's party. I had a bottle of wine I was drinking. Either I won in an office raffle or our loan officer gave it as a Christmas gift. It was a memorable New Years in part because of the generosity of Denis.

I waited until the day after New Years to get my money out of the bank and went straight to Denis to pay him back. One of my New Years Resolutions was to learn how to snow board, so I bought an $800 snowboard. Blew more money at the *Foxy Lady* and bought an *AFI*, a musical group, CD titled *Sing the Sorrow*. I was attracted to them after seeing one of their music videos a few times. I listened to the disc on my way to *Loon Mountain* to snowboard for the first time. The only problem was they didn't have night skiing and I got there around five o'clock. I then headed back to Rhode Island and more than likely the *Foxy Lady* to blow more money. On the way home I really got into the CD, especially the first track on the disk.

As I got into the music my imagination produced a globe and as the music shouted out I envisioned the migration across the ice bridge across the Bering Strait. The shouting pushed the travelers over the bridge and saw them settle along North and South American. Over and over again I watched this process in my mind. The best I could make of this was the Indians who where the first settlers arrived through being nomads from Asia, which crossed over the ice bridge thousands of years ago. I don't know if this has any scientific validity or maybe it was something I had learned in my schooling, which surfaced. With these visions came a image of Vincent D'Onofrio, detective on *Law and Order* or psycho cadet in *Full Metal Jack*, appearing to be listen to my thoughts on a head set, which would disturb him when I pushed the explorers over the ice bridge. James Gandolfini also entered my imagination at this time, but in a less active role. It was almost as if he were concerned for my welfare.

Some of this thinking led me to the selecting of some Visroi candidates. "The Donald" Donald Trump was an easy selection. The primer moneyman in the United States, dealing primarily in Real Estate, Castle or Rook. He is definitely a boy with a toy. Another candidate coming to mind was Mike Tyson. Mike has seen to good, the bad and the ugly of being famous and wealthy. He has risen from poverty, experienced the glory and wealth of being the Champion of the World, as well as the captivity of prison. I also like the circus atmosphere surrounding him when someone has to negotiate with him from a distant land or existence, it's kind of like saying we have a guy like this can you explain his behavior. He is kind of built like a castle or Rook, can still beat the hell out of 99.9% of the human population, a Visroi candidate.

By this time mania had all but taken control of my thoughts and imagination. The best I can do to convey the mental state would be to imagine being in a state of worship, prier, or meditation every minute of the day. Visuals and topics shift back and forth with out much logic, though thoughts are returned to work on from one time to another.

One such topic was the complaint I had filed against *CVS* for changing my medication from Lithobid to Lithium without consoling my doctor or myself. It was a reminder or return to this topic that lead to an idea to settle my complaint. I came up with the idea I would like to start a University in Rhode Island with the backing of *CVS*. Founding a University could also gain respectability for a young Massajah. I thought about this in great detail. I would call the institution the Rhodes University and would like to sprinkle the campus around the islands in Narragansett Bay. Having the campus spread around the islands would call for a ferry and bridge system. With this system I envisioned a Colossus of Rhodes to straddle over a bridge, appearing to be holding the bridge from falling into the ocean water. The idea came to me as I placed designs on a campus scattered around the islands, which reminded sailors of the bays islands of that of the Greek islands of Rhodes, which Rhode Island takes its name. The Colossus could become a national treasure and a strong male to impress the Statue of Liberty on the Northeastern Atlantic coast.

My wish would have a school built on Medicine and Art. I had hope of establishing a power in New England able to compete with other Universities and Colleges in athletics, as there are no schools in the region competing for National Titles. I realize this is a huge undertaking and only talented young recruits could make this happen. A strong Greek presence would be prescribed for the Rhodes University. Of all the grand schemes I have dreamed up, the Rhodes University most likely would give me the respect I craved to launch me into a strong government position and an accomplishment worthy of a Massajah.

I made another trip to go snow boarding, but this time to Watchusset Mountain in Massachusetts. They had night skiing and my first experience as a snowboarder came fast and with a lot of dumps. I was very surprised at the speed of the sport. I made four runs, all of which took me straight down the mountain on an easy trail with several biffs on the way down.

The following day I visited the *Foxwoods Casino* on the just over the Rhode Island boarder into Connecticut. I played some stud poker, ate at the buffet and even took time to bet on a horse named Fenway, I couldn't resist putting a bet on. The horse actually won the race and I won a few bucks. In fact I was up for the day before the race. While I was waiting for my commission checks to come in, the animosity toward my father grew. In my now eroding and clouded thought process, I held my father partially to blame for the snail like pace the checks where being processed. My logic at the time was the company was disrespecting me while my father stood by and watched.

After visiting the casino I traveled back to the office in Coventry to see if the second check had found its way into my mailbox. When I arrived in the late afternoon the office was empty with the exception of my father and low and behold the second check had surfaced. I began to taunt my father telling him I didn't need him to go through a transaction. I continued in my verbal bashing telling him he wasn't a good father and I was better than he was. The door to the office then opened and a couple came in and my father showed his clients into the conference room. This silenced my assault for the time being, but after a few a few minutes of silence, I chose to interrupt his meeting addressing the clients, with the verbal message he was an awful father and I was better than he was and they shouldn't deal with him. I was doing my best to blow his deal. After several moments of my verbal nonsense my dad called 9-11 telling the emergency operator I had a history of mental illness, was acting up and needed some help.

Witnessing this call I stayed in the office for a few minutes longer before exiting the office where I was met by three police officers in the parking lot. They had me sit down while all three surrounded me until a rescue arrived. Once in the rescue vehicle I began spewing information at one of the paramedics. I showed him my collection of what I told him where my playing cards. On the top was my ID, followed by my debit card. The next card down was my *Foxwoods* card and the *Foxy Lady* VIP card defiantly gave him a surprise. I also shared with him a theory I was working on the attack of space. I told him I put the United States Marine Corp. into the British Armada to pick up the pace of space travel and exploration. I'm also pretty sure I gave one of them if both weren't paying attention, some of my political philosophy. I never told them I was the Massajah, but I told the EMT works someone should have started filming my every move, to prove what I was up to, a while ago. I meant that in the context off my experiences over the course of the past few years. Soon enough I was dropped off at Kent County Hospital with a return trip to Butler Hospital looming.

CHAPTER 22

I found myself in a waiting room in Kent County Hospital with a more than curtain trip to Butler Hospital in my future. I waited alone in a small room with a Hospital employee guarding my door. The young man was dressed in a blue blazer and tie. His name was Joseph, which upset me, as my father's name is also Joseph. At one point when asked whom I would like to see. I commented, "Only Joe Paterno could help me now."

A new unexpected experience began when I was asked to get undressed, put my clothes in a bag, and jump into a jonnie. From there I had another considerable wait before I was admitted into a wing of Kent County Hospital. I was relegated to a bed in the hospital. A strange twist had been thrown my way. I was more than sure I would be shipped off to Butler, but I was informed they had no beds available at Butler Hospital. This was a queue, as I didn't enjoy my stays at Butler.

Seated by my side was a young lady. Not always the same girl, but a different set of eyes to ensure I didn't wander from my bed. Though it seemed the company of one of the girls was there almost every morning. It was your typical two-bedroom hospital room. I believe I had two different roommates during my stay.

I had unexpected doctor visits from time to time to check on my mental state. I remember answering their question of if I wanted to go to Butler with a smart, "I shouldn't take up a bed that could be better used by someone else." Another question I answered with honesty was "How do you feel about you father?" Again I gave my honest answer, "I would like to strangle him, but I realize there are laws against such a thing." Somehow these answers kept a few different doctors at bay? I can also recall not being medicated for the first few days of my stay. This was the first time marijuana was detected in my system, though it never became an issue, most likely due to the fact I had no sign of the drug in my system the first two hospitalizations I experienced.

I watched a lot of TV, as I was confined to my bed almost 24 hours of the day. They allowed me out of my room, chaperoned by the girl on duty, to fill a small pitcher of water just down the hall. Other than that I only left my bed for bathroom visits.

One of the movies I watched while laying there was *The Running Man* staring Arnold Schwarzenegger. Watching the movie sparked my imagination to consider Arnold as a possible Visroi. He has lived the American dream and is a large man, whose initial fame came as a body builder, Mister Universe in fact, before a wildly successful acting career. I couldn't resist a partnership between Arnold and the owner of the *World's Gym* I worked out at, Mike. Again Arnold is a massive individual, while Mike is vertically challenged.

My mind continued working overtime. I would like to share a theory I had been working on leading up to and during this hospitalization. I look out at the great number of universes that may exist in space and may have societies evolved a little further than ours while others may lag behind. For instance the automobile is old hat for earth, but may be a new innovation in another human experiment. Again there may exist a race starting colonize on planets other than their own. Another example would be film and the camera. I could see the advent of film and photography struggle behind other advances like flight. To me film has had the most influence on the human race since fire. Without film there are no movies, no photos, no glossy magazines and no TV. As they say, 'A picture says a thousand words.' On some level of evolving humans could still be struggling with fire out there. For what it's worth I consider fire to be the first example of technology. With out fire one cannot forge metals or mold plastics, as well as, burn fuel.

With our advancements in technology I suggest science has truly achieved a level of magic that can't be denied. Yes magic is being produced all around us. We put a liquid formula in our vehicles allowing them to travel without the power of horses. We talk to people thousands of miles away with the touch of a few buttons. The most mysterious instance of technology or magic I don't understand and would still more than likely not understand how a DVD or CD player works. There is a little glass dome in a box that when one puts in a magic circle (CD) either music is produced or a show is played out on a piece of glass on one side of a magic box (television). What perplexes me most is the fact the little dome in the box never makes contact with the CD, some how the wizards out there have reproduced theatre and music with, I guess, some kind of beam or light. I saved my favorite for last. The remote control somehow with a touch of a button changes the show on the glass surface of the TV box with no strings or need to leave ones chair. Again I guess some kind of beam or light switches what is being watched. It also allows for the sound to be raised or lowered. In my mind this reminds me of magic wands. All that needs to be done is to produce a remote in the shape of a wand, with the necessary buttons to be pushed along the side. I'd also love to see a remote in the shape of a toy gun to shoot the unentertaining shows away.

It is this theory that got me into trouble. The guillotine once existed on our planet and the fantasy I was producing envisioned space travelers who still had the guillotine as a method of capital punishment. My mind felt threatened by theses 'pirates', because I feared if they ever came to our planet they would reinstate the device with me first. I felt this because the Massajah is the governmental representative when it comes to negotiating with visitors and I don't think I could talk my way out of why we still don't have the guillotine, a governmental device, as part of our system of penalty. I didn't make these thoughts known to the doctors who probed my thought, but I do feel somehow during my visit I was able to convince these travelers not to bother earth.

A program on Abraham Lincoln was on TV one of the days and I enjoyed watching the documentary. These type shows fill one with patriotism. Another show I enjoyed while at the hospital was a program on the massive hangers produced to construct space shuttles.

Through my stay I made sure I told the doctors, "There is no need for me to take up a bed that someone else needs." After the first few days of my stay the hospital did start to medicate me, but they where not giving me the doses I was taking. They fell a little short. I really have to say this was about the length of my stay. My stay spanned roughly seven to nine days before I was released into my mothers' supervision.

I had a check in my pocket for around two grand and deposited it into the bank for the one day it needed to clear. For the mean time I still had money from the first check left. The first thing I recall doing after being let go from the hospital was going to a florist and putting some flowers together and I mean that literally. I asked the florist if I could pick the flowers and arrange them in the vase and she obliged. With a little guidance from the two women working at the flower shop I was able to arrange something. It cost me around $80, which left me with a hundred or less dollars to work with until the next day.

The flowers where for the nurses, especially the girls who sat by my bedside, and the doctors I encountered in my stay at Kent County Hospital. Flowers alone can't tell them how pleased I was not to be shipped out to Butler Hospital. I delivered them in the early afternoon and was hoping to see the young lady who was at my bedside most mornings. She wasn't there when I dropped off the bouquet to the ooh's and aah's from the nurses on the floor. Most of them had nothing to do with my pleasant stay, but I really didn't mind spreading good cheer to all of them. Luckily, on my way out I came across the girl who looked over me and I gave her the heads up, I had left some flowers.

The doctors at Kent County Hospital had scheduled an appointment for me to see someone at the Kent Mental Health Center where I had been seeing Dr. Koyfman and Jackie. I had been looking to switch them both to males the last time I mentioned a visit. I went to the appointment armed with a painting of the gentleman, 'Red'; I had met on the 4th of July. It was one of my better paintings and I hoped the gift would leave a favorable impression to start with. When I arrived at the Center there was no appointment scheduled for me, but the people at the front desk where good enough to locate my new case manager, Kevin, to meet with me for a few seconds. I showed him the painting; he was impressed and accepted the gift. He didn't have much time to see me, so we scheduled another time to visit.

The next day I emptied the bank account I had deposited the check into and headed to a fire station, which had a Jeep for sale parked out front. I had noticed the Jeep before I went into the hospital and it was still there when I left. The strangest coincidence occurred when I entered the fire department and was faced with the EMT worker who I spoke with in the back of the Rescue. I gave an awkward hello and quickly let it be known was interested in the Jeep for sale. One of the

AN AMERICAN MESSIAH

men left to get the Jeeps owner and I was then given a test run. He told me I would need to put a fluid into part of the Jeep and I was O.K. with that. The Jeep was $2,400 and I gave him $500 to hold onto the Jeep until I came back.

Something re-entering my thoughts over those next few days was the return of Hell and Heaven. Somehow I came up with the God of Fire, Thor, who more than likely resides in the flames of Hell for I don't think Heaven has fire. To me this meant Hell even had a God. I took this opportunity to conduct attacks on Heaven, for if Thor was a God he at least knew where Heaven was. I would use the accuracy of the sign of the Devil, 666, to line up attacks. I envisioned several strikes producing spoils from the most holy residence. This is how my mind was occupying its thought, no matter how outlandish they may seem. To provide another example of my minds processing of thought, I would tell myself, again and again as a joke, the bitter cold of the January nights was cold enough to freeze my eye balls, but it couldn't because I could see right throw it. I spent a lot of cash at the *Foxy Lady* over those few days with drinks and girls in the day and the night.

Visiting home, the sight of my father would fill me with uncontrollable anger. One day I came home and yelled and shouted at him. Yelling he was trying to turn my mother against me. I was shouting at the top of my lungs while cursing at him. I even knocked, not hit, at his head twice before leaving him. At this time I'm truly astonished he didn't call for help a second time, but that night while he and my mother watched the Presidential address to the nation I interrupted with verbal bashing of George W. and my father. Only George W. didn't have to endure my verbal abuse. I was calling my father a looser and I was using the example of Otto Graham as a winner. The assault only lasted but ten minutes before my father did call for a rescue.

I prepared myself for the police and rescues arrival. I put the *AFI* CD in the CD player getting it ready to play when they arrived. I also grabbed the box of computer disks holding the start of this book, to take with me. When they arrived I turned on the music and held onto my computer disks and went without an altercation or conflict. I was curtain I would be headed to Butler Hospital after dodging a visit days ago.

DAVID MICHAEL

As usual, I was taken to Kent County Hospital to wait before a decision was made on what to do with me. The embracing thing about waiting this time was Ginnie, who I had sold her and Matt's house, was a nurse and was on duty to see me boxed into the small waiting room. I had already started shouting things out of the room before she saw me there. She more than likely knew I suffered from Bi-Polar illness through roomers in the Youth Football League, but it was embracing to be seen in this situation. She stayed her distance, but did acknowledge I was there at one point. My stay there came to an end after some time where I was given the option of going to Butler Hospital or Landmark Hospital in Woonsocket. It took only seconds before I chose the unfamiliar Landmark. It had to be better than Butler.

After the half hour or so ride to Landmark Hospital, I was admitted into the Hospital psychiatric unit. It was late at night by the time I was introduces to the facility. My first memory is of a woman I met in the kitchen. She mentioned she was visiting her mother from Arizona, but not at the hospital. I immediately thought she was in a strange situation, being committed while visiting someone. She went on to tell me and her husband had been involving her in awkward sexual scenarios with him and other men. The topic did shift from her confession to other ordinary topics. Over the two days she was there we bonded quickly. The night she was released we exchanged hugs before she left.

The psychiatric wing at Landmark was a large rectangle, with the nurse's offices in the center of the rectangle. The kitchen ran off one end of the rectangle and a lounge area extended down a sort hall. I smoking booth resided in that lounge. Another common area sat along one of the longer sides of the rectangle. I would have to estimate 9 to 10 double bedrooms housed the close to 20 patients. The two doctors offices lay on opposite sides of the unit.

Again the fact I had marijuana in my system wasn't an issue. The reason they gave for my relapse was I wasn't taking my med's. My Lithium levels where lower than they should have been. I agreed there where a few times I miss taking my medication, that's not to say one day I decided to stop taking my med's all together. I accepted the diagnosis again only because I was aware of a few instances I did miss a prescribed time I was to take them.

I spent a lot of the first few days walking around the rectangle or one might say circle, over and over again. There where group meetings every morning, which I have to truly judge as much more relaxed and enjoyable. Every morning we would go around the room for personal updates or to answer a question supplied to us. I also noticed after a few days I was meeting with my doctor every day for about a half hour.

I really began taking advantage of these visits with my doctor. I took the opportunity to start to unload my thoughts, memory and mind. At Butler the doctor meets with a patient for five minutes in the morning and then took off. The half hour visits with the doctor Landmark provides allowed me to open up for the first time.

I told Dr. Elhi about the Leagues of Nations, with the brief explanation of three powerful Nations existed on each continent. I told him I was a man of government and wrote down I believed I was a Massajah. I opened up about my anger to my father. On one particular day it snowed and I told him I hoped my father would get a heart attack from shoveling heavy snow. I told him I thought I was being left behind only to sling shot my way to the front. I explained the chessboard of test cells I theorized might exist in space. Along with this I mentioned my loyalty to the British crown and the positions of business minded Visroi's and the position of Rook, as well as the Pope and maybe Jew as religious bishops. I talked about a governmental minded woman, a Massajahess to go along with my Massajah position on the board. I mentioned I thought I was more than likely from Hell and believed that's where I would be found after this life. I talked about my new version of football. I spoke about a desire to start a Rhodes University and the Colossus appearing to hoist up a bridge. It wasn't at one specific visit I unloaded; rather these confessions came little by little each days half hour visit. I grew to anticipate my visits being toward the end of group.

After a few days of keeping to myself outside Dr. Elhi's office, a new patient was admitted. He was around 50 years old in fact I believe he turned 50 during his stay. His name was Ken and we hit it off rather quickly. We shared a common interest in politics. The Democrats primaries for President were being conducted during our stay and we shared opinions and views. So much so he shared with me he had ran for Lieutenant Governor. I let it be known I wanted to start a political party. He was somewhat interested in such an endeavor. When he told me he worked for the Bridge and Port authority I immediately told him about my vision of a Colossus in the Bay. He thought it was off the wall and had no chance of being erected. We got along well through out our stays. If my memory serves me correctly he had been hospitalized for alcohol abuse.

It was the constant coverage of the Democrats searching for a Presidential candidate that had me reconsider my choice for a possible first women President and first black President. I'm not a big fan of George W. though some good was coming from his administration. I find there to be a very qualified woman in his cabinet, as well as, a black candidate. This woman and black candidate are the same person. I think Condilieza Rice has been exposed first hand to how a White House is conducted, as well as, having occupied an important position in an administration. The first black and woman President could be covered by the same individual, who almost all would agree is a smart cookie.

Another advantage Landmark had over Butler was a patient could order off the daily menu. There was always a choice of cheeseburgers, grilled cheese, and pizza or for breakfast egg muffin as a meal substitute. They weighed us once a week and I did gain some weight from ordering meals off the menu and decided to eat less each meal. The following week I had lost seven or more pounds by curbing my diet. The clothes my brother had brought me at the beginning of my stay then fit much better.

Speaking of my brother, the decision was made by my family and the doctors to release me into my brothers' supervision. That didn't mean I would be staying with my brother Mark, but rather he would be the contact person in an attempt to maintain my wellness. My release was well off, though my brother had been introduced as my contact person and meeting with him and a case manager began mid-way through my hospitalization.

The first meeting was with my brother, a case manager named Jackie and myself, a different Jackie from my earlier treatment outside of Landmark. I can recall the meeting growing out of control. In an attempt to convince my brother our father was no good I accused my dad of possibly molesting my brothers two children. This was in my thoughts and was unfounded, but this was at a time I was unloading what was on my conscience and this was something I wanted to get out.

The Patriots where in the Super bowl for the second time in three years during my Landmark experience. I called my friend Eddy the week before the game to let him know I was in the hospital, for basically two reasons. One to have him let my other friends know not to ask me to a Super bowl party and two to get some visitors out of my friends. I had no visitors other than supervised meetings with my brother and later family.

The day of the Super Bowl Ken put out a spread. He ordered out and treated all the patients to a Super Bowl party. There was pizza and sandwiches and chips and soda, everything one would expect at a Super Bowl party. It was a good game. The Pats beat the Carolina Panthers in a close game. I was still smarting from the tuck rule game the Patriots beat the Raiders in and was rooting against the Pats, so was Ken. Ken also handed out Patriot championship T-shirts to almost every one. I past on a Pats T-shirt. I'm a loyal Raiders fan and hold the tuck rule game against the Pats. That was like Ken who on other occasions splurged for pizza for the unit. Ken also through himself a birthday party, at which I met his wife and kids. Ken was released before I was and we exchanged numbers before he departed, though Ken gave out his contact information to quite a few patients on his way out.

After Ken left I spent some time talking with another patient, whose name I believe was Roger, but I can't say that with any certainty. He was a little strange, but aren't all the people in a mental facility. I looked passed his somewhat bizarre behavior and got to know him. He talked me about how he had produced a film and I thought this might be a chance to get into movie making. I exchanged names and numbers with him before I left.

I had an epiphany one day for why I had the strong feelings toward my father. I told the doctor I believed my father didn't take care for himself health wise. He had had a triple bye pass in the not to distant past and was again not taking care of himself. I had developed the belief he was going to die and I was preparing for it and it made me angry he didn't care. I was carrying around his possible death for several years and for the first time I was letting my feelings known. I believe it was at this point the wheels began getting greased on my release date.

The days at Landmark had past by much quicker than jail or Butler. Before I knew it I was there for a month or so. The doctor had medicated to a point he wanted and meetings with my family picked up. There was a meeting with my entire family where I felt they where painting me into a corner so I left in a huff telling them I would rather go to a shelter than give in to them.

Even with this cloud Dr. Elhi contested I was ready to be released. Valentines Day was approaching and I got word I was going to be released shortly. I was hoping to be released before V-Day so I could visit the girls at the *Foxy Lady*. I never let the doctor know this, when low and behold I was let free two days before the holiday. Believe it or not my father picked me up and took me back home. On the way home I did something I hadn't done to anyone a single time. I apologized to my dad.

The first thing I remember doing after being released was visiting the *Foxy Lady* on Valentines Day. I wore a red *Foxy Lady* shirt I had. I spent some money that night, nothing like I was spending before I was committed to Landmark. Still I had spent all of the money from my commission checks and had to rely on the two disability checks, for around $600 dollars each, coming in the mail during my stay at the hospital.

I contacted the Department of Business Regulations fresh out of the hospital to see where my complaint against *CVS* was. I was informed the complaint was dropped because they found my doctor failed to specify Lithobid instead of the generic Lithium. It wouldn't be until a months later I made a connection between my relapse and the change in medications, I accepted the fact I wasn't consistently taking my meds for a long time.

Almost immediately after my trip to Landmark ended, I was introduced to the Coldwell Banker in Narragansett. Again my manager Coreen was both the manager in Coventry and Narragansett and she had O.K.ed a move for me to Narragansett that Fall. She was aware that I was in the hospital with Bi-Polar over the stretch I was out of commission. The one property I had listed, the large Philip's property, Coreen handed over to another agent while I was being treated. I really wasn't ready to take on the responsibility. My confidence was low after what is always a somewhat humiliating experience of being found mentally unfit. It takes some time to feel ones way back into a mainstream situation.

That weekend I received a phone call from the owner of the Jeep I had put $500 down on. He informed me the Jeep was still for sale at a reduced price of $1800. This meant I had to come up with $1300, which I was short $100 or more if I handed over all my money. Somehow I shared my situation with my mother, who mentioned it to my father and my father lent me the money to pay for the Jeep. He told me to pay him back a hundred dollars a month until the $1300 was paid back. We went and purchased the Jeep for the $1800 that day.

Shortly after I put my snowboard in the Jeep and went snowboarding at Watchusset Mountain. My second time on the slopes was during the day and the sport was no easier than my first. I took maybe five trips falling all the way down one of the easier runs before heading home. On the way home the shifting of the gears became inconstant on the Jeep, I was still able to make it all the way home with the emerging problem.

I met with Dr. Koyfman following the hospitalization and I agreed to keep seeing her instead of switching to a new doctor. I also began visits to my new male case manager Kevin. He was a nice enough guy who somewhat dictated the time spent with him.

I met with Roger a few times out side of the hospital. He never really got around to showing me any film he had directed or made and after a few visits we stopped contact with one another. I didn't contact Ken at all. I didn't want to bother him, as I knew the other patients probably where.

My mother and father went on a trip, I believe to Las Vegas and my father left me in charge of his Real Estate business while he was gone. It took a lot of energy for me to keep things afloat and I was able to keep everything at bay until he returned.

The Jeep stayed parked in front of the house with the gear and shifting problem until my dad erased the debt I owed him. He also brought the Jeep in to get fixed, because I had maintained his Real Estate business.

Spring emerged from winter and I had no luck in Real Estate, until my father handed over a buyer to me. She was a relative of a friend of the family looking for a condo. We made an offer on one condominium, which went to a higher bidder. This experience frustrated her enough she decide to rent an apartment instead of purchasing a Condo. I really didn't have activity other than that all the way through the 2004 year.

On my visits with Kevin he would suggest Real Estate might not be my cup of tea. Around that same time I received information on how to get back to work from the State government. They offered someone to meet with to get me going. So I did meet with him and we went over my situation and he thought he would be able to help me. When it came around the time I was getting serious about finding work and had started working on a new design portfolio, the guy I was seeing got promoted and I had no contact which through my plans of getting a new job into the trash.

At the start of summer another case manager in the same office as Kevin, who had a Rhode Island School of Design degree, noticed my painting of 'Red' in the office. She made me aware of an art exhibition the mental health community was putting on. The show would be made up of works from individuals living with mental illness. Gene asked me if I wanted to enter a few pieces into the show and I agreed to show some of my stuff. The art exhibition would be conducted in Pawtucket at the Travel Center. I felt my work was on a different level from the others. I considered most of the other artists work to be possibly something they picked up as therapeutic and lacked a natural talent. Though there where some works I considered pretty good. I enjoyed participating in the gallery of art even though I was somewhat disappointed in the skill level of the majority of works. I hope I don't sound to condescending, that's just my honest opinion.

I had been waiting for the summer for sometime. I was in Narragansett at least twice a week and could skip out to the beach after visiting the office. Sadly enough I only visited the beach once that summer. Though I did go door to door through one of the beach communities to try and drum up business, it was the most I had tried up until that point, nothing came out of the door knocking.

I took the top off the Jeep and drove it as often as I could. The vehicle was a 1989 and had some life left in it over that summer. I can recall taking it down to the *Foxy Lady*. I had no money to spend at the gentleman's club, though I still had a VIP card to get me in for free. I would sit and smoke a cigar most of my visits to the club and then leave. The card expired in October and I really didn't have the extra

AN AMERICAN MESSIAH

money to purchase another one.

Fall brought the end of the regular season for baseball, which brought the play-offs. The Red Sox made it into the play-offs as a wild card in 2004. In the first round Boston faced the formidable Anaheim Angeles. In a close five game series the Red Sox eliminated the Angeles and advanced to the next round. The bitter rival New York Yankees would be matched up against the Red Sox in the next best of seven game series, with a trip to the World Series on the line.

Before I get into the match up between the hated Yankees and cursed Red Sox., I'd like to give a brief history on how the Red Sox became cursed and the Yankees 26 time World Champs.

The Red Sox acquired a pitcher in 1914, George Herman Ruth or the Babe as he is widely known. The Sox would win three Word Series Championships with the Babe. Due to WWI and the absence of players Ruth started to play some time in the field. After new ownership and Ruth didn't see eye-to-eye the Babe was traded in 1918 to the Yankees for $200,000, so the owner could fund a play. Ruth would go on to rewrite the home run record books and the Yankees would win 26 World Championships and the Red Sox would experience heart breaking loses in the playoffs and World Series, especially to the Yanks.

The 2004 playoff match up between the two teams looked like this would be just another year the Sox would fall victim to the New York Yankees. The Yankees took a decisive three games to none lead in the best of seven series; with a particularly humiliating game three lose of 19 to 8.

The Red Sox earned the right to extend the series with a close 6 to 4 win in game four. With a lopsided 3 game to 1 lead the Yankees fell short of advancing to the Series in game 5 with a 5 to 4 lose to the Red Sox. The Sox then come back to even this round of the playoffs with a 4 to 2 win. In the final game seven, with a trip to the World Series on the line, the Sox did 'believe' and closed out the series with a 10 to 3 victory sending them and Curt Schillings bloody sock into the World Series. Curt produced one of the more famous images in playoff history when he pitched a game with a detached tendon in his ankle. While Curt pitched blood seeped through his sox, do to the injection he received to help block the pain to get him out there.

The team entered the World Series with extreme confidence,

knowing they had extinguished many demons by eliminating the Yankees in a come from behind fashion. The Sox made quick work of the World Series, sweeping a strong St. Louis Cardinals team 4 games to none. After an absence of 86 years the team were crowned the 2004 World Champion Boston Red Sox, putting the 'Curse of the Bambino' to rest.

I was never sure I would get to witness a championship from the Sox in my lifetime. This event gave me something to feel good about. Not just me, but all of Red Sox Nation for that matter. The common experience of this victory transplanted me back into society and I can trace it back to my current recovery and wellness. The Red Sox BELIEVE approach has re-enforced my strong belief, 'If one truly believes in themselves, anything is possible.'

Printed in the United States
92120LV00004B/34-42/A